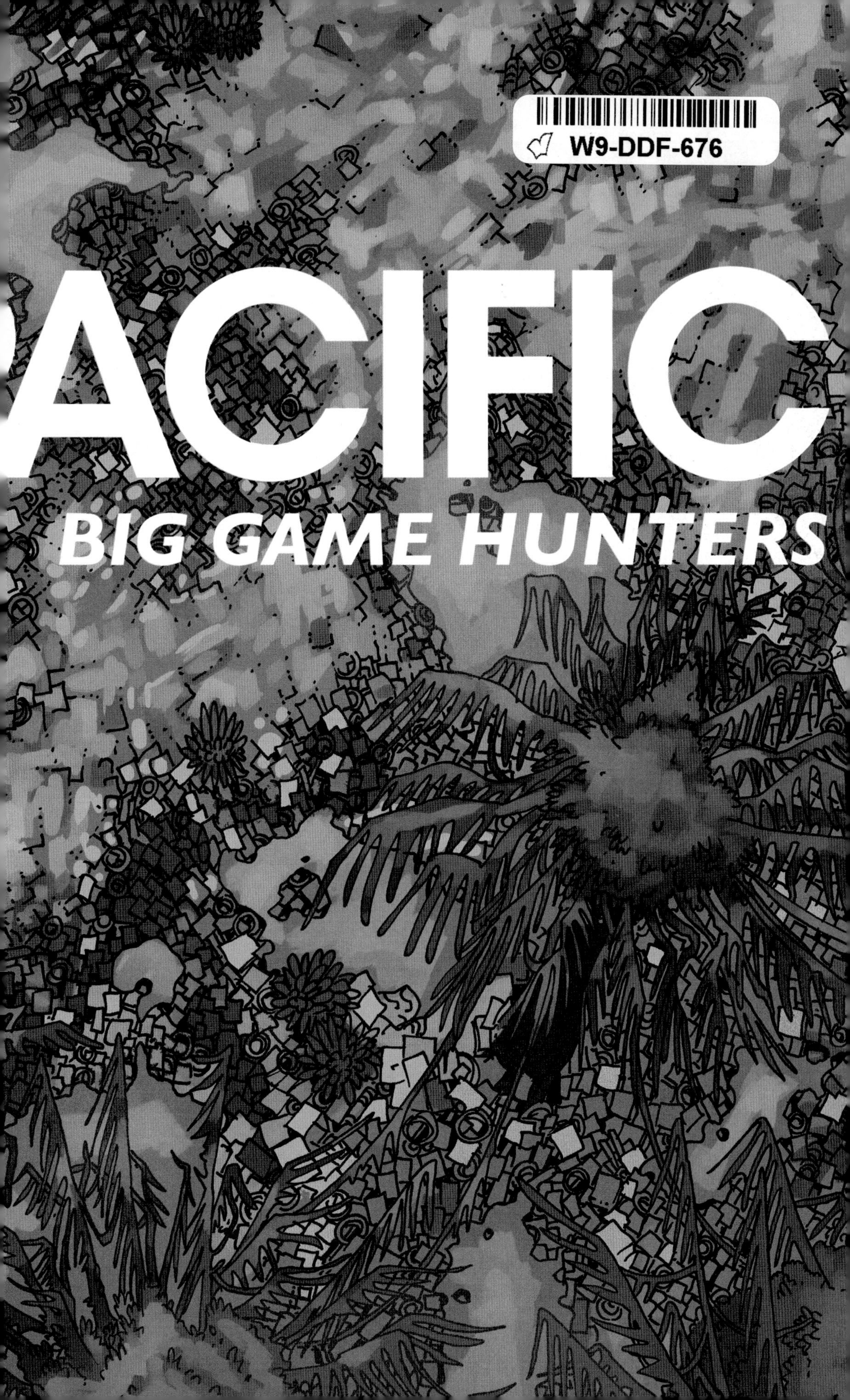
ACIFIC
BIG GAME HUNTERS

CREATED BY
JOE**HARRIS** AND
MARTÍN**MORAZZO**

WRITTEN BY
JOE**HARRIS**

ART BY
MARTÍN**MORAZZO**

COLORS BY
TIZA**STUDIO**

LETTERS BY
MICHAEL DAVID**THOMAS**

DESIGN BY SEAN**DOVE**
EDITED BY SHAWNA**GORE**

WWW. GREATPACIFICCOMICS.COM
WWW.IMAGECOMICS.COM

PUBLISHED BY IMAGE COMICS, INC.

This book collects issues **13-18** of the
Image Comics series GREAT PACIFIC

First edition January 2015
ISBN — 978-1-63215-104-9

IMAGE COMICS, INC.
Robert Kirkman – Chief Operating Officer
Erik Larsen – Chief Financial Officer
Todd McFarlane – President
Marc Silvestri – Chief Executive Officer
Jim Valentino – Vice-President
Eric Stephenson – Publisher
Ron Richards – Director of Business Development
Jennifer de Guzman – Director of Trade Book Sales
Kat Salazar – Director of PR & Marketing
Corey Murphy – Director of Retail Sales
Jeremy Sullivan – Director of Digital Sales
Emilio Bautista – Sales Assistant
Branwyn Bigglestone – Senior Accounts Manager
Emily Miller – Accounts Manager
Jessica Ambriz – Administrative Assistant
Tyler Shainline – Events Coordinator
David Brothers – Content Manager
Jonathan Chan – Production Manager
Drew Gill – Art Director
Meredith Wallace – Print Manager
Monica Garcia – Senior Production Artist
Addison Duke – Production Artist
Vincent Kukua – Production Artist
Tricia Ramos – Production Assistant
IMAGECOMICS.COM

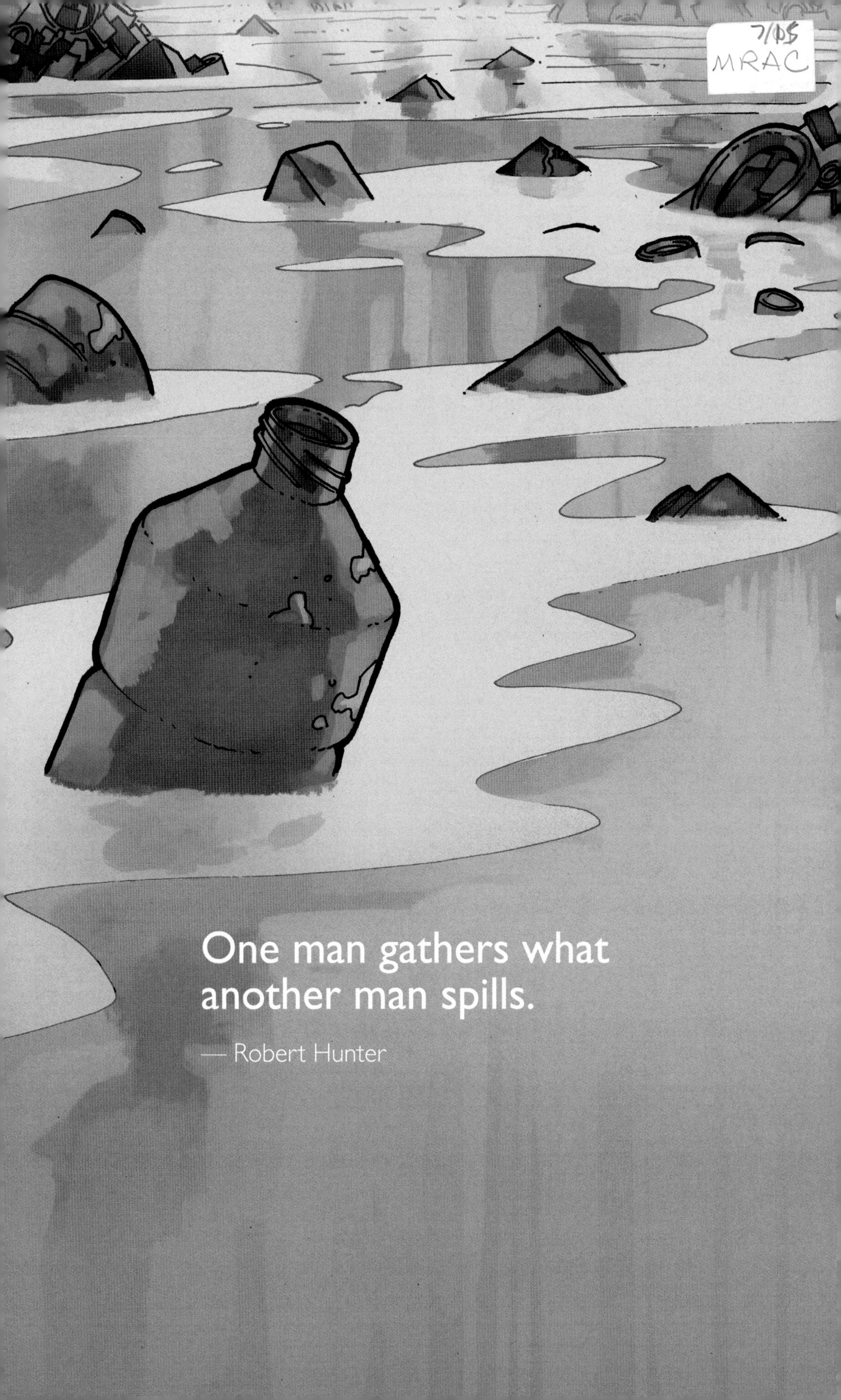

One man gathers what another man spills.

— Robert Hunter

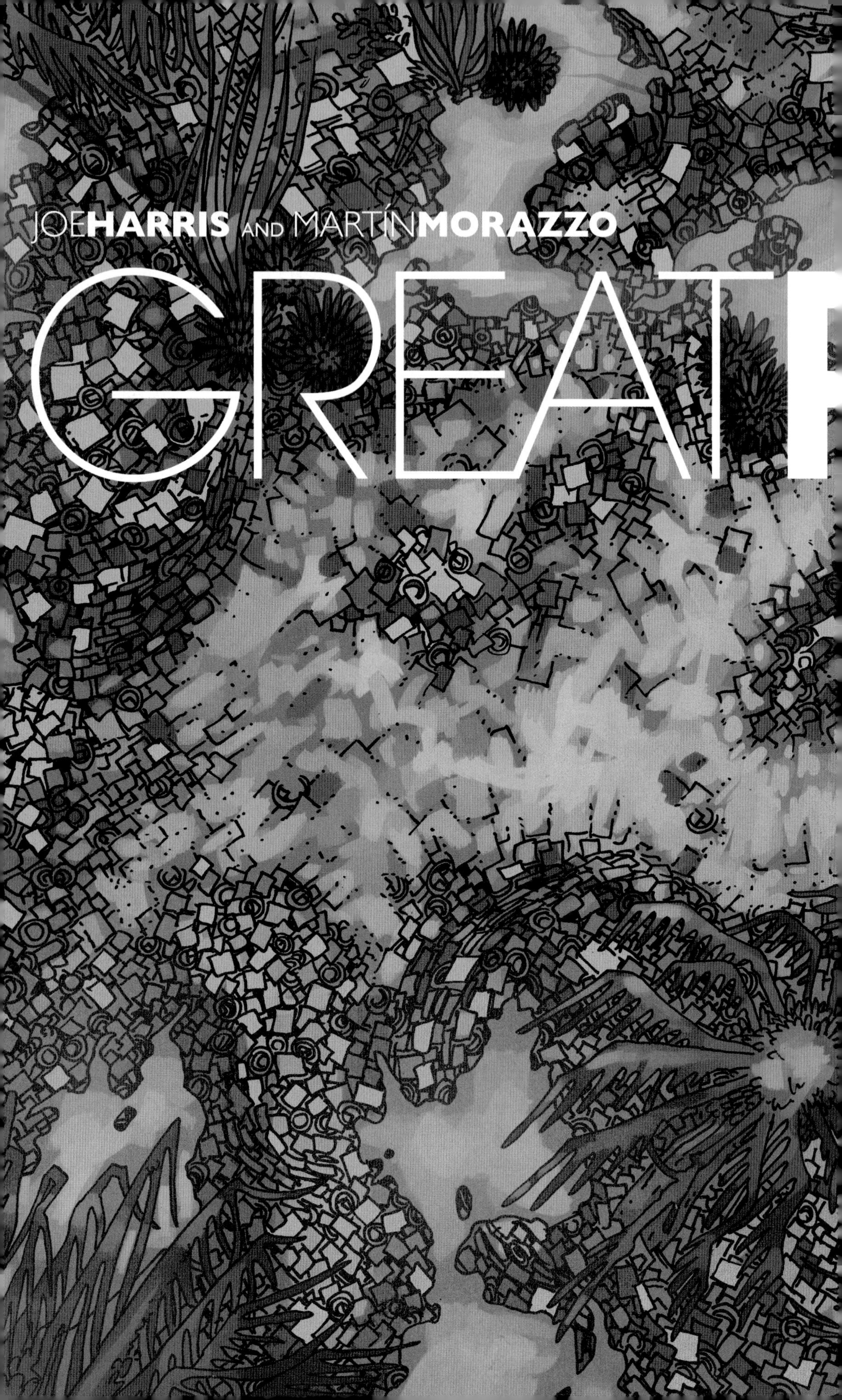
JOE HARRIS AND MARTÍN MORAZZO
GREAT

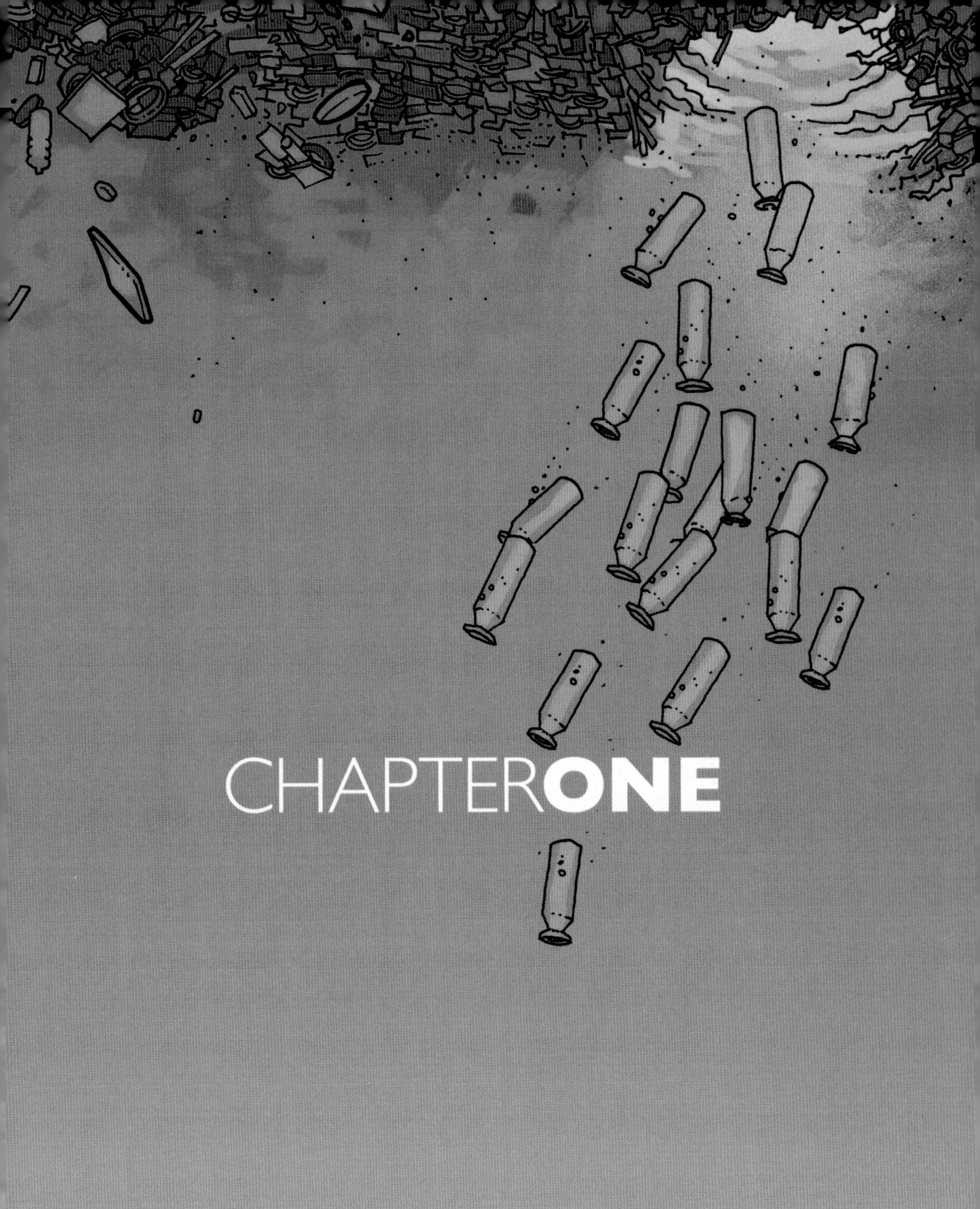

CHAPTER ONE

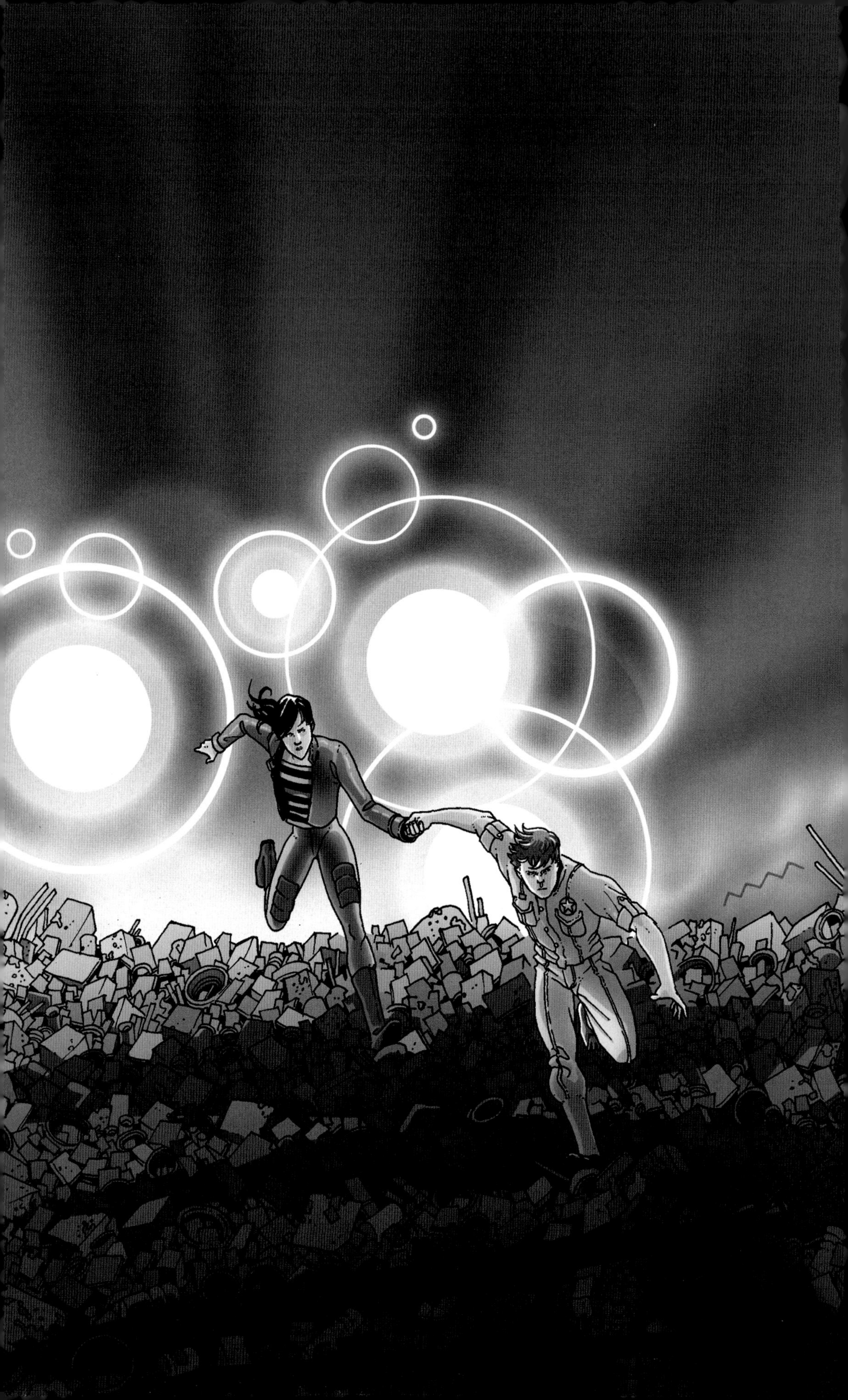

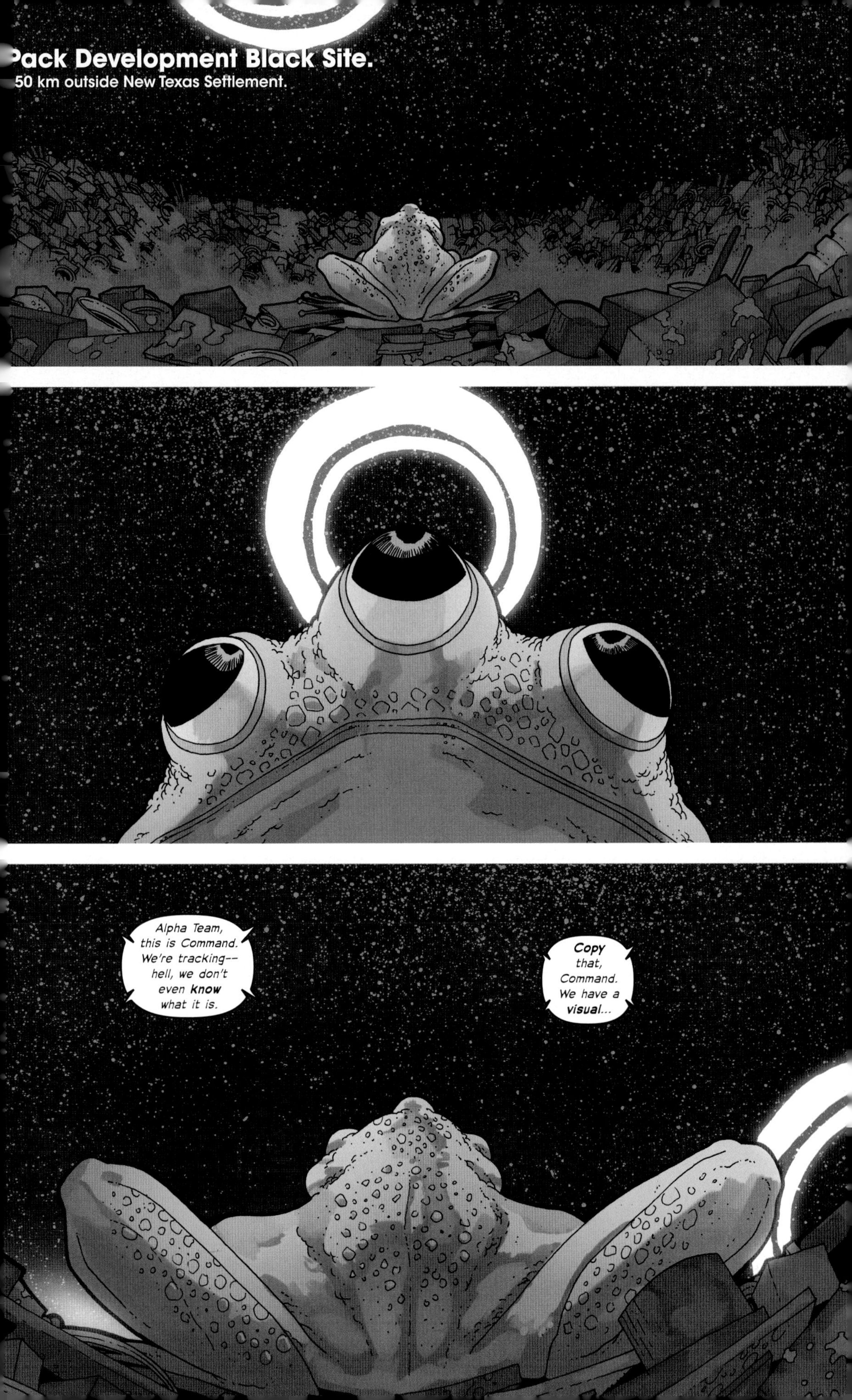
Pack Development Black Site.
50 km outside New Texas Settlement.
Alpha Team, this is Command. We're tracking-- hell, we don't even **know** what it is.
Copy that, Command. We have a **visual**...

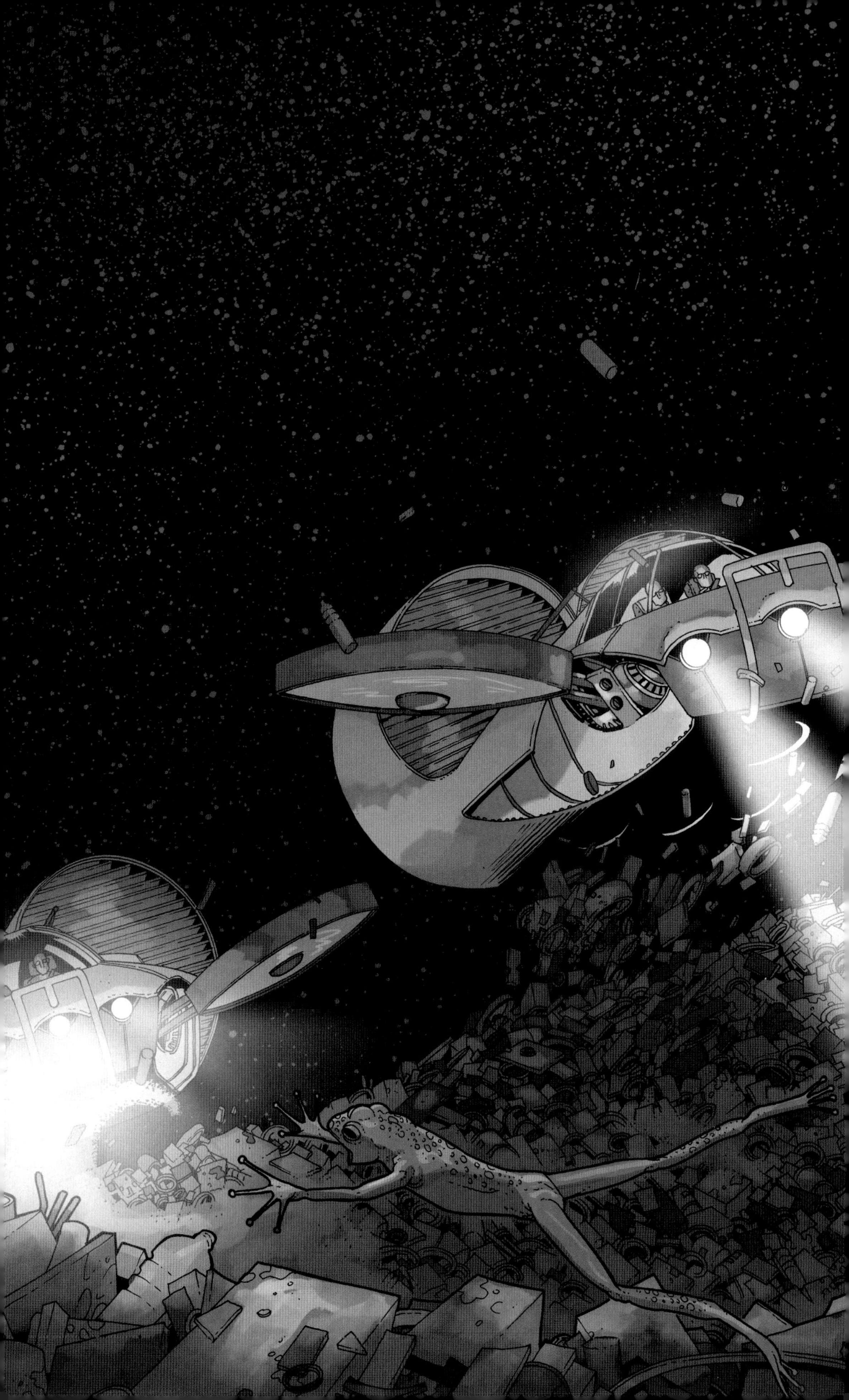

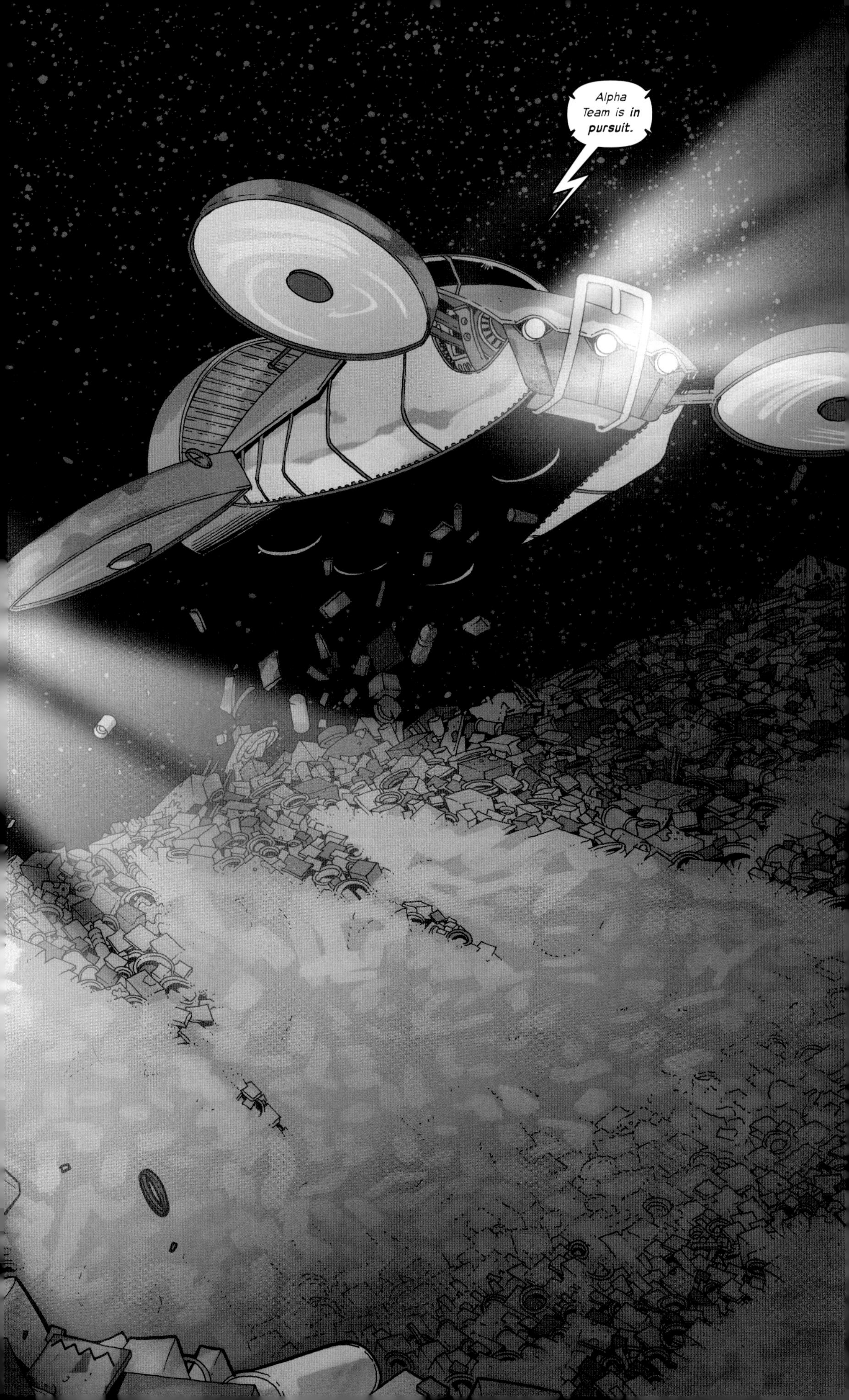
Alpha Team is in pursuit.

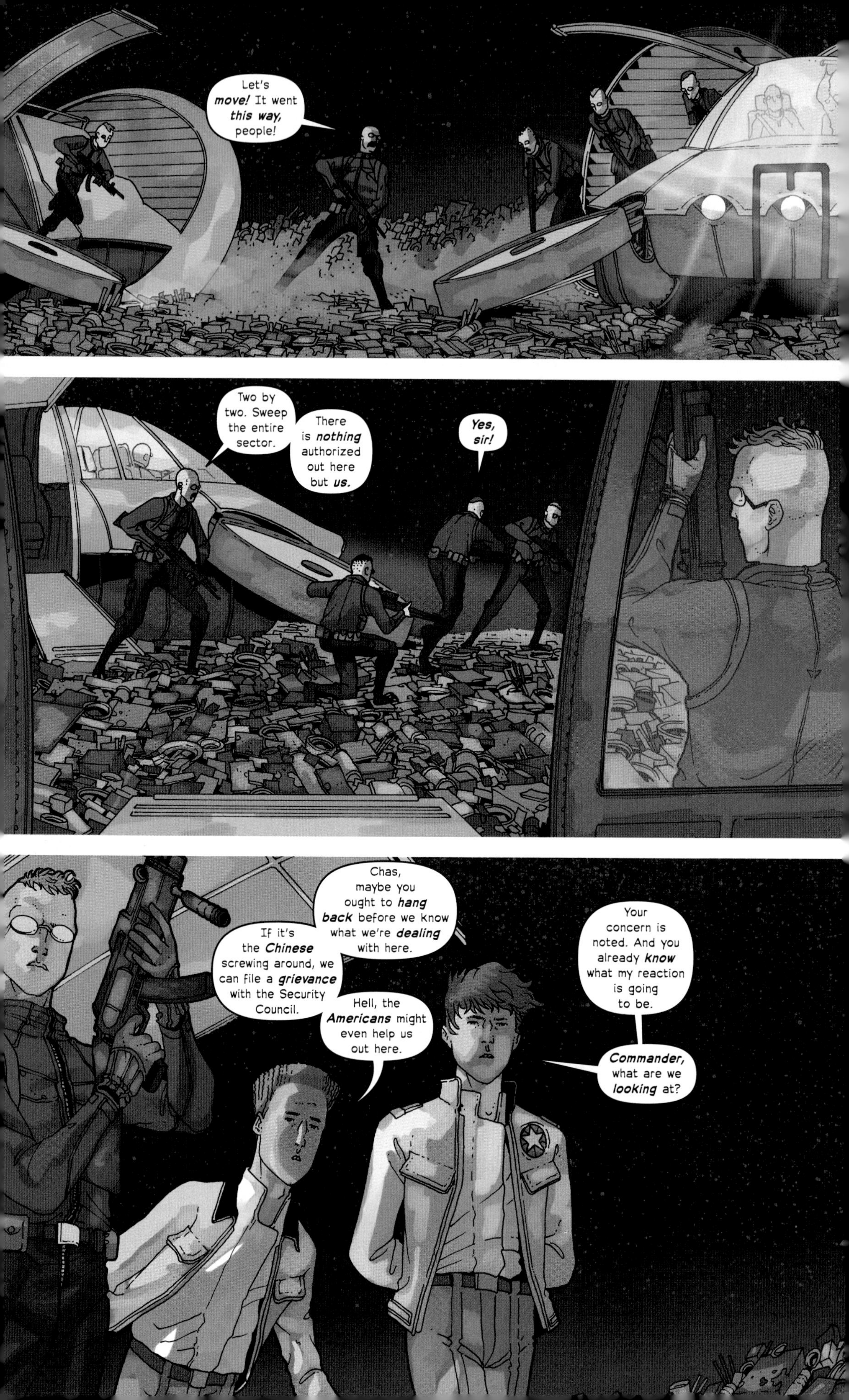
Let's move! It went this way, people!
Two by two. Sweep the entire sector.
There is nothing authorized out here but us.
Yes, sir!
Chas, maybe you ought to hang back before we know what we're dealing with here.
If it's the Chinese screwing around, we can file a grievance with the Security Council.
Hell, the Americans might even help us out here.
Your concern is noted. And you already know what my reaction is going to be.
Commander, what are we looking at?

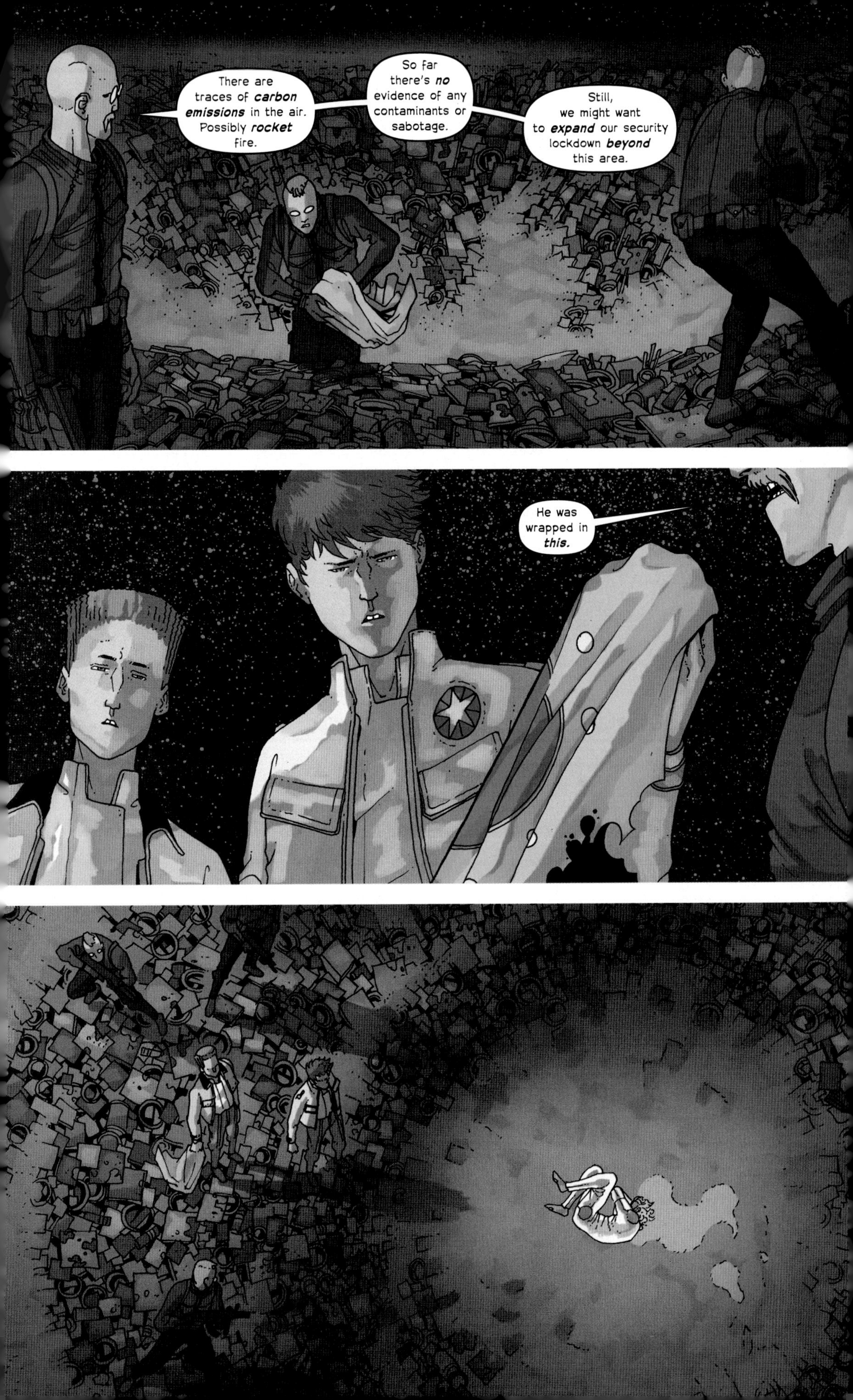
There are traces of **carbon emissions** in the air. Possibly **rocket** fire.
So far there's **no** evidence of any contaminants or sabotage.
Still, we might want to **expand** our security lockdown **beyond** this area.
He was wrapped in **this.**

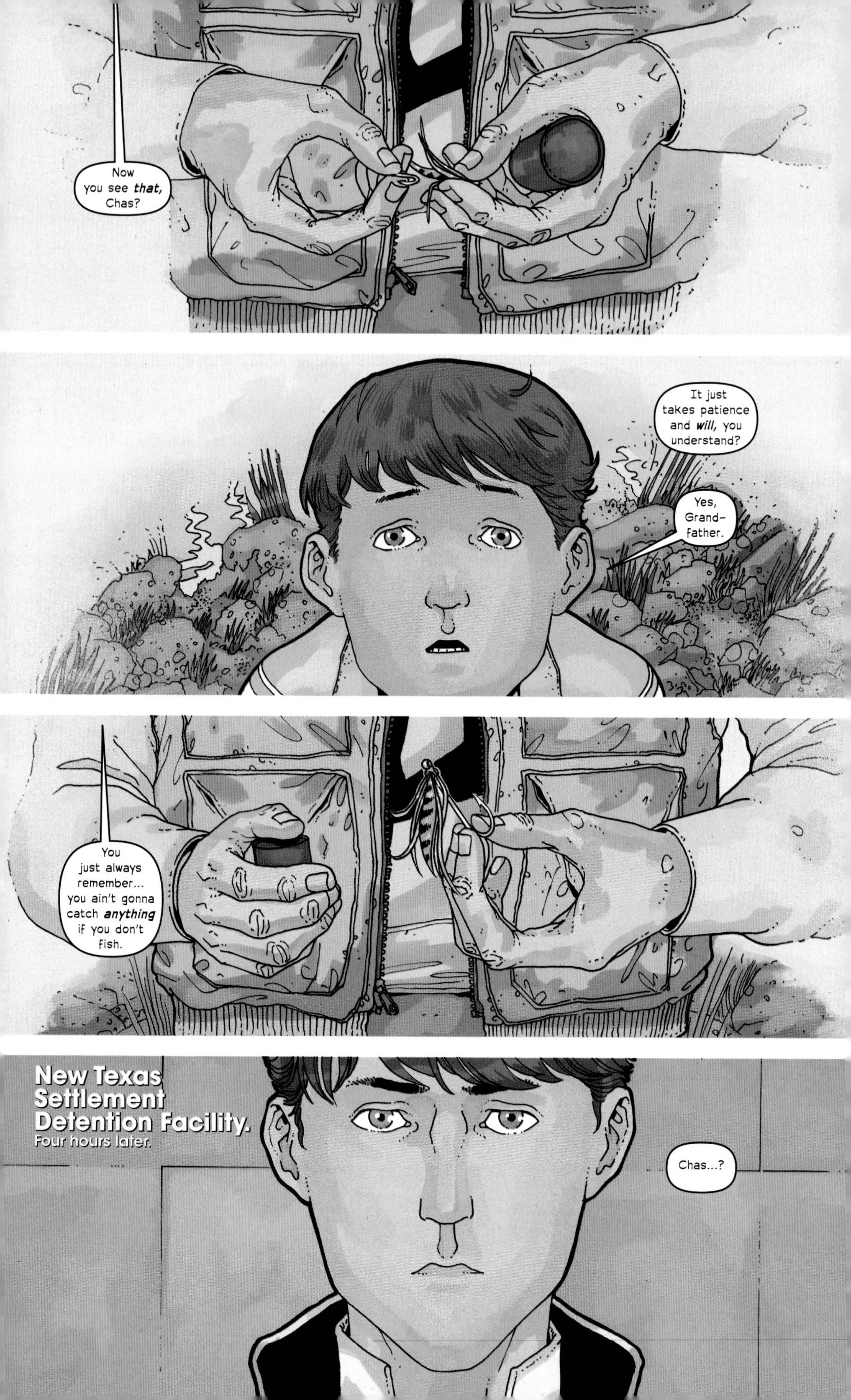
Now you see *that,* Chas?
It just takes patience and *will,* you understand?
Yes, Grand-father.
You just always remember... you ain't gonna catch *anything* if you don't fish.
New Texas Settlement Detention Facility.
Four hours later.
Chas...?

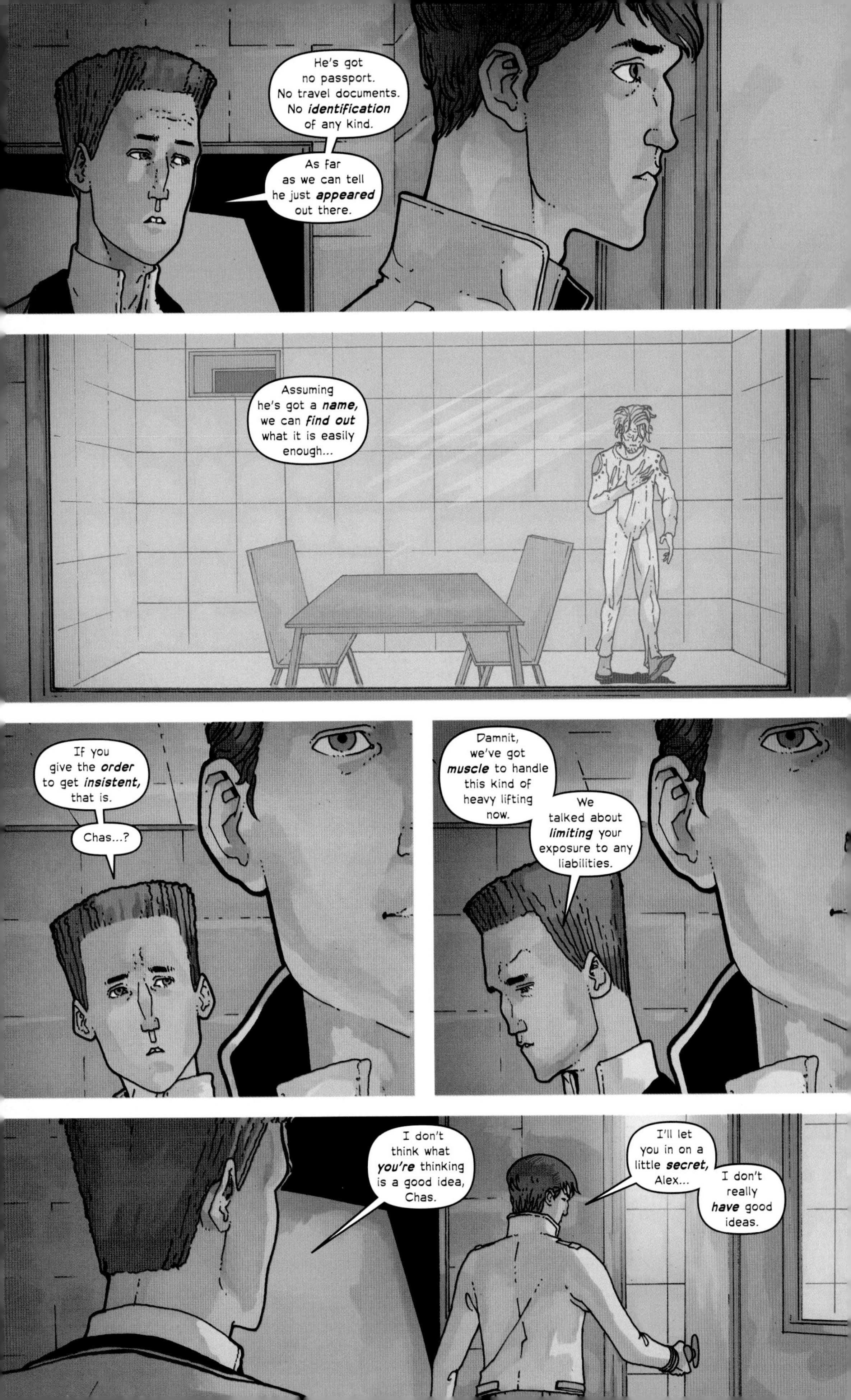

He's got no passport. No travel documents. No *identification* of any kind.
As far as we can tell he just *appeared* out there.
Assuming he's got a *name,* we can *find out* what it is easily enough...
If you give the *order* to get *insistent,* that is.
Chas...?
Damnit, we've got *muscle* to handle this kind of heavy lifting now.
We talked about *limiting* your exposure to any liabilities.
I don't think what *you're* thinking is a good idea, Chas.
I'll let you in on a little *secret,* Alex...
I don't really *have* good ideas.

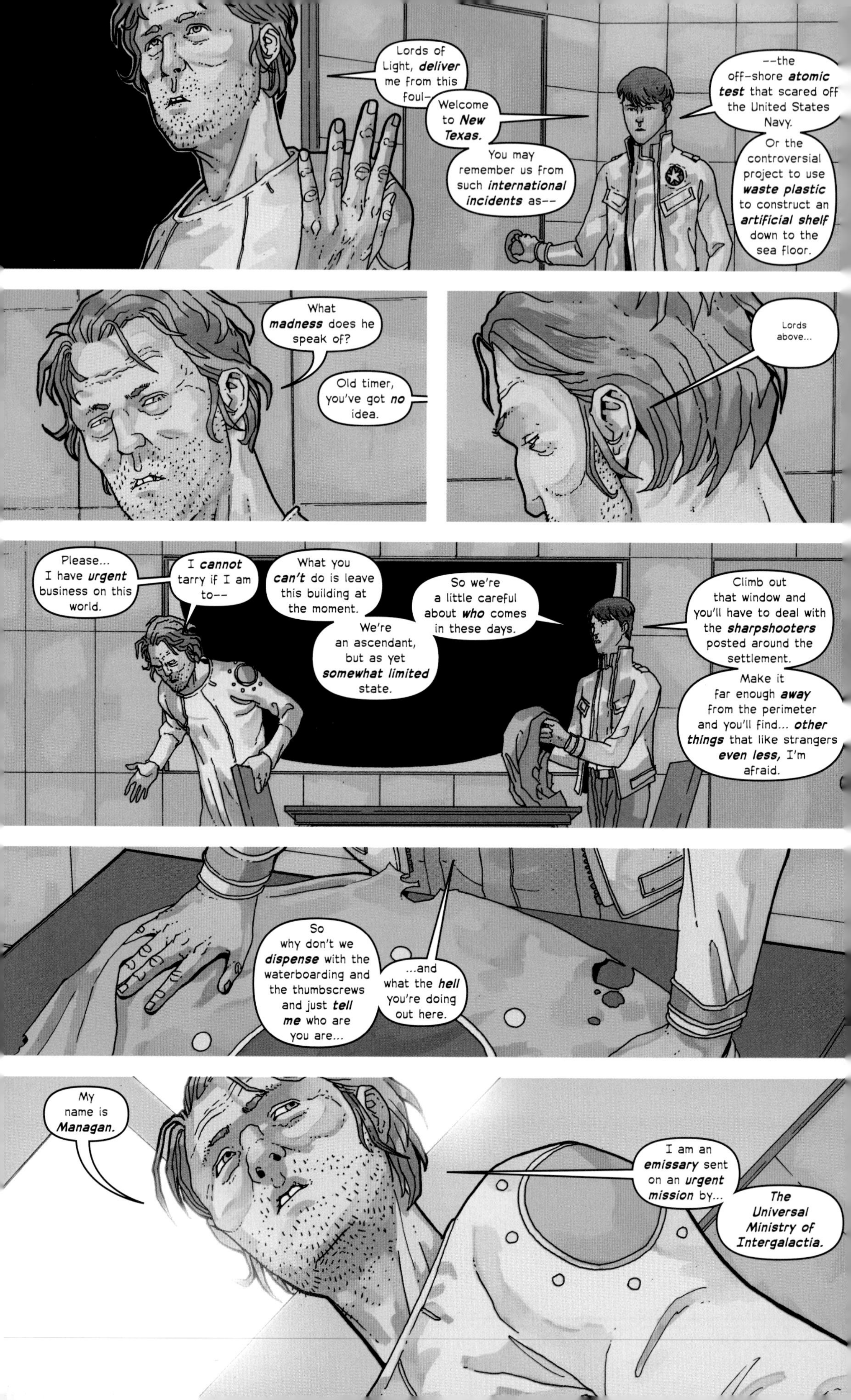
Lords of Light, *deliver* me from this foul–
Welcome to *New Texas.*
You may remember us from such *international incidents* as--
--the off-shore *atomic test* that scared off the United States Navy.
Or the controversial project to use *waste plastic* to construct an *artificial shelf* down to the sea floor.
What *madness* does he speak of?
Old timer, you've got *no* idea.
Lords above...
Please... I have *urgent* business on this world.
I *cannot* tarry if I am to--
What you *can't* do is leave this building at the moment.
We're an ascendant, but as yet *somewhat limited* state.
So we're a little careful about *who* comes in these days.
Climb out that window and you'll have to deal with the *sharpshooters* posted around the settlement.
Make it far enough *away* from the perimeter and you'll find... *other things* that like strangers *even less,* I'm afraid.
So why don't we *dispense* with the waterboarding and the thumbscrews and just *tell me* who are you are...
...and what the *hell* you're doing out here.
My name is *Managan.*
I am an *emissary* sent on an *urgent mission* by...
The Universal Ministry of Intergalactia.

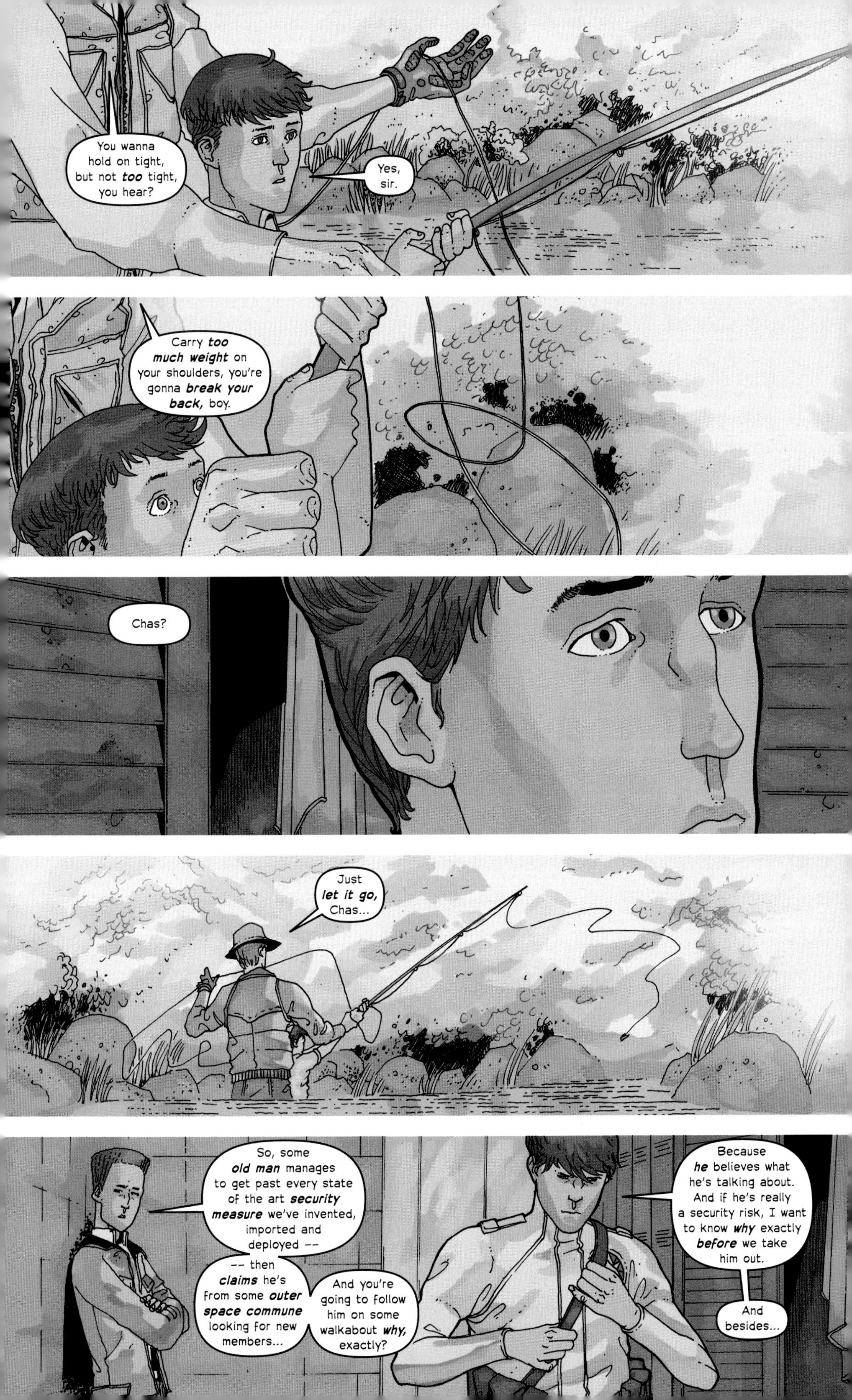
You wanna hold on tight, but not *too* tight, you hear?
Yes, sir.
Carry *too much weight* on your shoulders, you're gonna *break your back,* boy.
Chas?
Just *let it go,* Chas...
So, some *old man* manages to get past every state of the art *security measure* we've invented, imported and deployed --
-- then *claims* he's from some *outer space commune* looking for new members...
And you're going to follow him on some walkabout *why,* exactly?
Because *he* believes what he's talking about. And if he's really a security risk, I want to know *why* exactly *before* we take him out.
And besides...

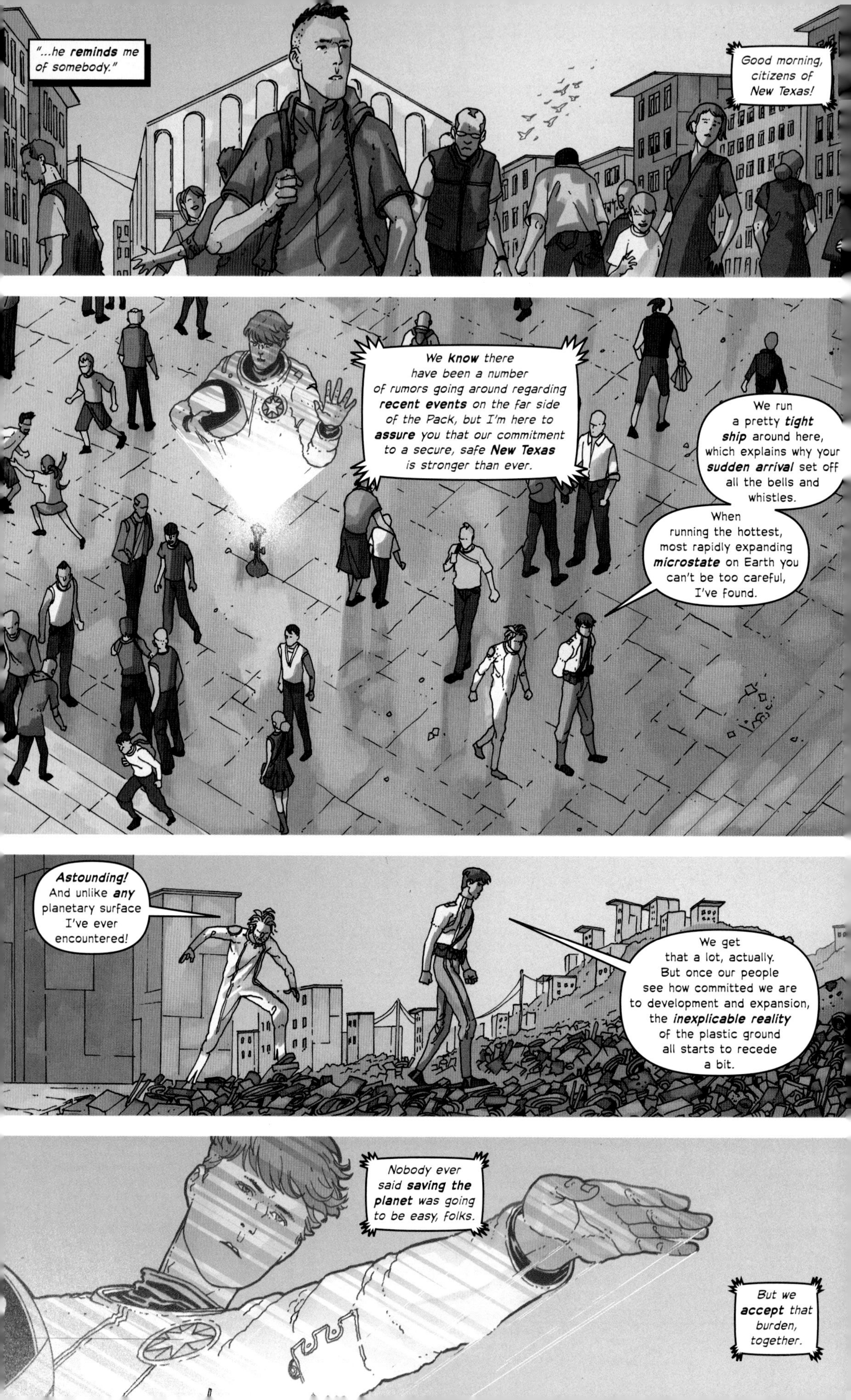
"...he reminds me of somebody."
Good morning, citizens of New Texas!
We know there have been a number of rumors going around regarding recent events on the far side of the Pack, but I'm here to assure you that our commitment to a secure, safe New Texas is stronger than ever.
We run a pretty tight ship around here, which explains why your sudden arrival set off all the bells and whistles.
When running the hottest, most rapidly expanding microstate on Earth you can't be too careful, I've found.
Astounding! And unlike any planetary surface I've ever encountered!
We get that a lot, actually. But once our people see how committed we are to development and expansion, the inexplicable reality of the plastic ground all starts to recede a bit.
Nobody ever said saving the planet was going to be easy, folks.
But we accept that burden, together.

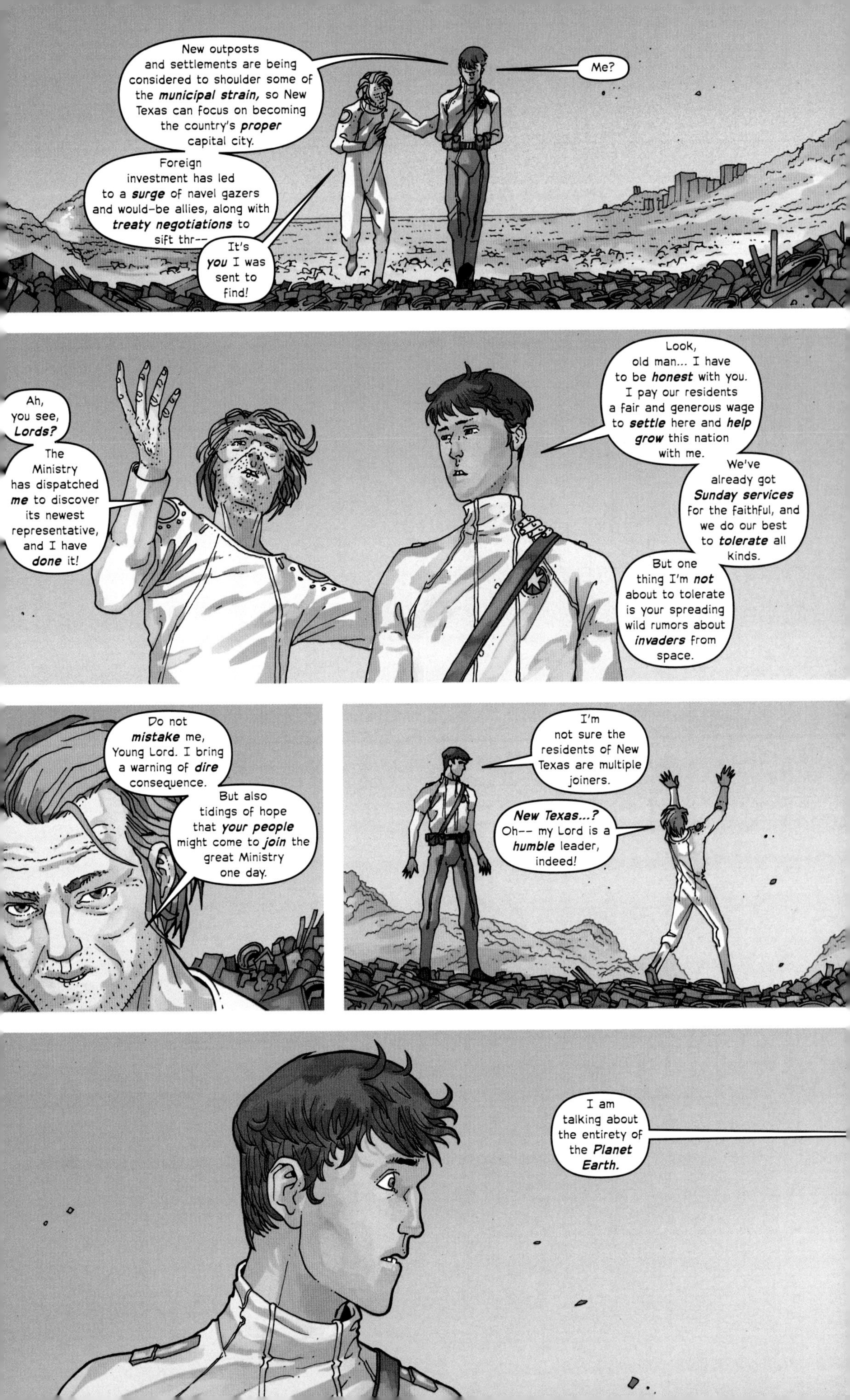
New outposts and settlements are being considered to shoulder some of the municipal strain, so New Texas can focus on becoming the country's proper capital city.
Me?
Foreign investment has led to a surge of navel gazers and would-be allies, along with treaty negotiations to sift thr--
It's you I was sent to find!
Ah, you see, Lords?
The Ministry has dispatched me to discover its newest representative, and I have done it!
Look, old man... I have to be honest with you. I pay our residents a fair and generous wage to settle here and help grow this nation with me.
We've already got Sunday services for the faithful, and we do our best to tolerate all kinds.
But one thing I'm not about to tolerate is your spreading wild rumors about invaders from space.
Do not mistake me, Young Lord. I bring a warning of dire consequence.
But also tidings of hope that your people might come to join the great Ministry one day.
I'm not sure the residents of New Texas are multiple joiners.
New Texas...? Oh-- my Lord is a humble leader, indeed!
I am talking about the entirety of the Planet Earth.

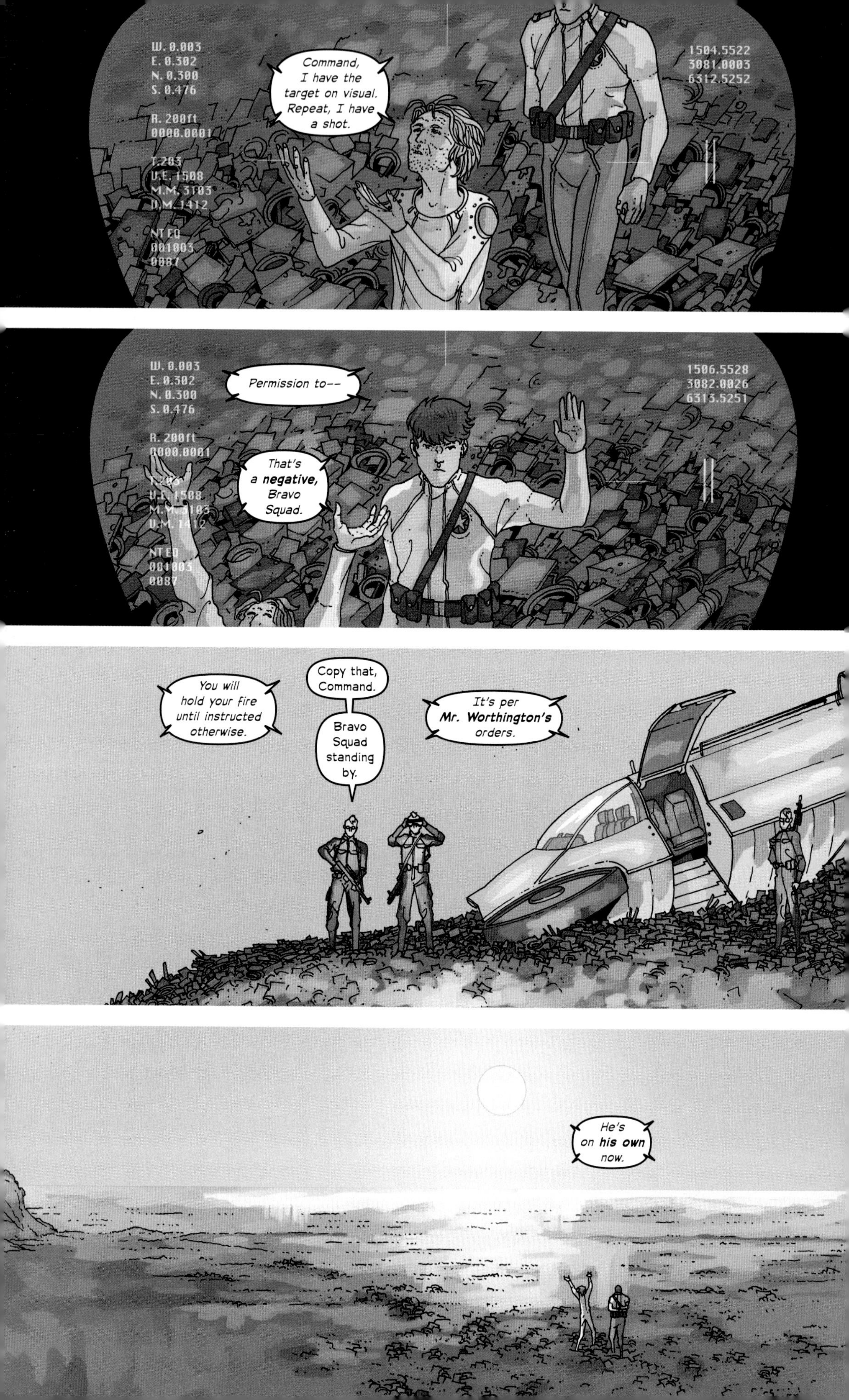
W. 0.003
E. 0.302
N. 0.300
S. 0.476
R. 200ft
0008.0001
1504.5522
3081.0003
6312.5252
Command, I have the target on visual. Repeat, I have a shot.
W. 0.003
E. 0.302
N. 0.300
S. 0.476
R. 200ft
0000.0001
1506.5528
3082.0026
6313.5251
Permission to--
That's a **negative,** Bravo Squad.
You will hold your fire until instructed otherwise.
Copy that, Command.
Bravo Squad standing by.
It's per **Mr. Worthington's** orders.
He's on **his own** now.

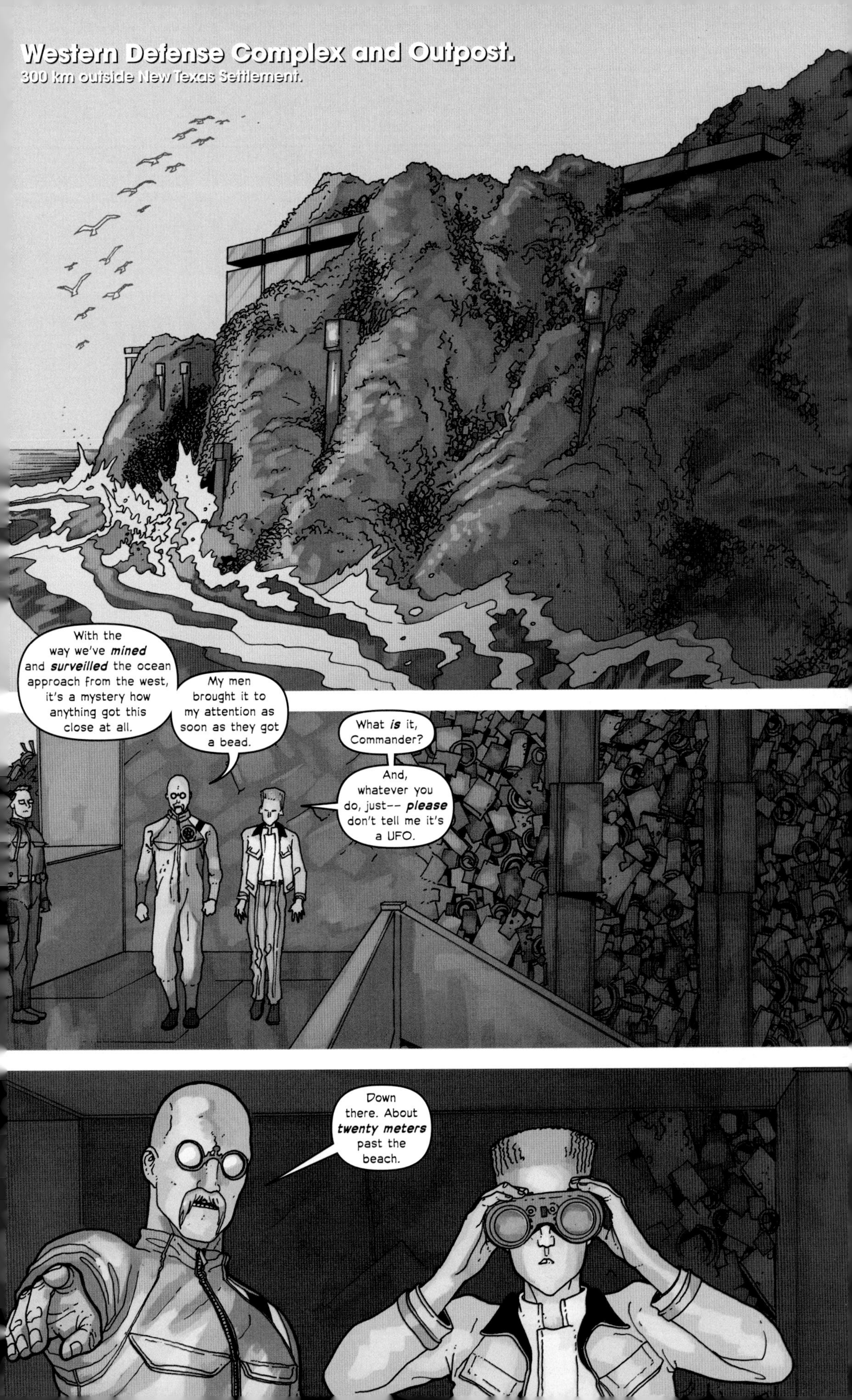
Western Defense Complex and Outpost.
300 km outside New Texas Settlement.
With the way we've *mined* and *surveilled* the ocean approach from the west, it's a mystery how anything got this close at all.
My men brought it to my attention as soon as they got a bead.
What *is* it, Commander?
And, whatever you do, just-- *please* don't tell me it's a UFO.
Down there. About *twenty meters* past the beach.

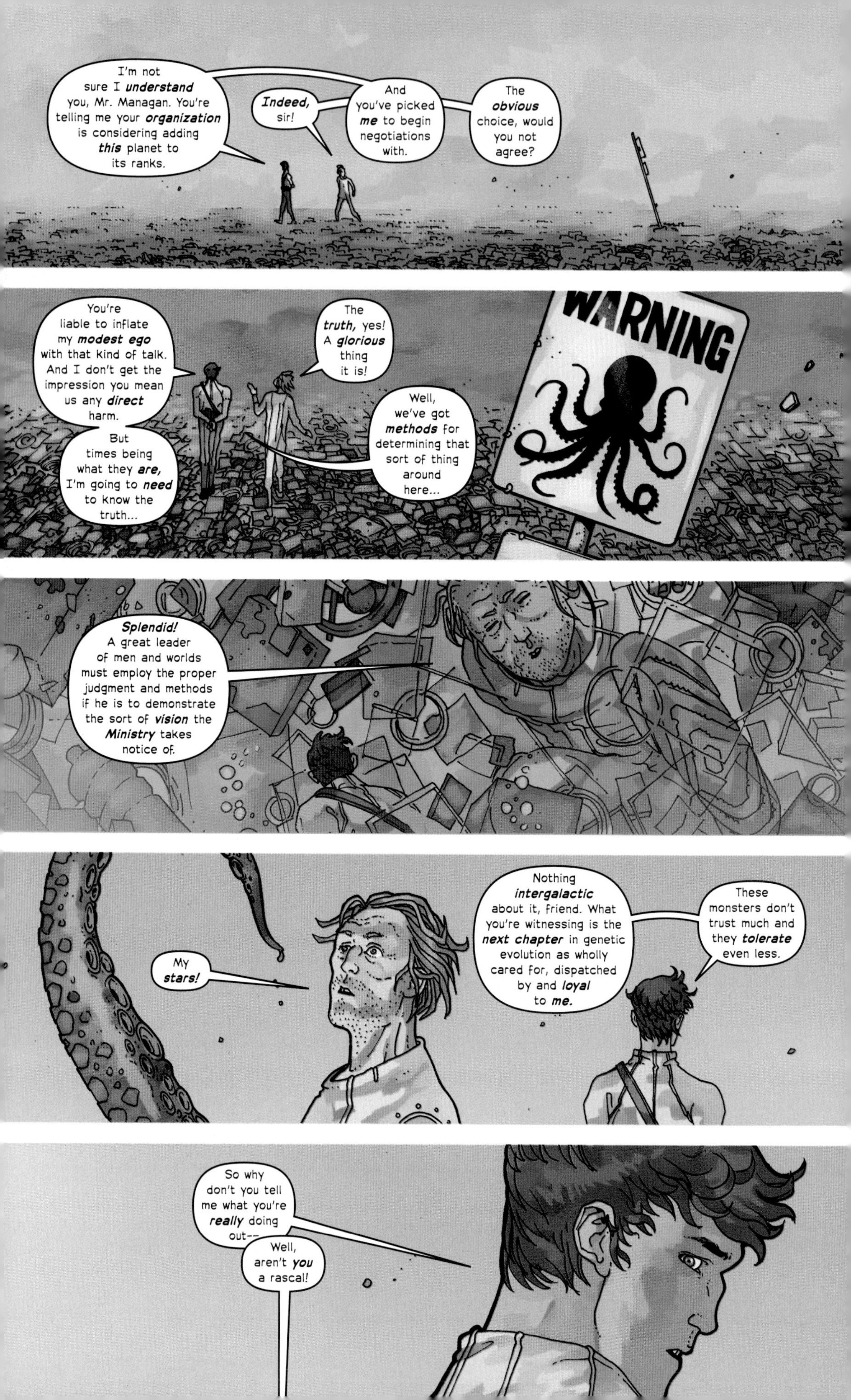
I'm not sure I understand you, Mr. Managan. You're telling me your organization is considering adding this planet to its ranks.
Indeed, sir!
And you've picked me to begin negotiations with.
The obvious choice, would you not agree?
You're liable to inflate my modest ego with that kind of talk. And I don't get the impression you mean us any direct harm.
But times being what they are, I'm going to need to know the truth...
The truth, yes! A glorious thing it is!
Well, we've got methods for determining that sort of thing around here...
WARNING
Splendid! A great leader of men and worlds must employ the proper judgment and methods if he is to demonstrate the sort of vision the Ministry takes notice of.
My stars!
Nothing intergalactic about it, friend. What you're witnessing is the next chapter in genetic evolution as wholly cared for, dispatched by and loyal to me.
These monsters don't trust much and they tolerate even less.
So why don't you tell me what you're really doing out--
Well, aren't you a rascal!

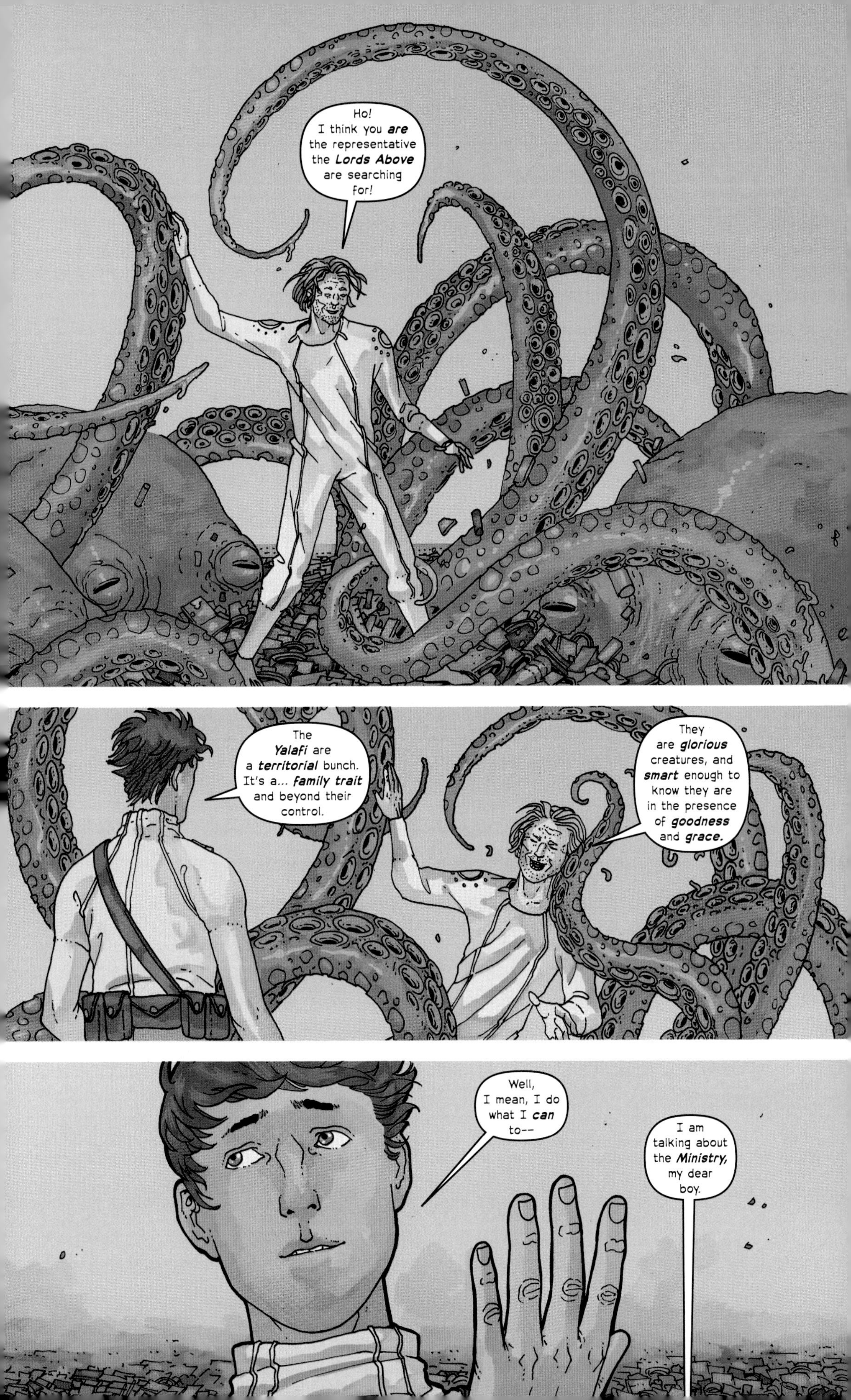
Ho! I think you ***are*** the representative the ***Lords Above*** are searching for!
The ***Yalafi*** are a ***territorial*** bunch. It's a... ***family trait*** and beyond their control.
They are ***glorious*** creatures, and ***smart*** enough to know they are in the presence of ***goodness*** and ***grace.***
Well, I mean, I do what I ***can*** to--
I am talking about the ***Ministry,*** my dear boy.

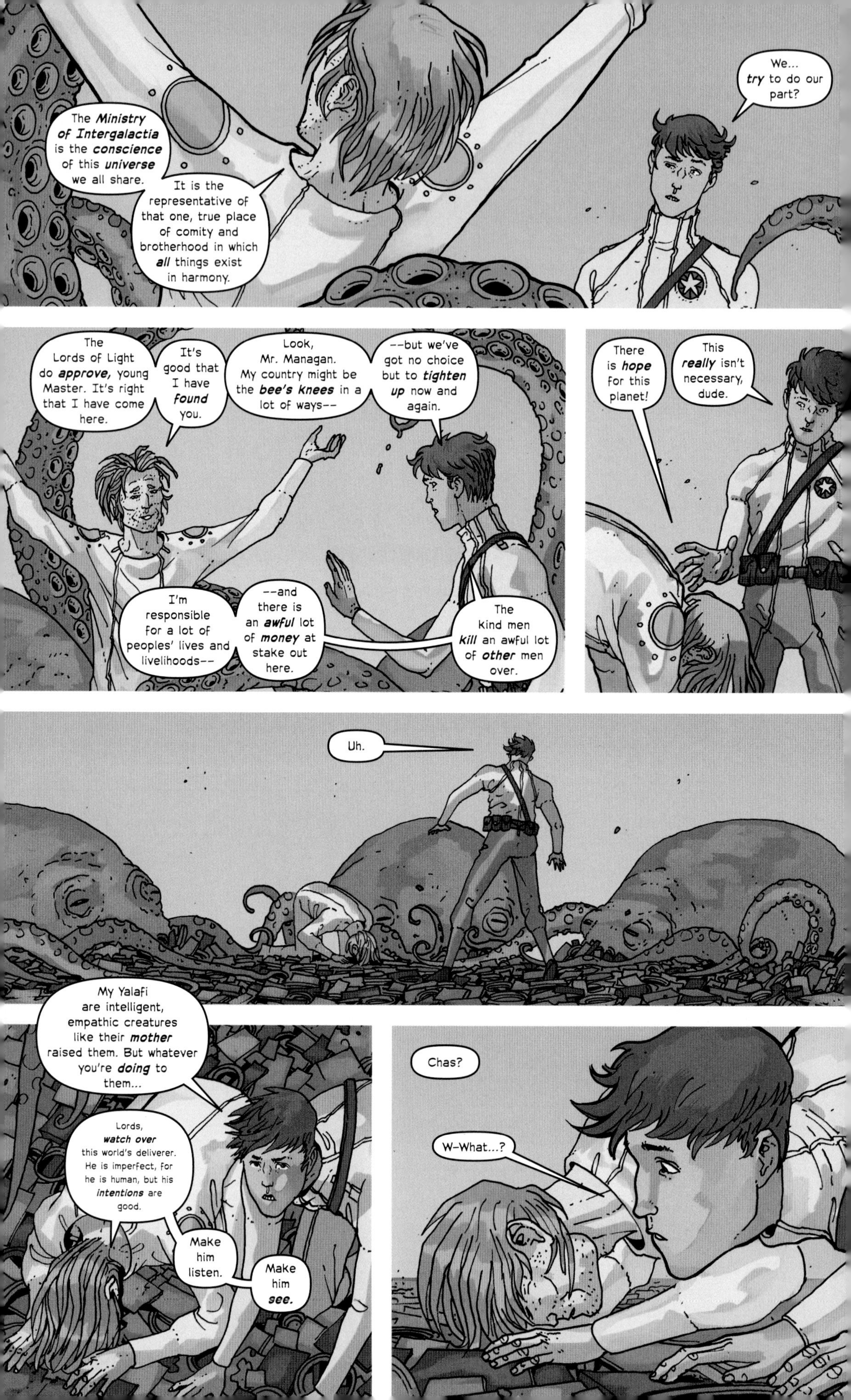
The Ministry of Intergalactia is the conscience of this universe we all share.
It is the representative of that one, true place of comity and brotherhood in which all things exist in harmony.
We... try to do our part?
The Lords of Light do approve, young Master. It's right that I have come here.
It's good that I have found you.
Look, Mr. Managan. My country might be the bee's knees in a lot of ways--
--but we've got no choice but to tighten up now and again.
I'm responsible for a lot of peoples' lives and livelihoods--
--and there is an awful lot of money at stake out here.
The kind men kill an awful lot of other men over.
There is hope for this planet!
This really isn't necessary, dude.
Uh.
My Yalafi are intelligent, empathic creatures like their mother raised them. But whatever you're doing to them...
Lords, watch over this world's deliverer. He is imperfect, for he is human, but his intentions are good.
Make him listen.
Make him see.
Chas?
W-What...?

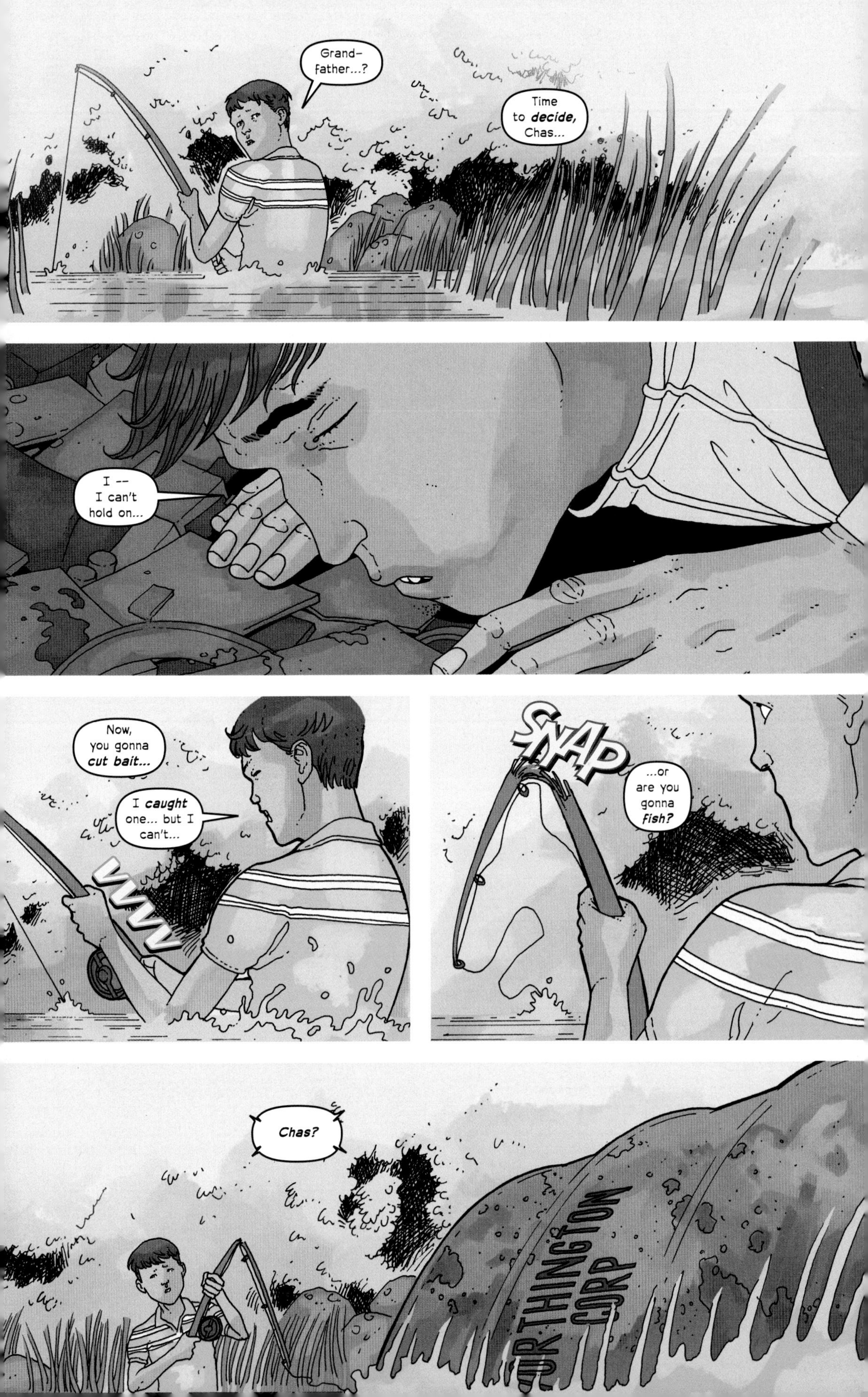
Grand-father...?
Time to decide, Chas...
I -- I can't hold on...
Now, you gonna cut bait...
I caught one... but I can't...
VVVV
SNAP
...or are you gonna fish?
Chas?
CORP

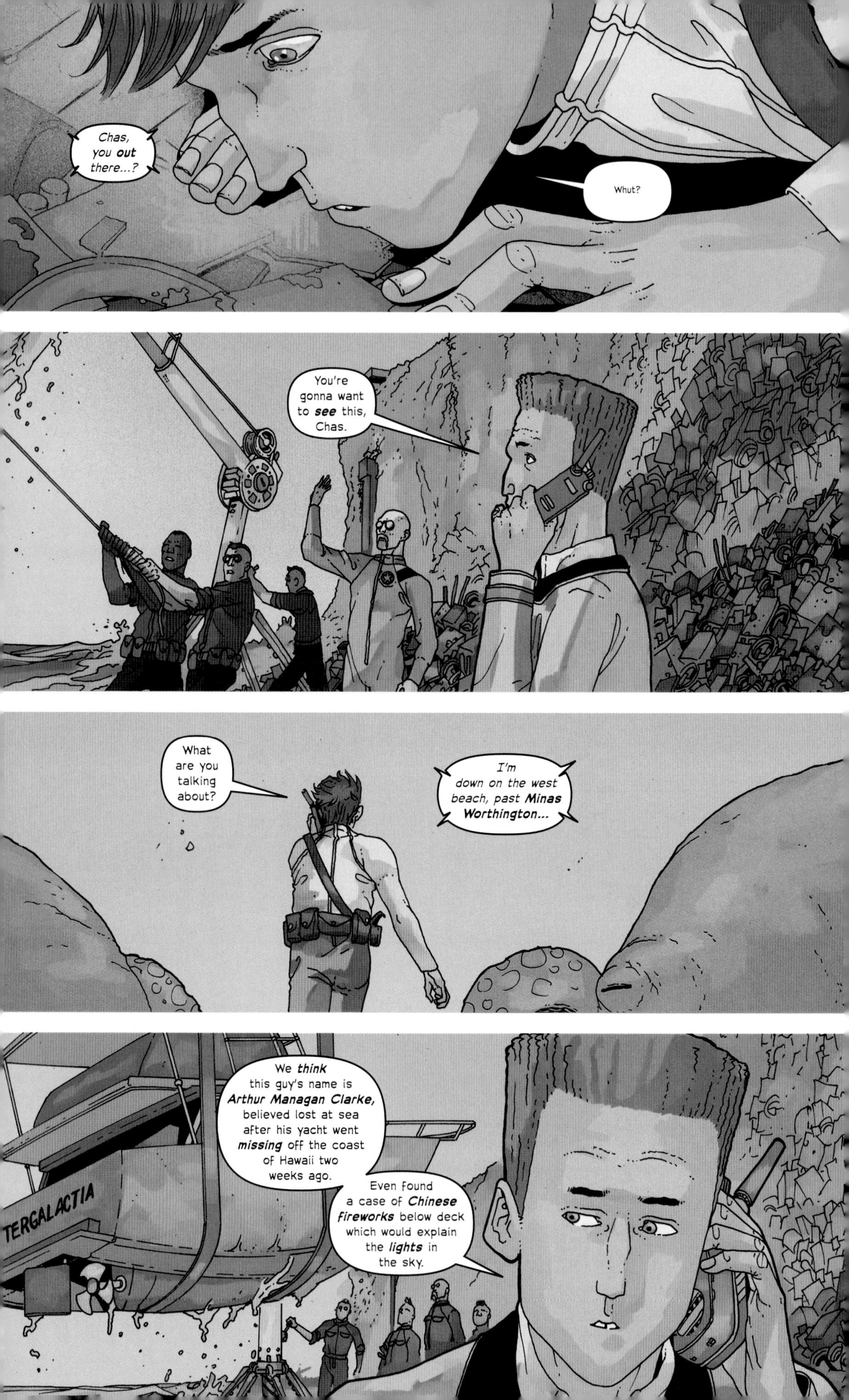
Chas, you out there...?
Whut?
You're gonna want to see this, Chas.
What are you talking about?
I'm down on the west beach, past Minas Worthington...
We think this guy's name is Arthur Managan Clarke, believed lost at sea after his yacht went missing off the coast of Hawaii two weeks ago.
Even found a case of Chinese fireworks below deck which would explain the lights in the sky.
TERGALACTIA

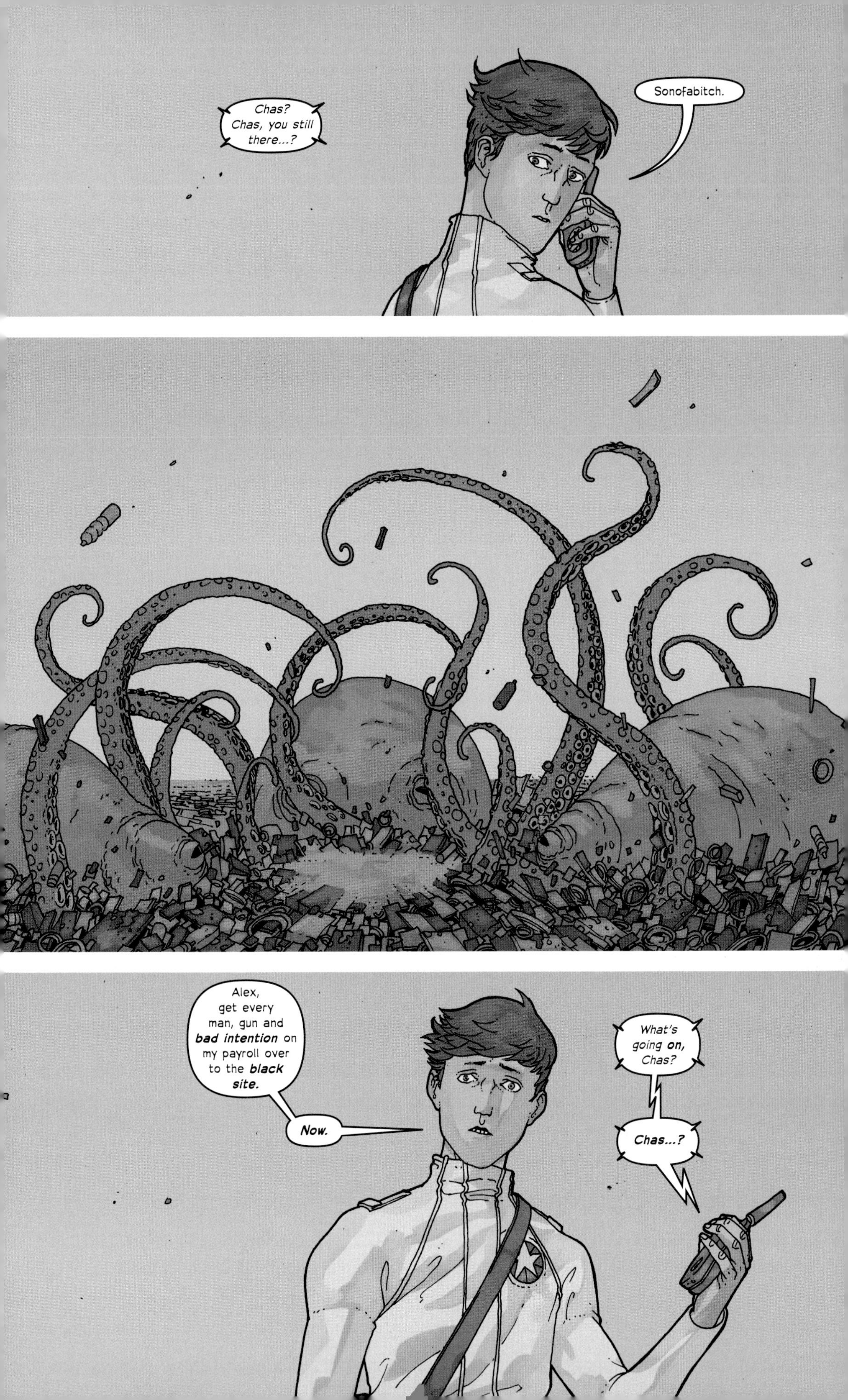
Chas? Chas, you still there...?
Sonofabitch.
Alex, get every man, gun and bad intention on my payroll over to the black site.
Now.
What's going on, Chas?
Chas...?

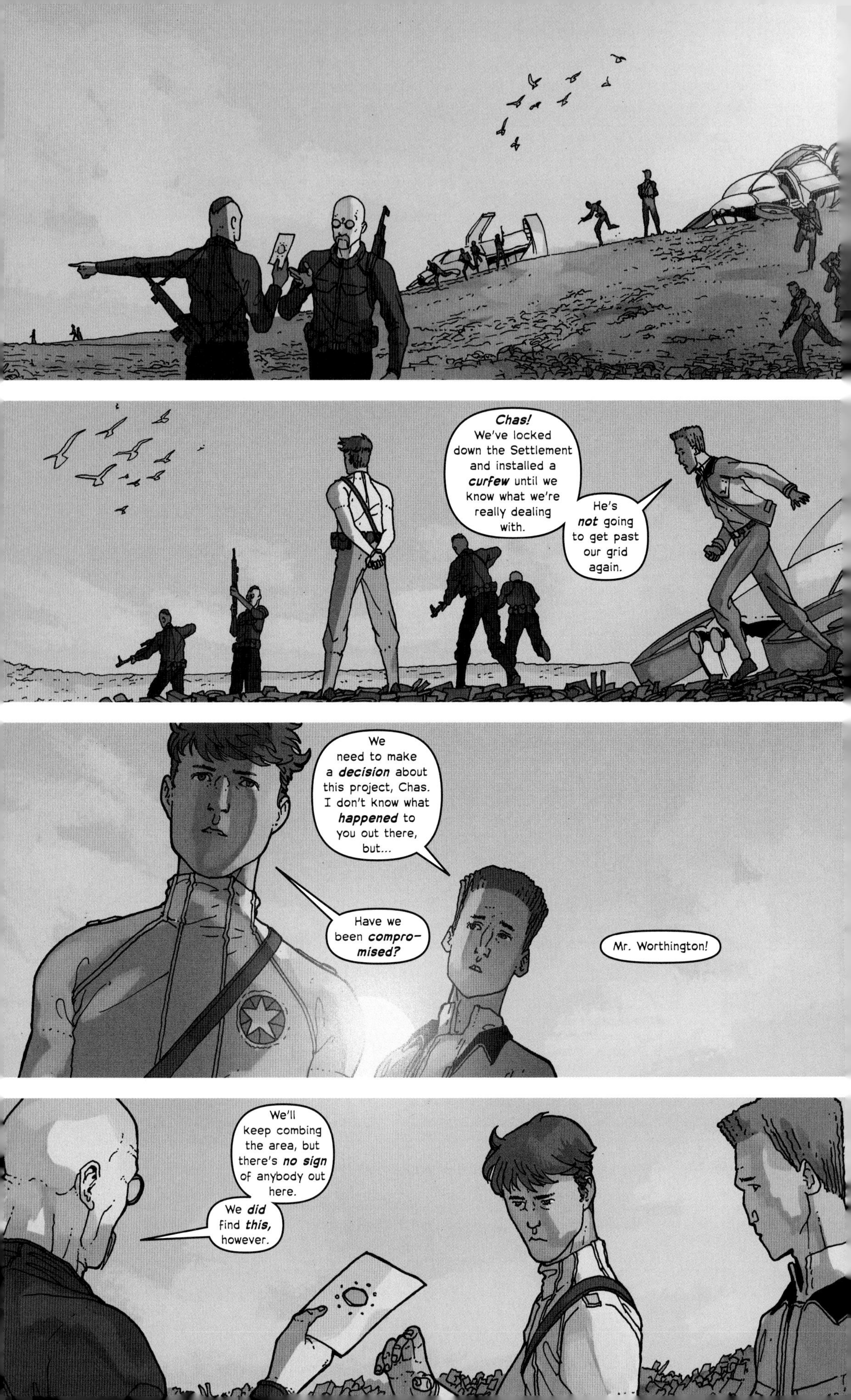
Chas! We've locked down the Settlement and installed a curfew until we know what we're really dealing with.
He's not going to get past our grid again.
We need to make a decision about this project, Chas. I don't know what happened to you out there, but...
Have we been compromised?
Mr. Worthington!
We'll keep combing the area, but there's no sign of anybody out here.
We did find this, however.

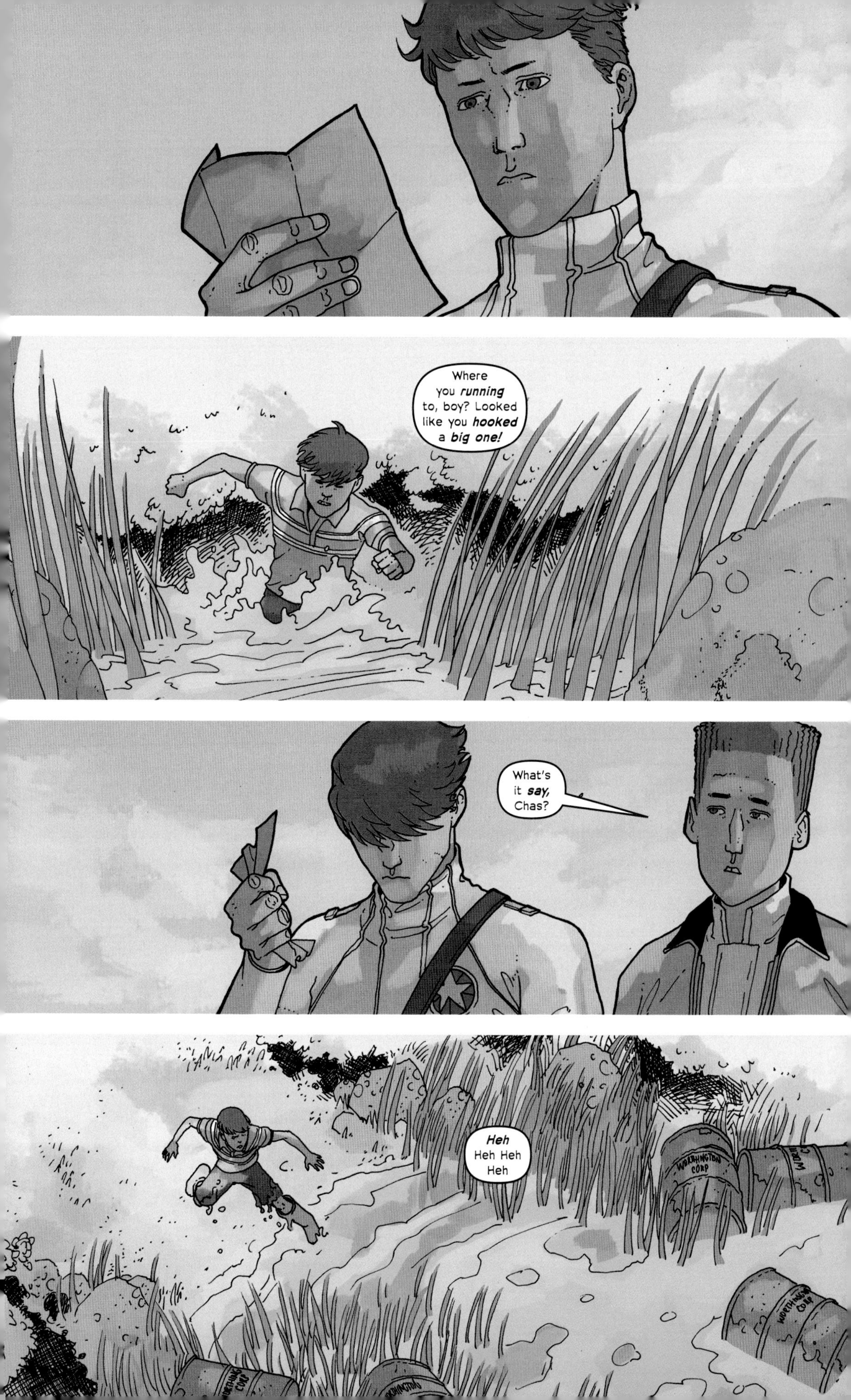
Where you *running* to, boy? Looked like you *hooked* a *big one!*
What's it *say,* Chas?
Heh Heh Heh Heh
WORTHINGTON CORP

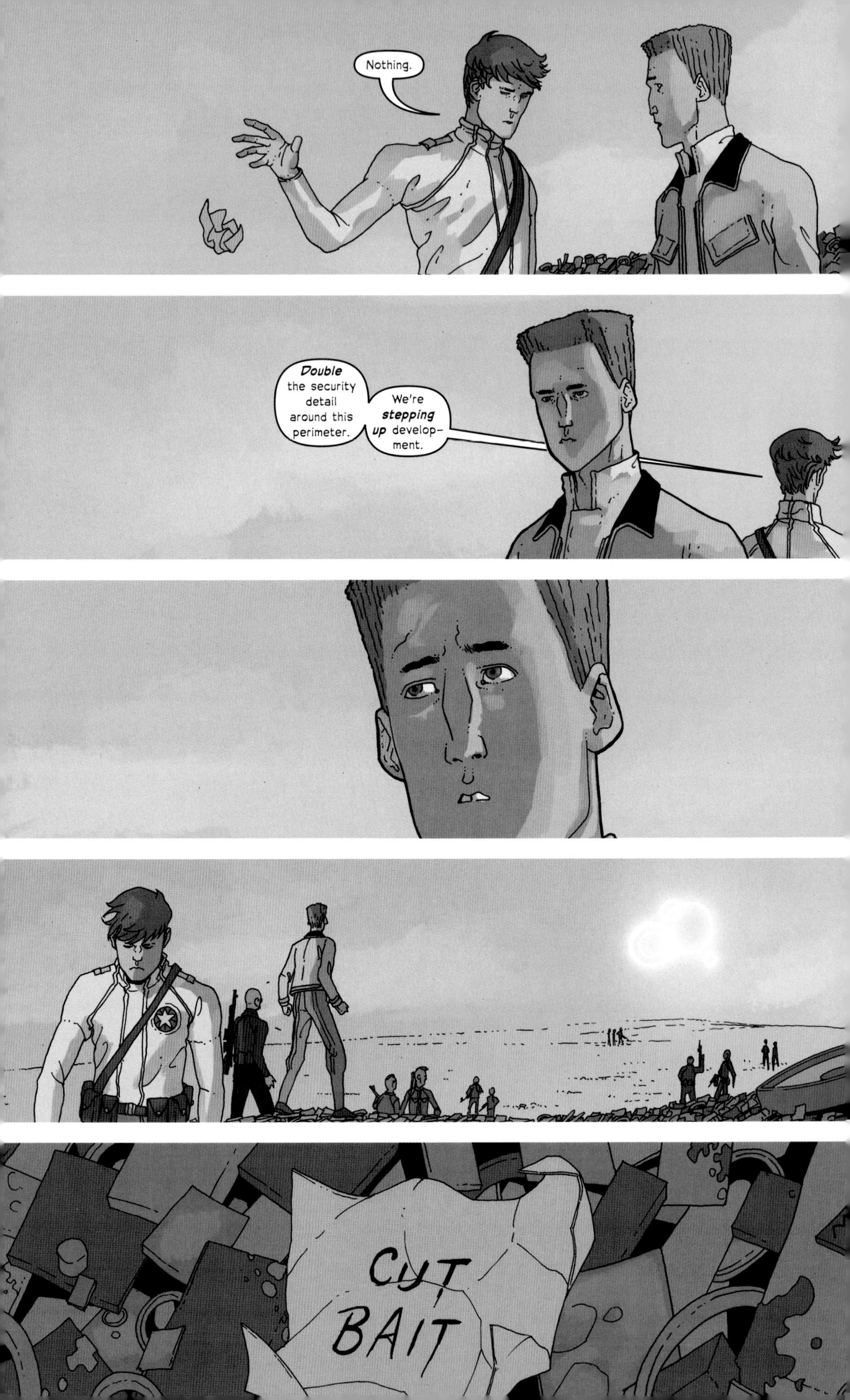
Nothing.
Double the security detail around this perimeter.
We're *stepping up* development.
CUT BAIT

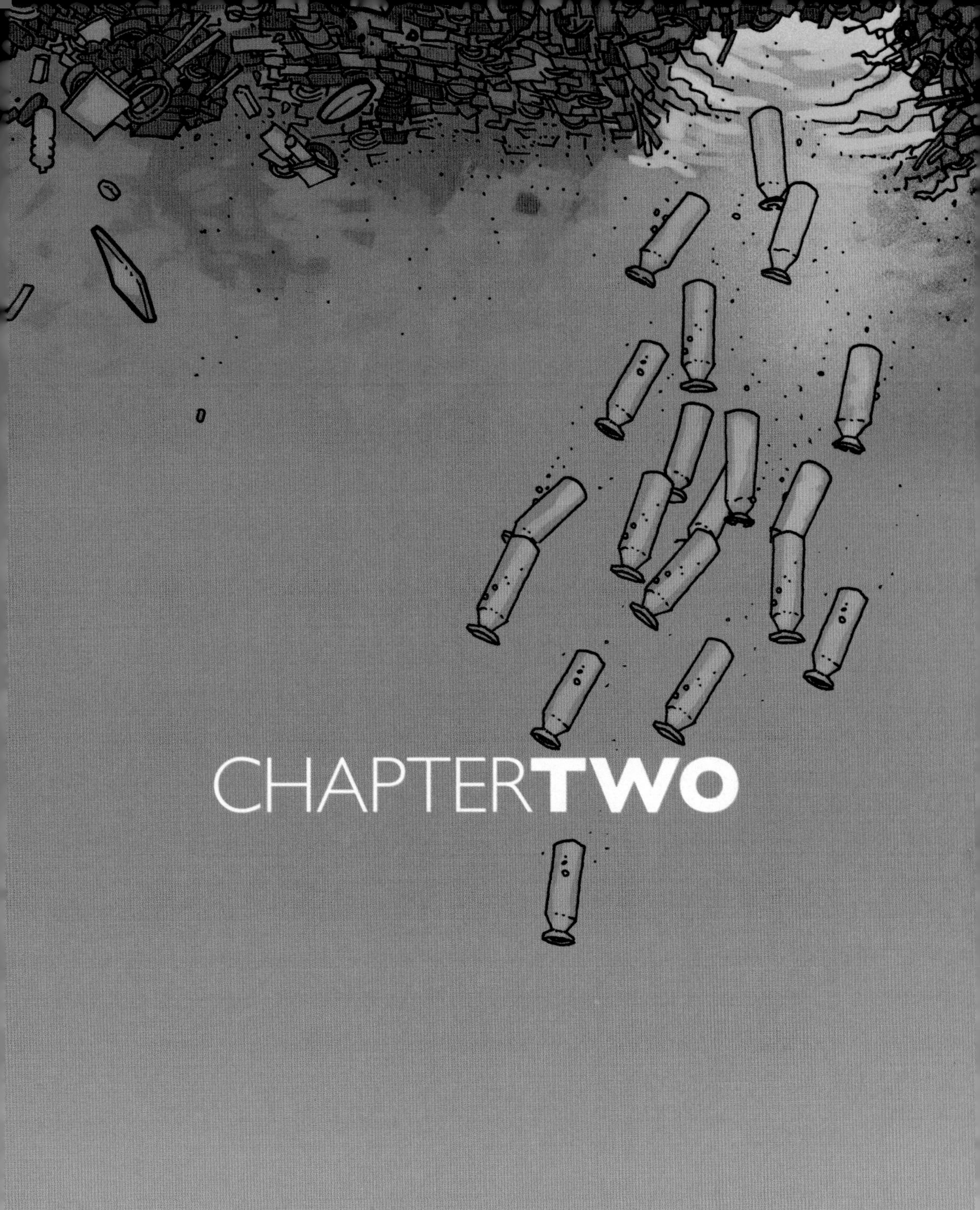

CHAPTER**TWO**

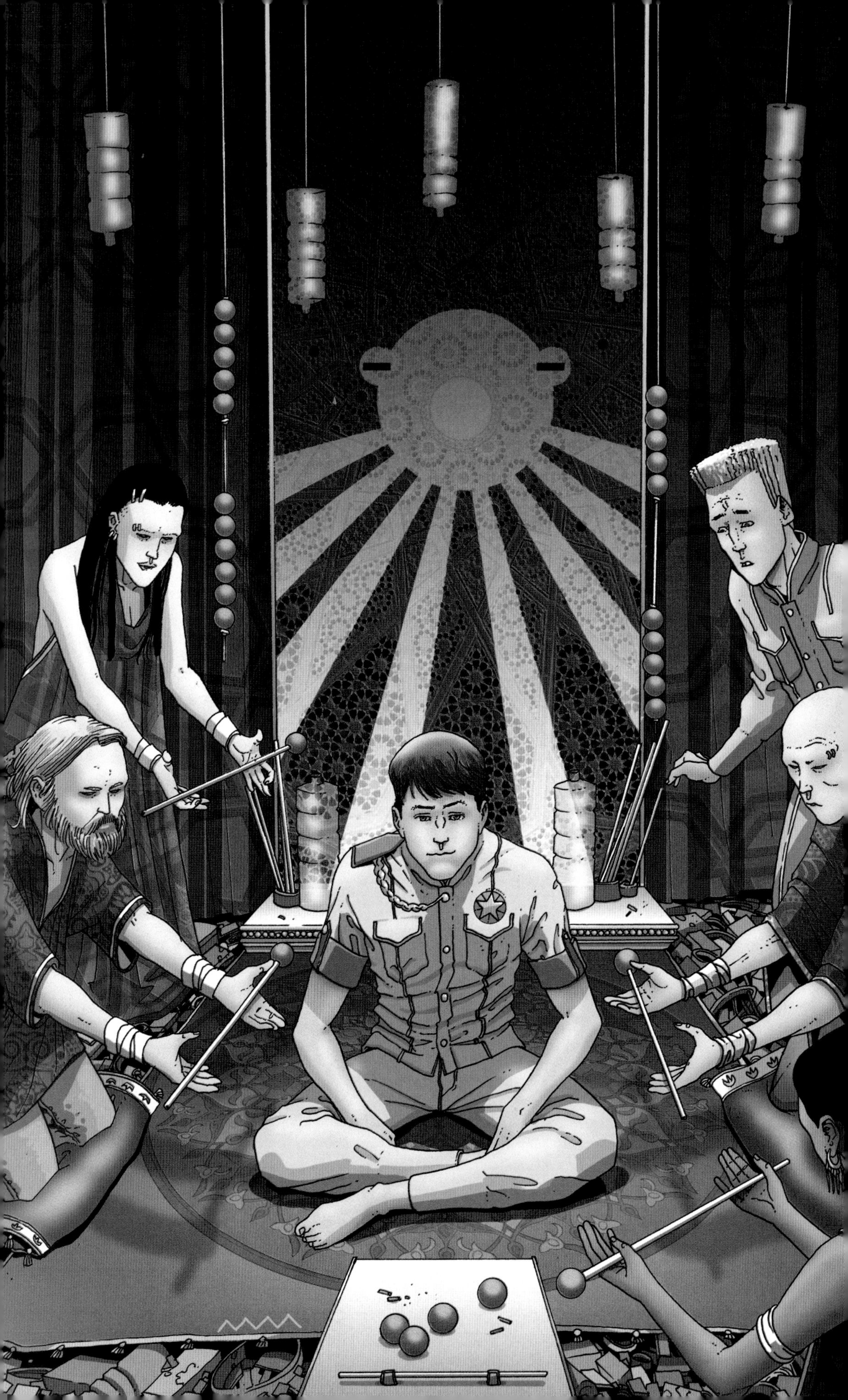

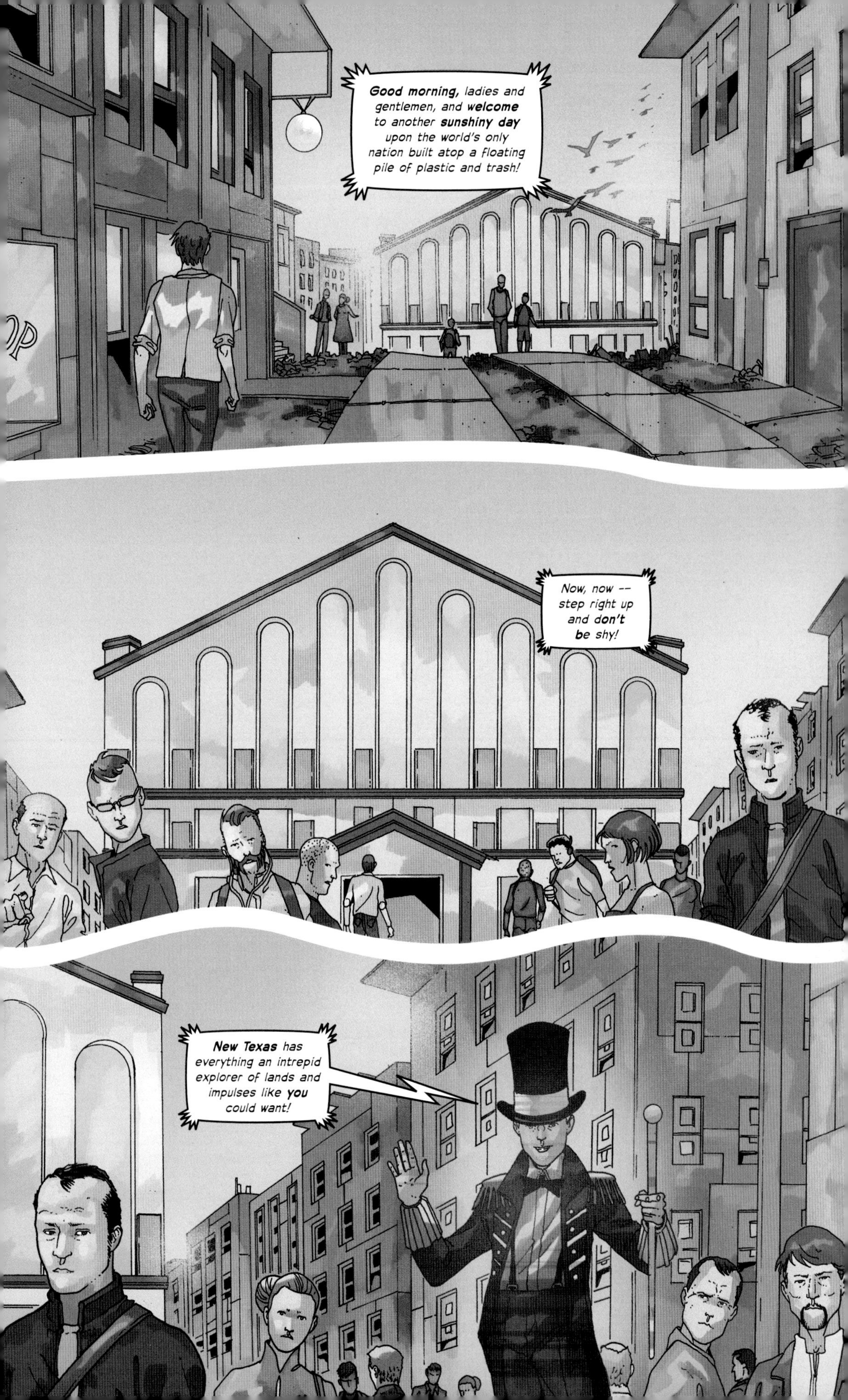
Good morning, ladies and gentlemen, and welcome to another sunshiny day upon the world's only nation built atop a floating pile of plastic and trash!
Now, now -- step right up and don't be shy!
New Texas has everything an intrepid explorer of lands and impulses like you could want!

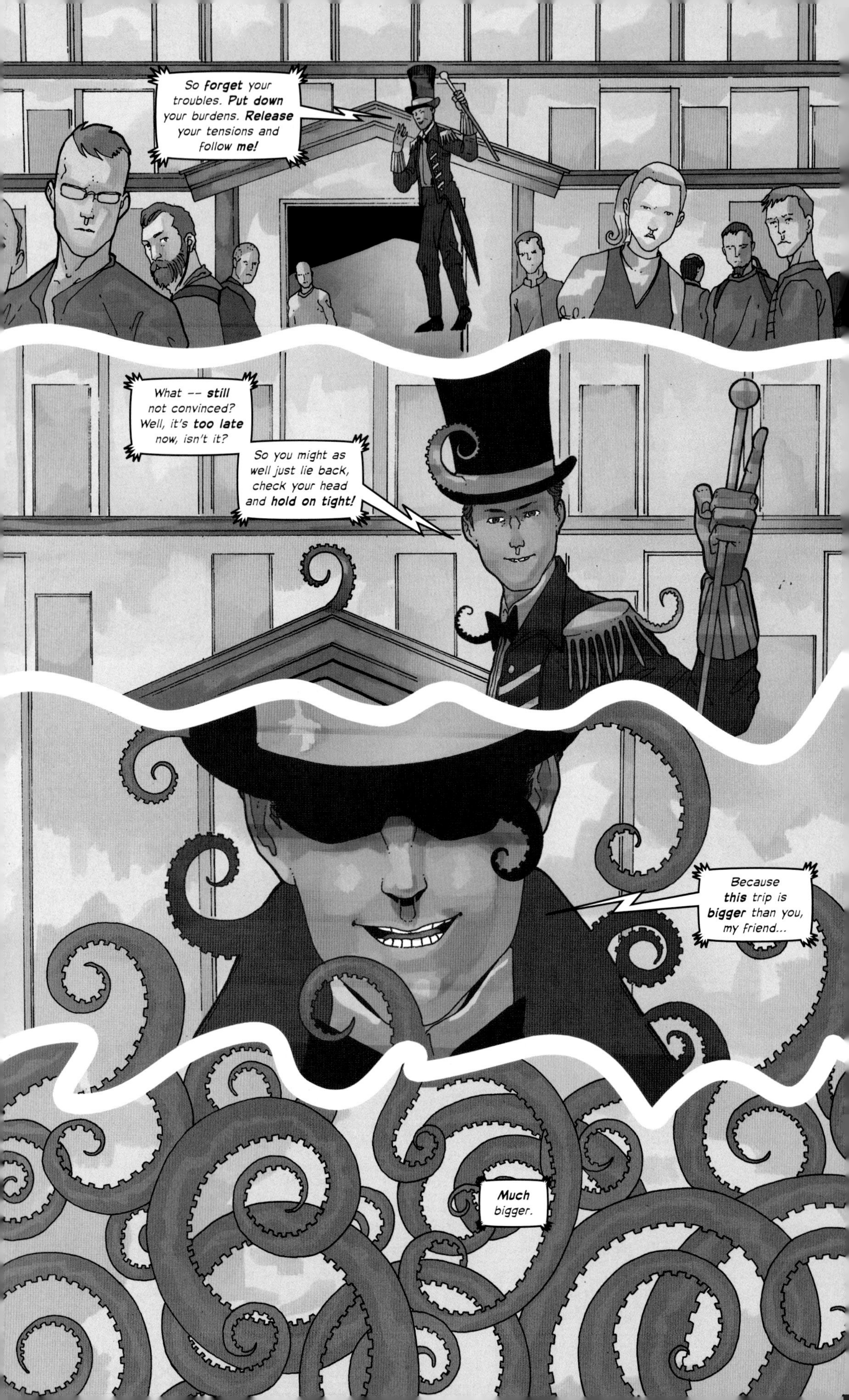
So **forget** your troubles. **Put down** your burdens. **Release** your tensions and follow **me!**
What -- **still** not convinced? Well, it's **too late** now, isn't it?
So you might as well just lie back, check your head and **hold on tight!**
Because **this** trip is **bigger** than you, my friend...
Much bigger.

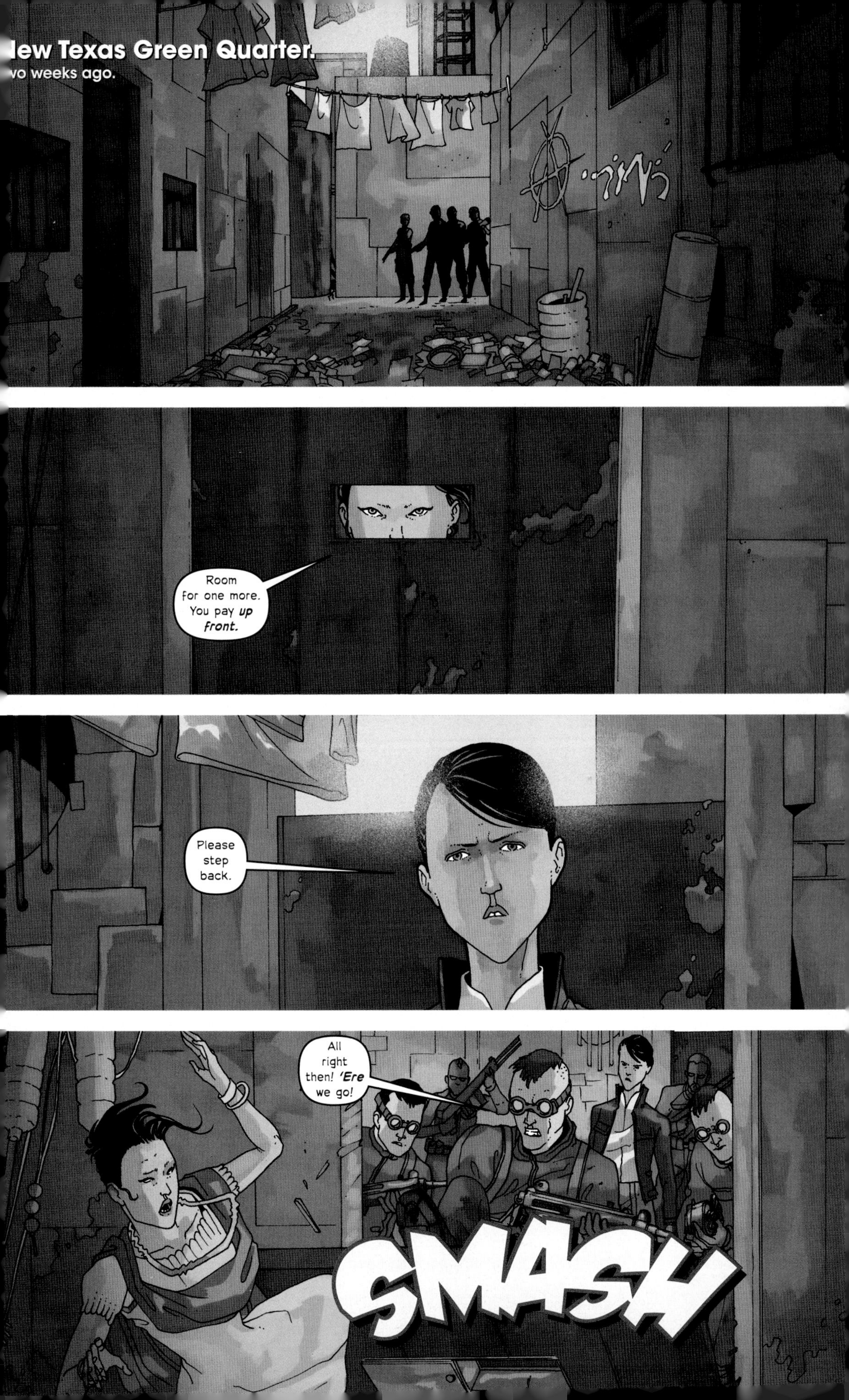
New Texas Green Quarter.
wo weeks ago.
Room for one more. You pay *up front.*
Please step back.
All right then! *'Ere* we go!
SMASH

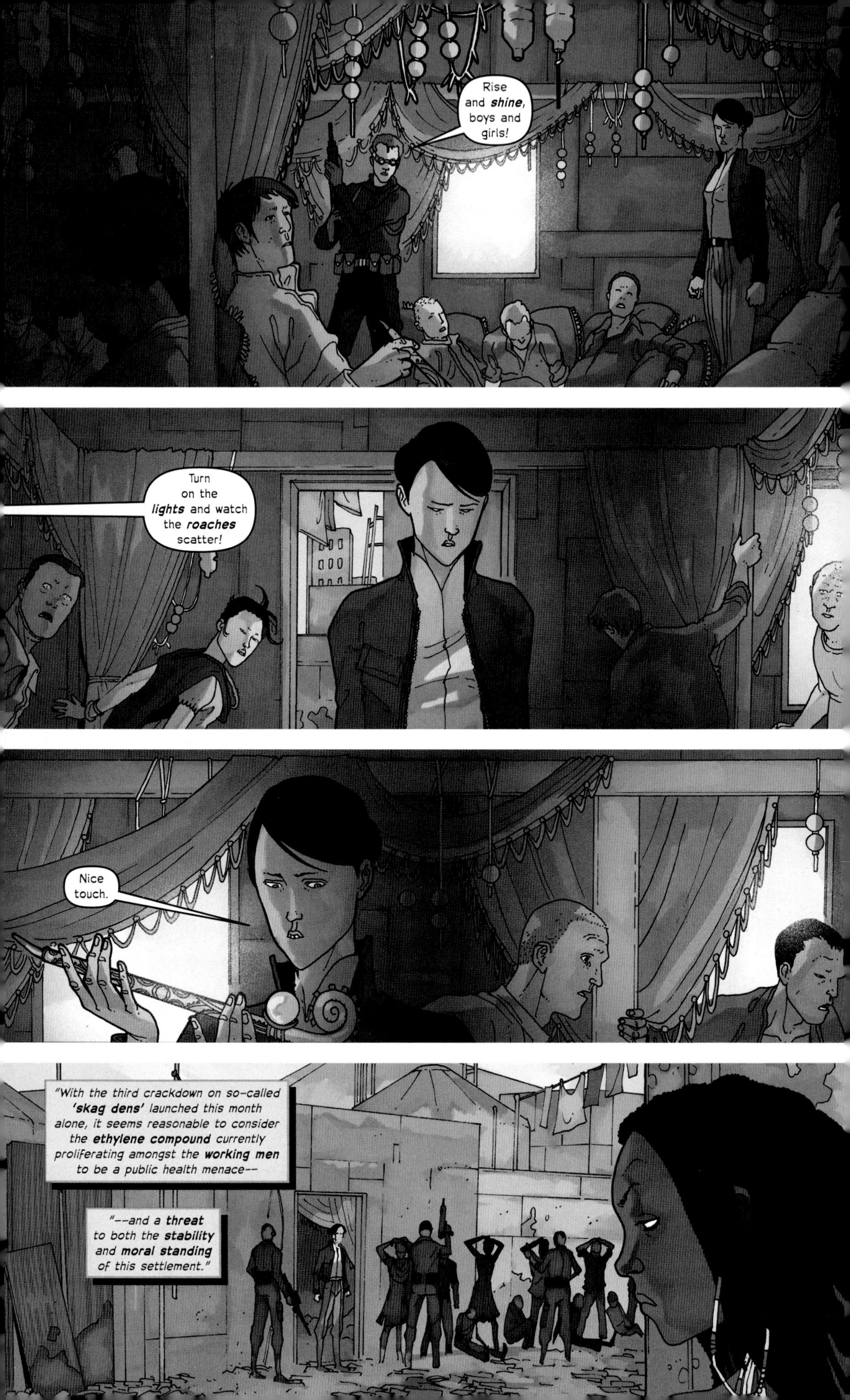
Rise and shine, boys and girls!
Turn on the lights and watch the roaches scatter!
Nice touch.
"With the third crackdown on so-called 'skag dens' launched this month alone, it seems reasonable to consider the ethylene compound currently proliferating amongst the working men to be a public health menace--
"--and a threat to both the stability and moral standing of this settlement."

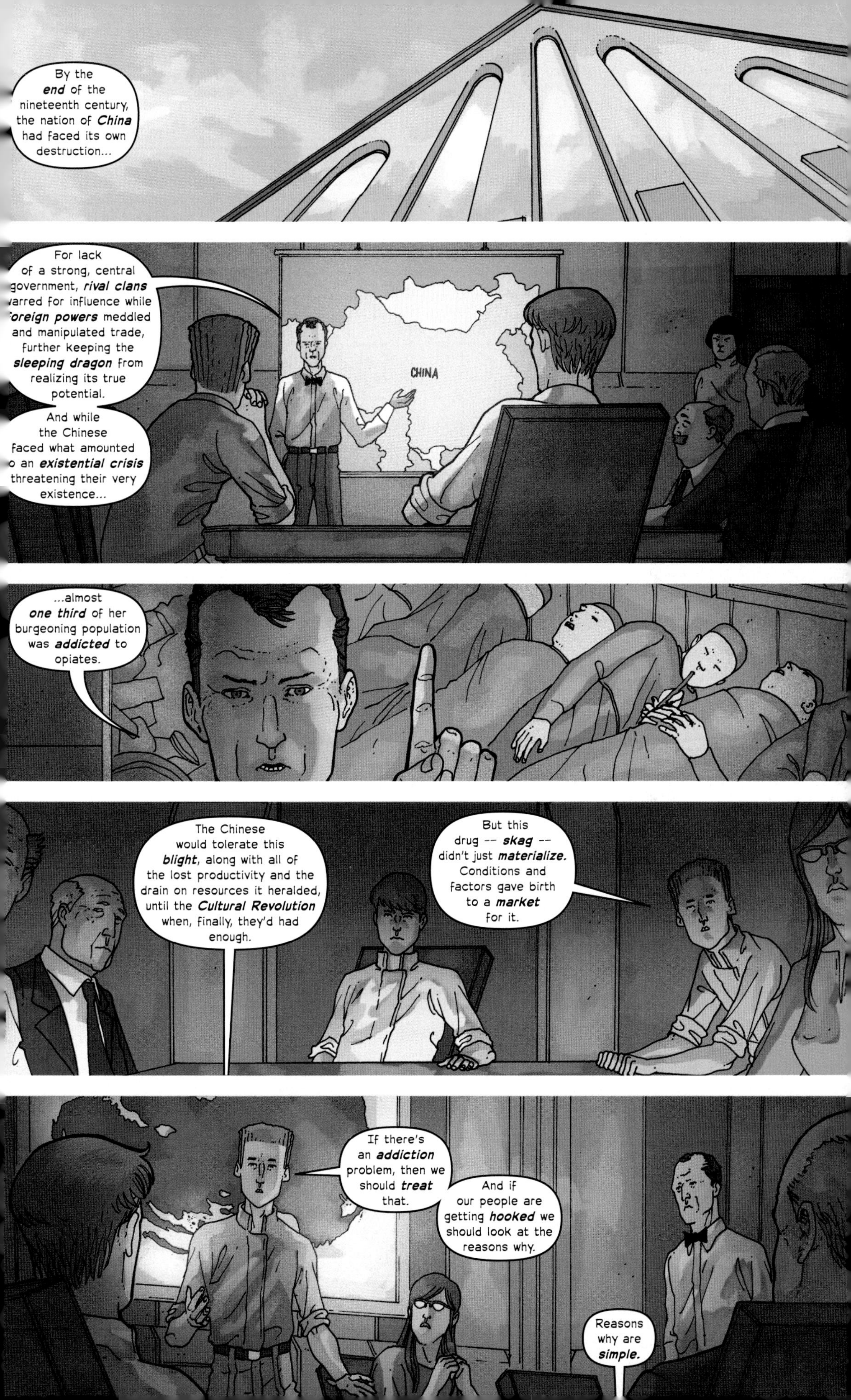
By the end of the nineteenth century, the nation of China had faced its own destruction...
For lack of a strong, central government, rival clans varred for influence while oreign powers meddled and manipulated trade, further keeping the sleeping dragon from realizing its true potential.
CHINA
And while the Chinese faced what amounted o an existential crisis threatening their very existence...
...almost one third of her burgeoning population was addicted to opiates.
The Chinese would tolerate this blight, along with all of the lost productivity and the drain on resources it heralded, until the Cultural Revolution when, finally, they'd had enough.
But this drug -- skag -- didn't just materialize. Conditions and factors gave birth to a market for it.
If there's an addiction problem, then we should treat that.
And if our people are getting hooked we should look at the reasons why.
Reasons why are simple.

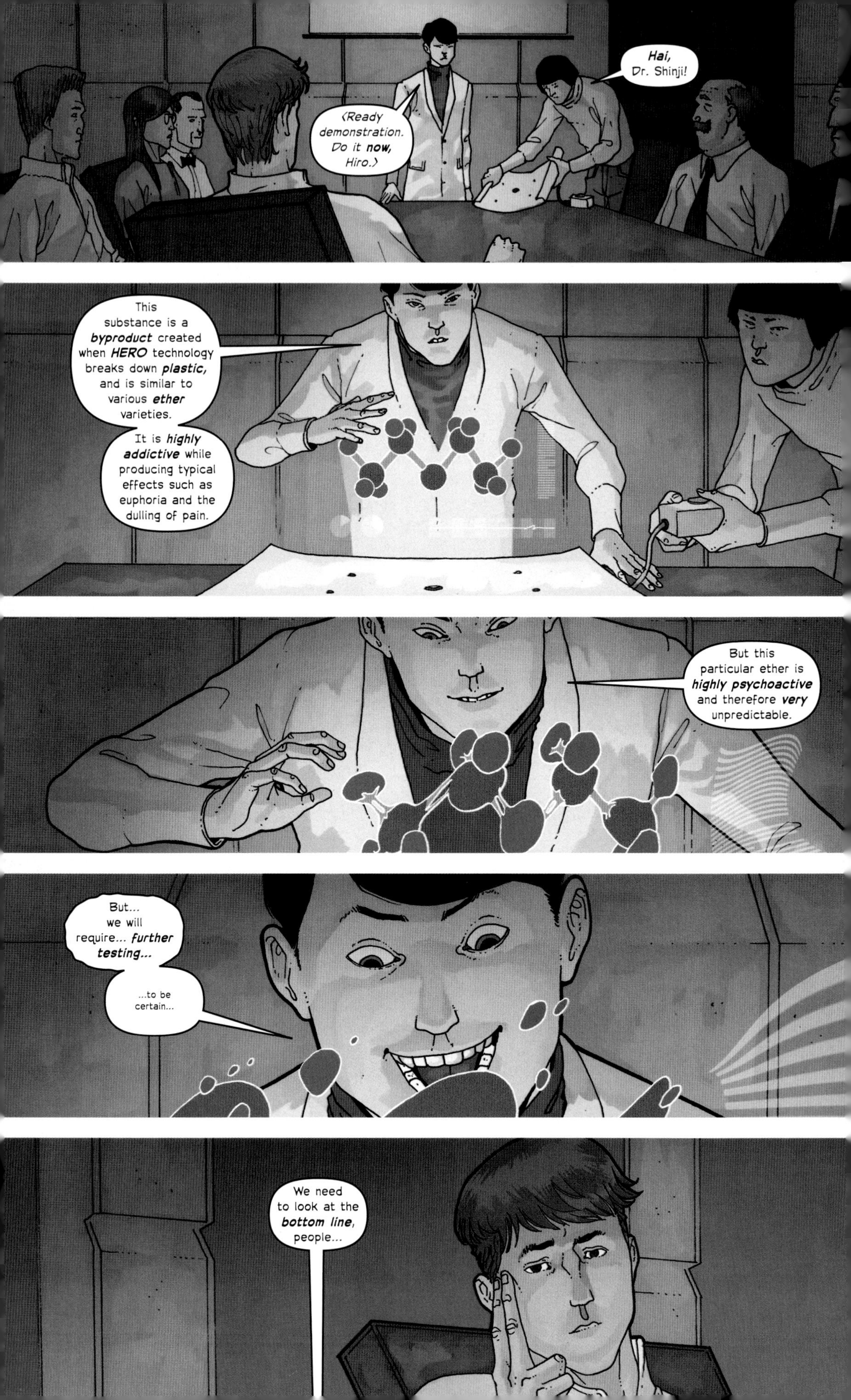
‹Ready demonstration. Do it **now,** Hiro.›
Hai, Dr. Shinji!
This substance is a ***byproduct*** created when ***HERO*** technology breaks down ***plastic,*** and is similar to various ***ether*** varieties.
It is ***highly addictive*** while producing typical effects such as euphoria and the dulling of pain.
But this particular ether is ***highly psychoactive*** and therefore ***very*** unpredictable.
But... we will require... ***further testing...***
...to be certain...
We need to look at the ***bottom line,*** people...

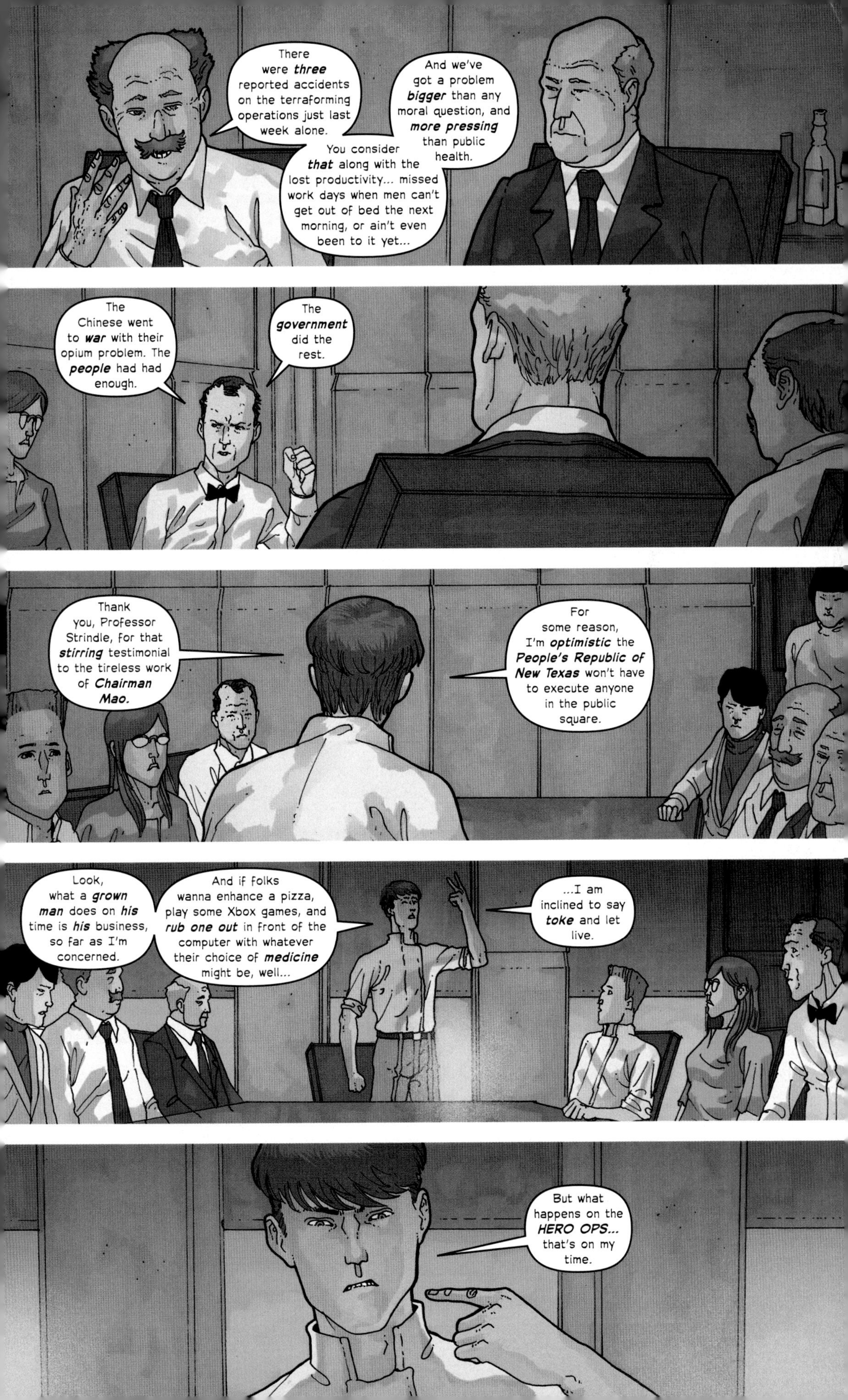
There were *three* reported accidents on the terraforming operations just last week alone.
You consider *that* along with the lost productivity... missed work days when men can't get out of bed the next morning, or ain't even been to it yet...
And we've got a problem *bigger* than any moral question, and *more pressing* than public health.
The Chinese went to *war* with their opium problem. The *people* had had enough.
The *government* did the rest.
Thank you, Professor Strindle, for that *stirring* testimonial to the tireless work of *Chairman Mao.*
For some reason, I'm *optimistic* the *People's Republic of New Texas* won't have to execute anyone in the public square.
Look, what a *grown man* does on *his* time is *his* business, so far as I'm concerned.
And if folks wanna enhance a pizza, play some Xbox games, and *rub one out* in front of the computer with whatever their choice of *medicine* might be, well...
...I am inclined to say *toke* and let live.
But what happens on the *HERO OPS...* that's on my time.

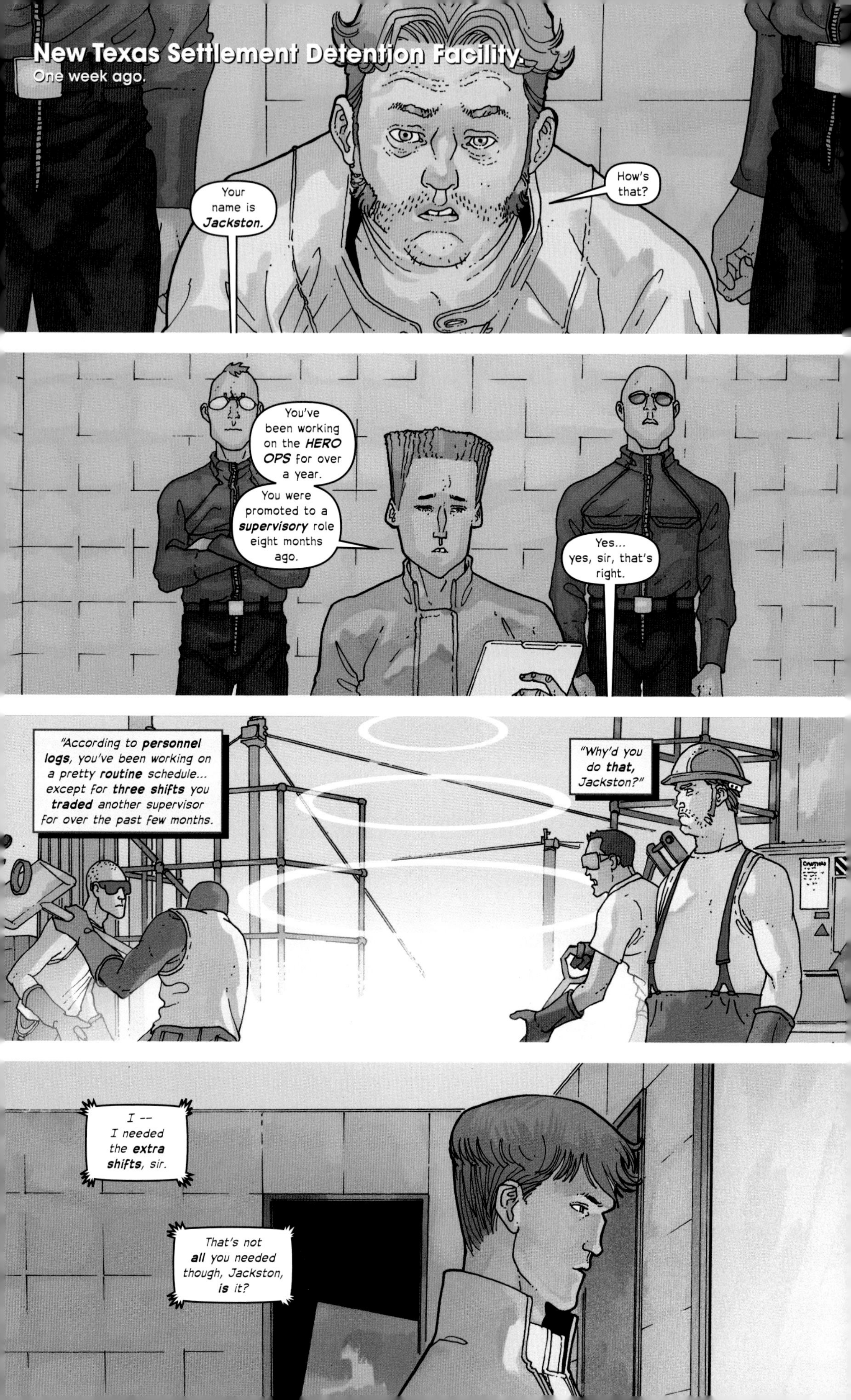
New Texas Settlement Detention Facility.
One week ago.
Your name is Jackston.
How's that?
You've been working on the HERO OPS for over a year.
You were promoted to a supervisory role eight months ago.
Yes... yes, sir, that's right.
"According to personnel logs, you've been working on a pretty routine schedule... except for three shifts you traded another supervisor for over the past few months.
"Why'd you do that, Jackston?"
I -- I needed the extra shifts, sir.
That's not all you needed though, Jackston, is it?

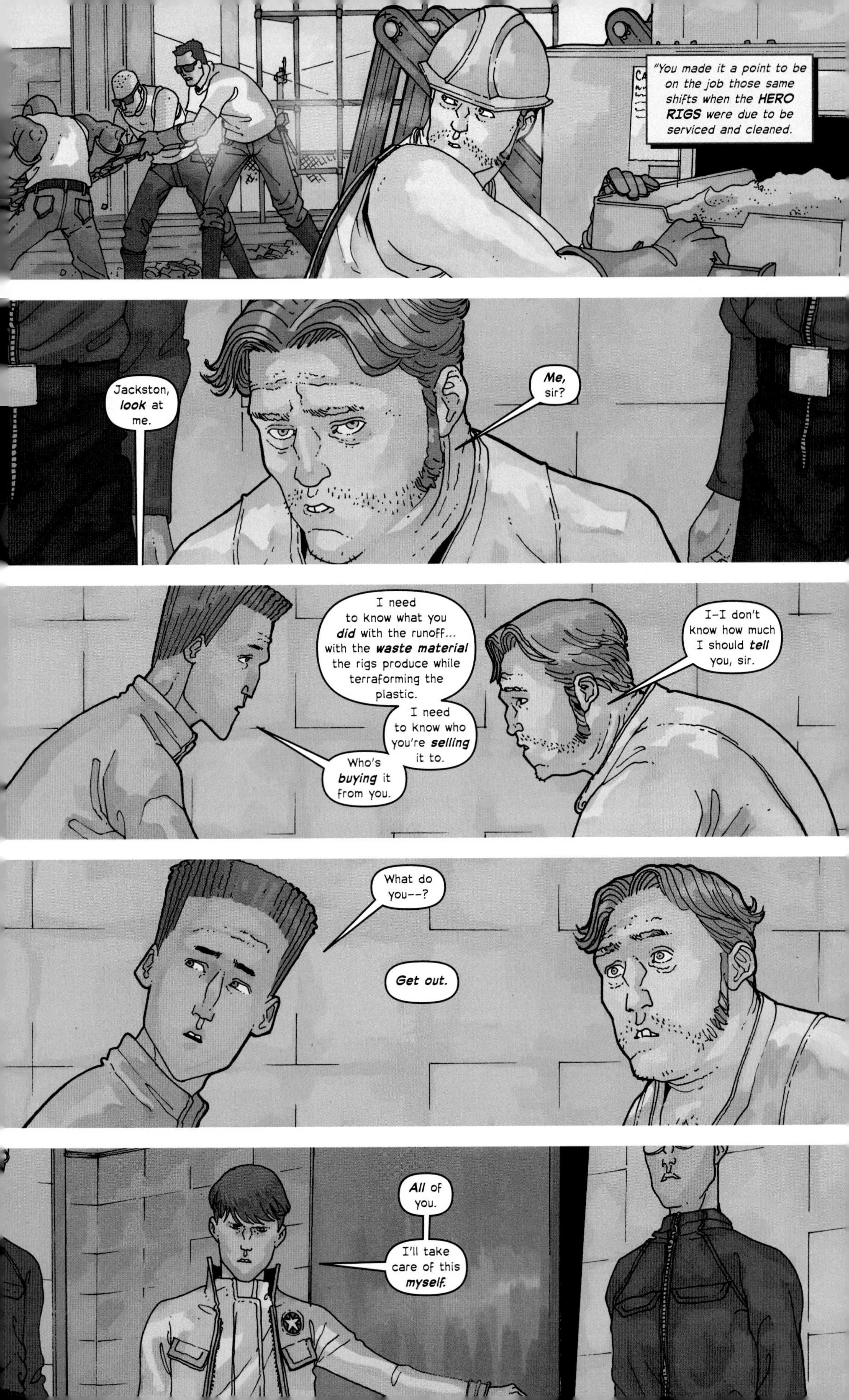
"You made it a point to be on the job those same shifts when the HERO RIGS were due to be serviced and cleaned.
Jackston, look at me.
Me, sir?
I need to know what you did with the runoff... with the waste material the rigs produce while terraforming the plastic.
I need to know who you're selling it to.
Who's buying it from you.
I-I don't know how much I should tell you, sir.
What do you--?
Get out.
All of you.
I'll take care of this myself.

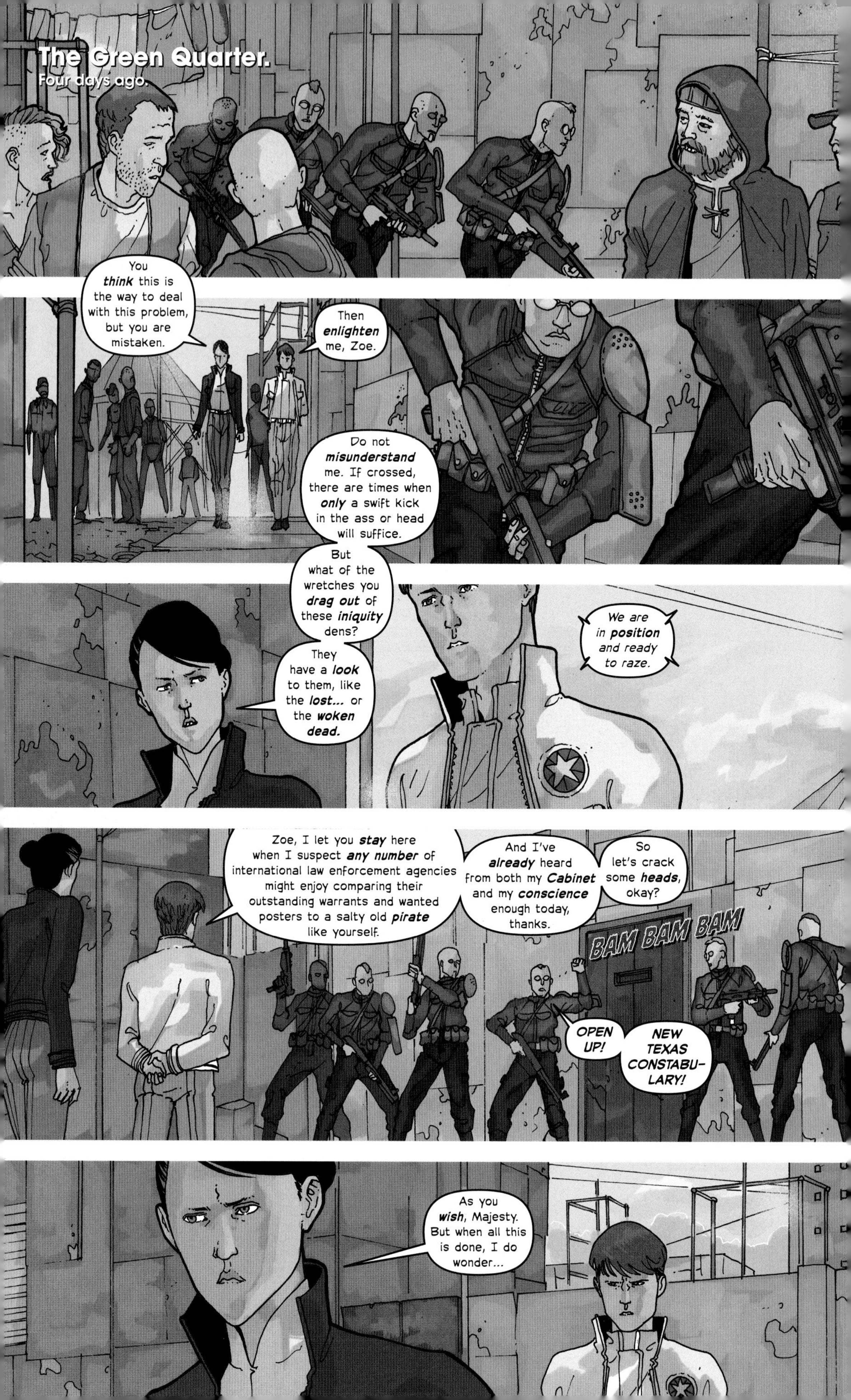
The Green Quarter.
Four days ago.
You think this is the way to deal with this problem, but you are mistaken.
Then enlighten me, Zoe.
Do not misunderstand me. If crossed, there are times when only a swift kick in the ass or head will suffice.
But what of the wretches you drag out of these iniquity dens?
They have a look to them, like the lost... or the woken dead.
We are in position and ready to raze.
Zoe, I let you stay here when I suspect any number of international law enforcement agencies might enjoy comparing their outstanding warrants and wanted posters to a salty old pirate like yourself.
And I've already heard from both my Cabinet and my conscience enough today, thanks.
So let's crack some heads, okay?
BAM BAM BAM
OPEN UP!
NEW TEXAS CONSTABULARY!
As you wish, Majesty. But when all this is done, I do wonder...

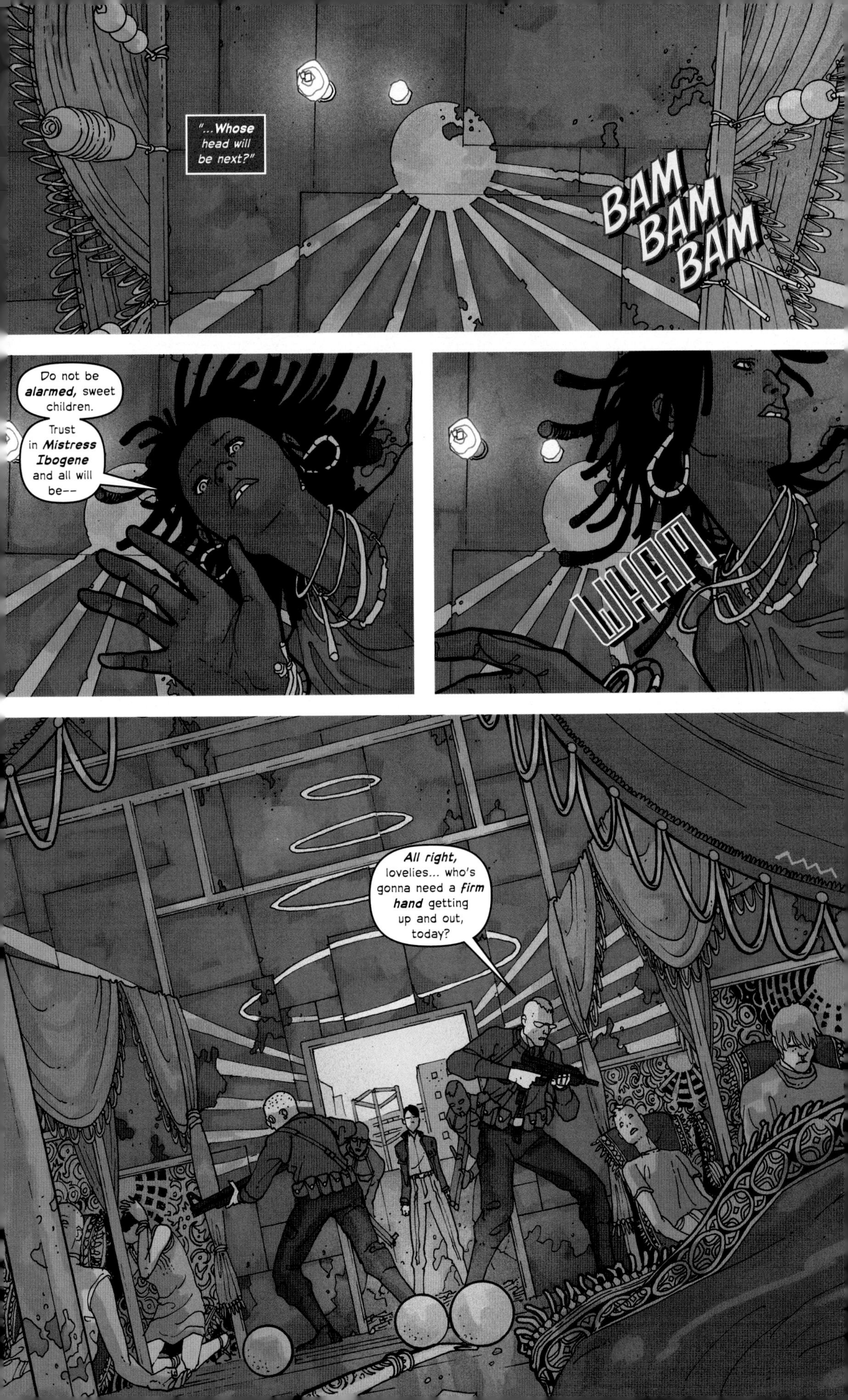
"...Whose head will be next?"
BAM BAM BAM
Do not be alarmed, sweet children.
Trust in Mistress Ibogene and all will be--
WHAM
All right, lovelies... who's gonna need a firm hand getting up and out, today?

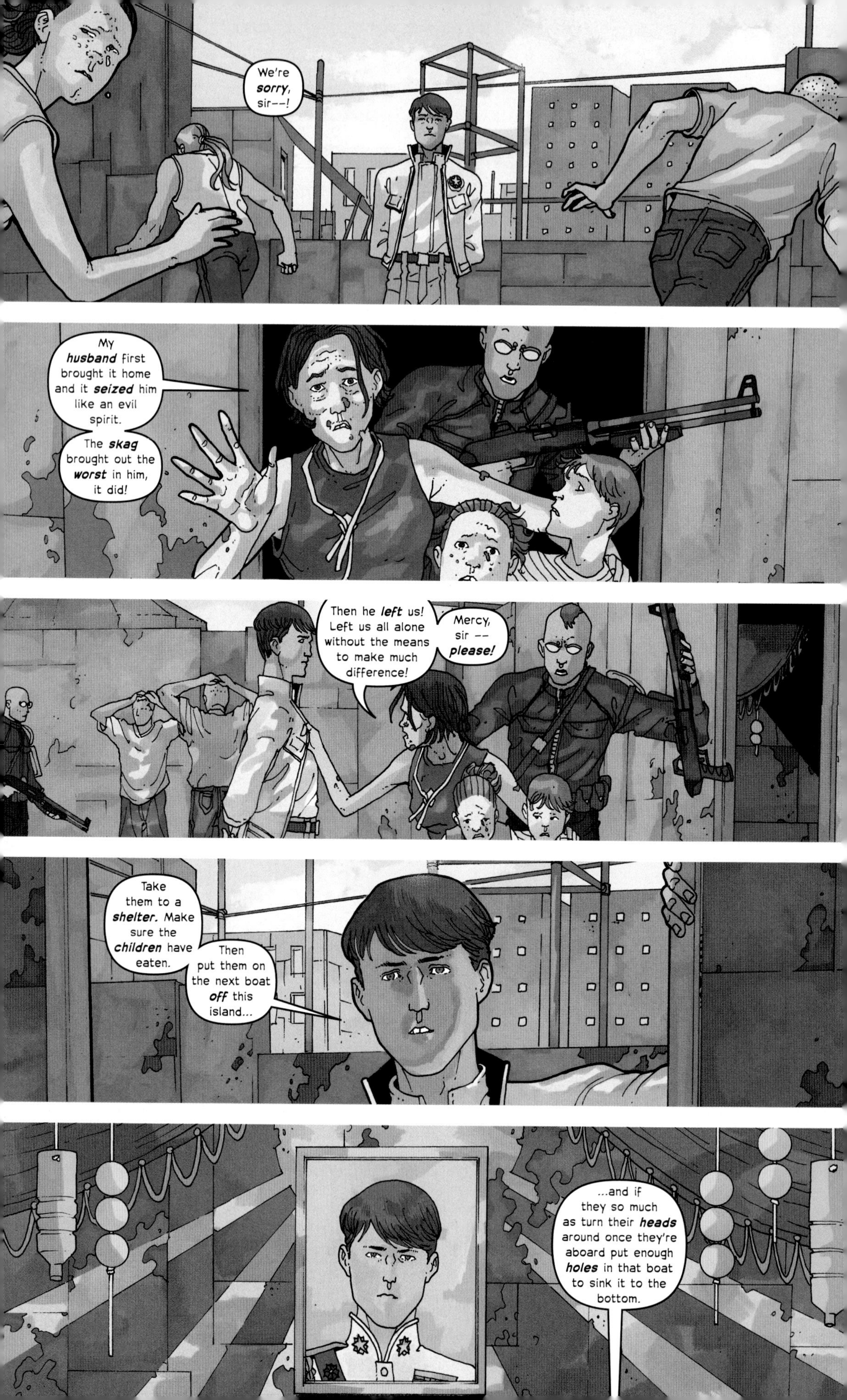
We're *sorry*, sir--!
My *husband* first brought it home and it *seized* him like an evil spirit.
The *skag* brought out the *worst* in him, it did!
Then he *left* us! Left us all alone without the means to make much difference!
Mercy, sir -- *please!*
Take them to a *shelter.* Make sure the *children* have eaten.
Then put them on the next boat *off* this island...
...and if they so much as turn their *heads* around once they're aboard put enough *holes* in that boat to sink it to the bottom.

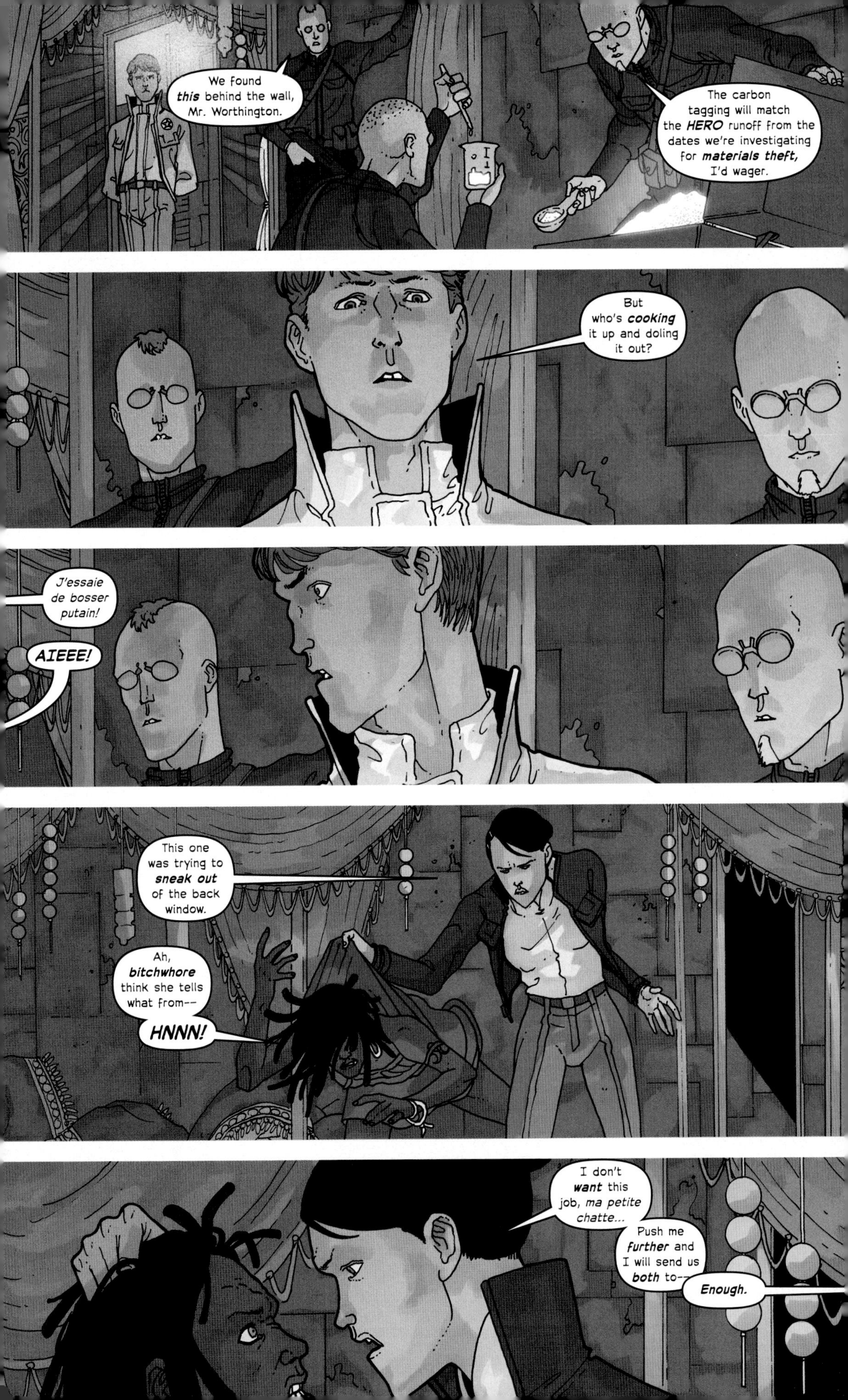
We found *this* behind the wall, Mr. Worthington.
The carbon tagging will match the *HERO* runoff from the dates we're investigating for *materials theft,* I'd wager.
But who's *cooking* it up and doling it out?
J'essaie de bosser putain!
AIEEE!
This one was trying to *sneak out* of the back window.
Ah, *bitchwhore* think she tells what from--
HNNN!
I don't *want* this job, *ma petite chatte...*
Push me *further* and I will send us *both* to--
Enough.

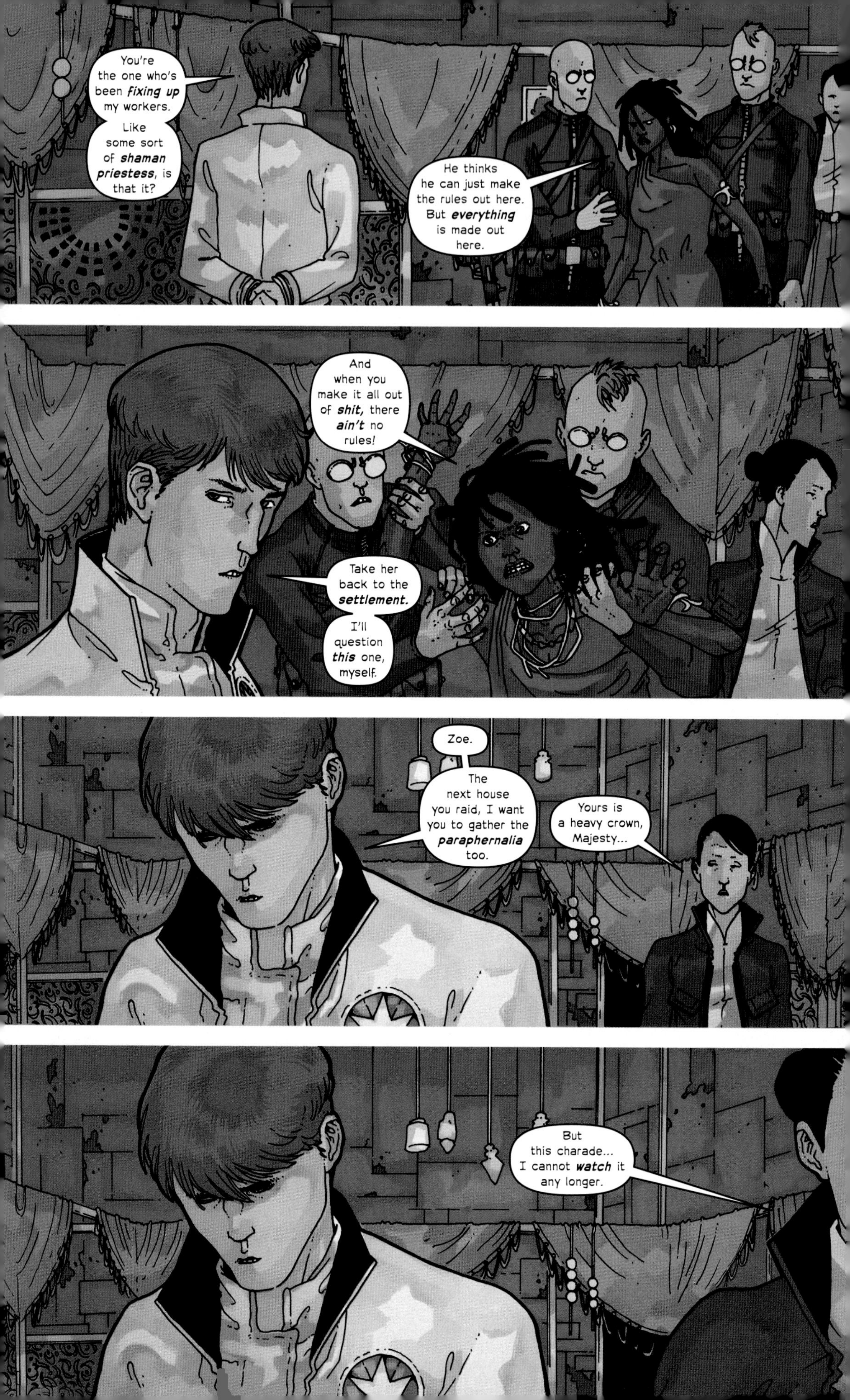

You're the one who's been *fixing up* my workers.
Like some sort of *shaman priestess*, is that it?
He thinks he can just make the rules out here. But *everything* is made out here.
And when you make it all out of *shit,* there *ain't* no rules!
Take her back to the *settlement.*
I'll question *this* one, myself.
Zoe.
The next house you raid, I want you to gather the *paraphernalia* too.
Yours is a heavy crown, Majesty...
But this charade... I cannot *watch* it any longer.

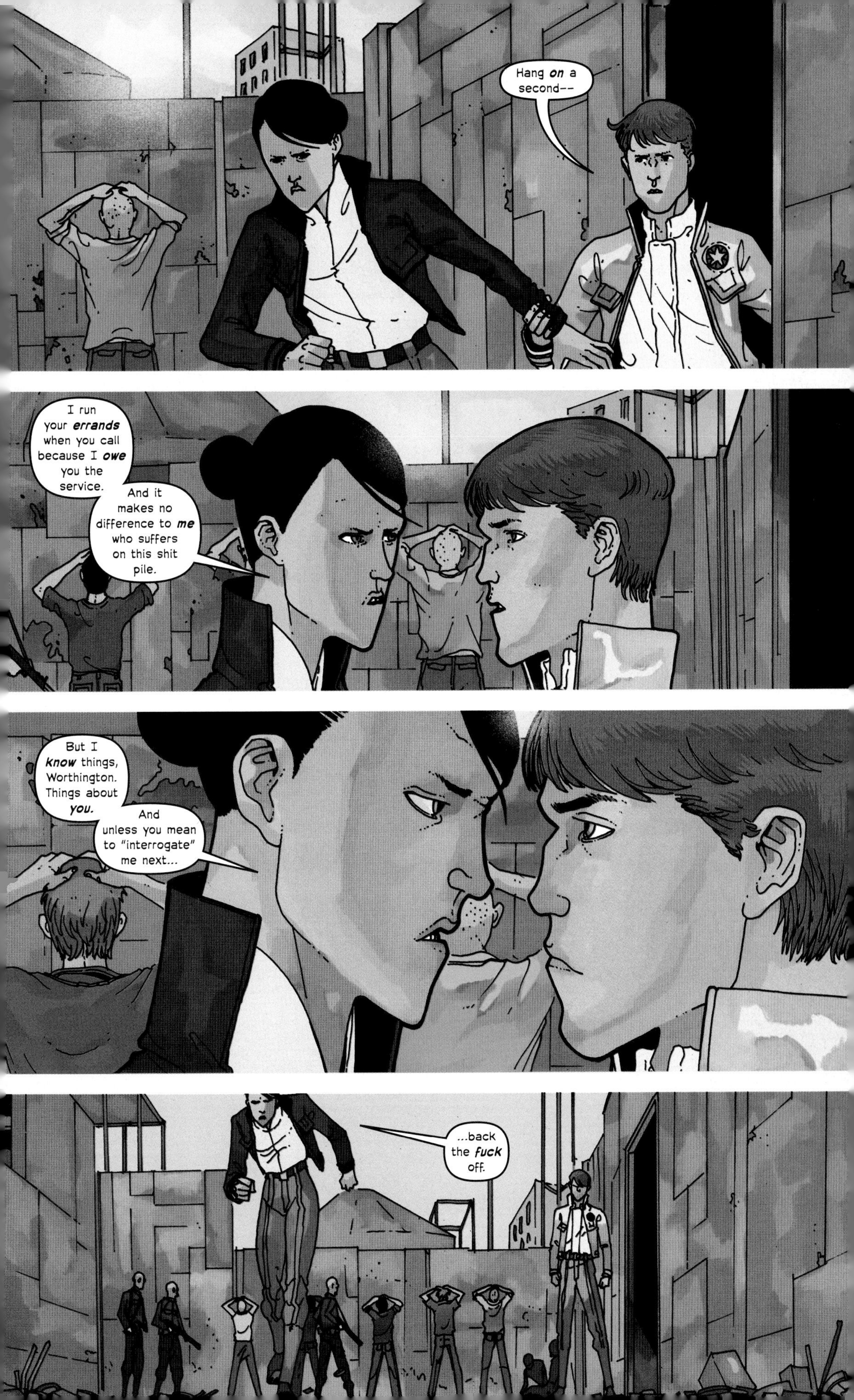
Hang on a second--
I run your errands when you call because I owe you the service.
And it makes no difference to me who suffers on this shit pile.
But I know things, Worthington. Things about you.
And unless you mean to "interrogate" me next...
...back the fuck off.

Chas?

We need to make some *decisions* now, Chas. The *cabinet* is looking to move on your agenda, but we need to plan for any sort of *fallout* with the people.

Those sanctimonious *gasbags* couldn't give *one fuck* for what the people are going through...

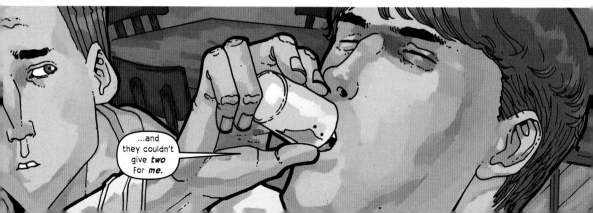

...and they couldn't give *two* for *me*.

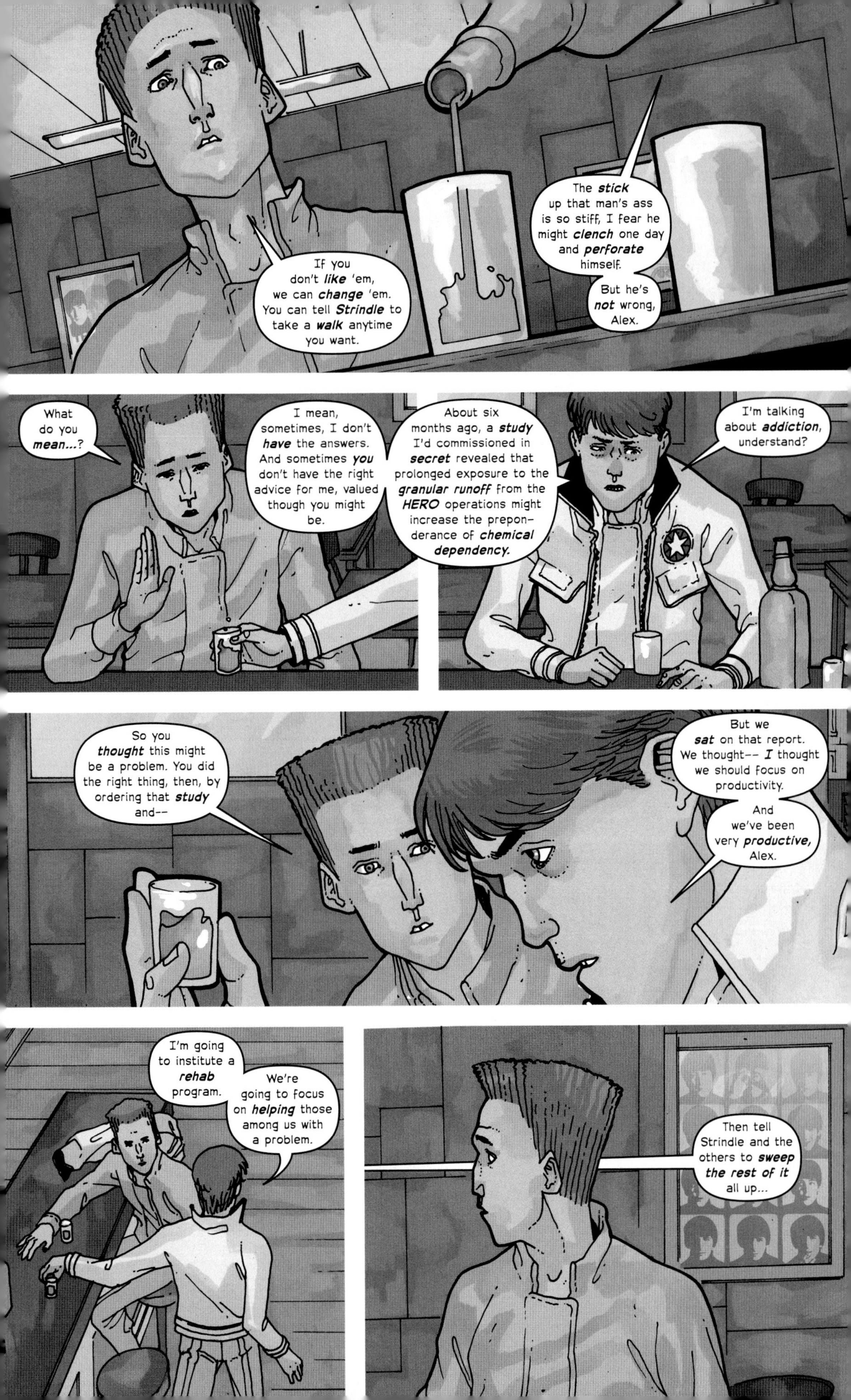
If you don't like 'em, we can change 'em. You can tell Strindle to take a walk anytime you want.
The stick up that man's ass is so stiff, I fear he might clench one day and perforate himself.
But he's not wrong, Alex.
What do you mean...?
I mean, sometimes, I don't have the answers. And sometimes you don't have the right advice for me, valued though you might be.
About six months ago, a study I'd commissioned in secret revealed that prolonged exposure to the granular runoff from the HERO operations might increase the prepon-derance of chemical dependency.
I'm talking about addiction, understand?
So you thought this might be a problem. You did the right thing, then, by ordering that study and--
But we sat on that report. We thought-- I thought we should focus on productivity.
And we've been very productive, Alex.
I'm going to institute a rehab program.
We're going to focus on helping those among us with a problem.
Then tell Strindle and the others to sweep the rest of it all up...

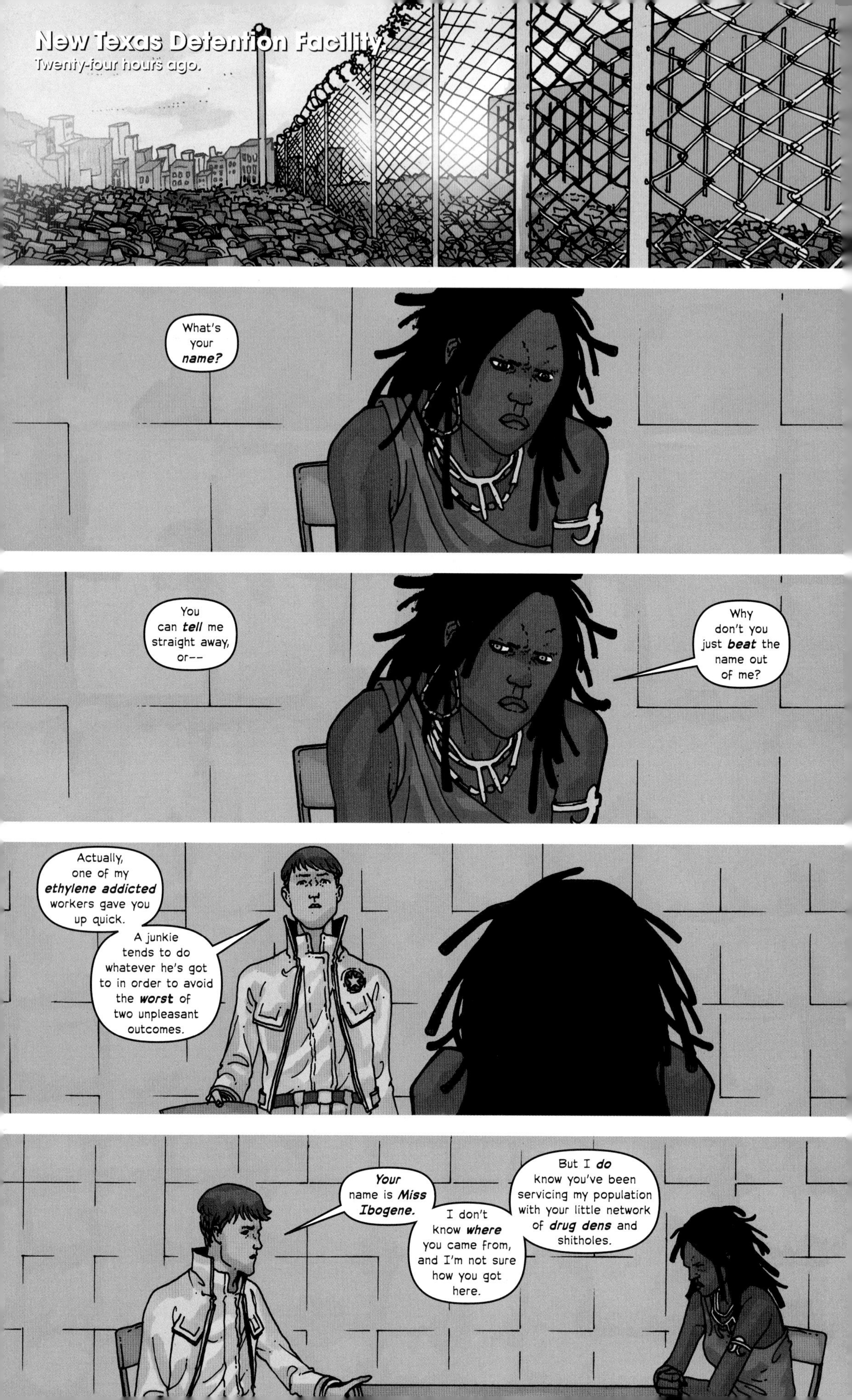
New Texas Detention Facility.
Twenty-four hours ago.
What's your name?
You can tell me straight away, or--
Why don't you just beat the name out of me?
Actually, one of my ethylene addicted workers gave you up quick.
A junkie tends to do whatever he's got to in order to avoid the worst of two unpleasant outcomes.
Your name is Miss Ibogene.
I don't know where you came from, and I'm not sure how you got here.
But I do know you've been servicing my population with your little network of drug dens and shitholes.

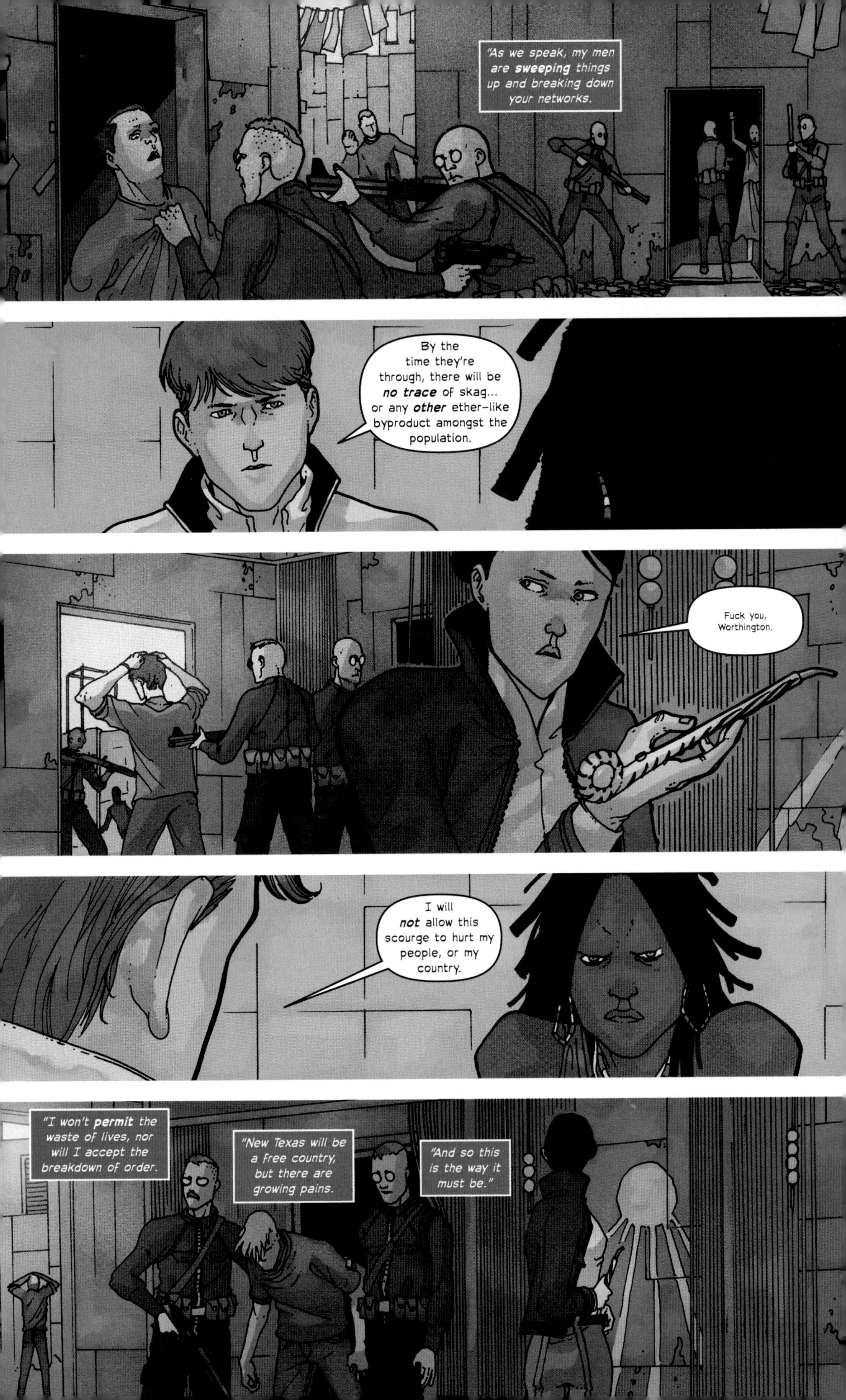
"As we speak, my men are **sweeping** things up and breaking down your networks.
By the time they're through, there will be ***no trace*** of skag... or any ***other*** ether-like byproduct amongst the population.
Fuck you, Worthington.
I will ***not*** allow this scourge to hurt my people, or my country.
"I won't **permit** the waste of lives, nor will I accept the breakdown of order.
"New Texas will be a free country, but there are growing pains.
"And so this is the way it must be."

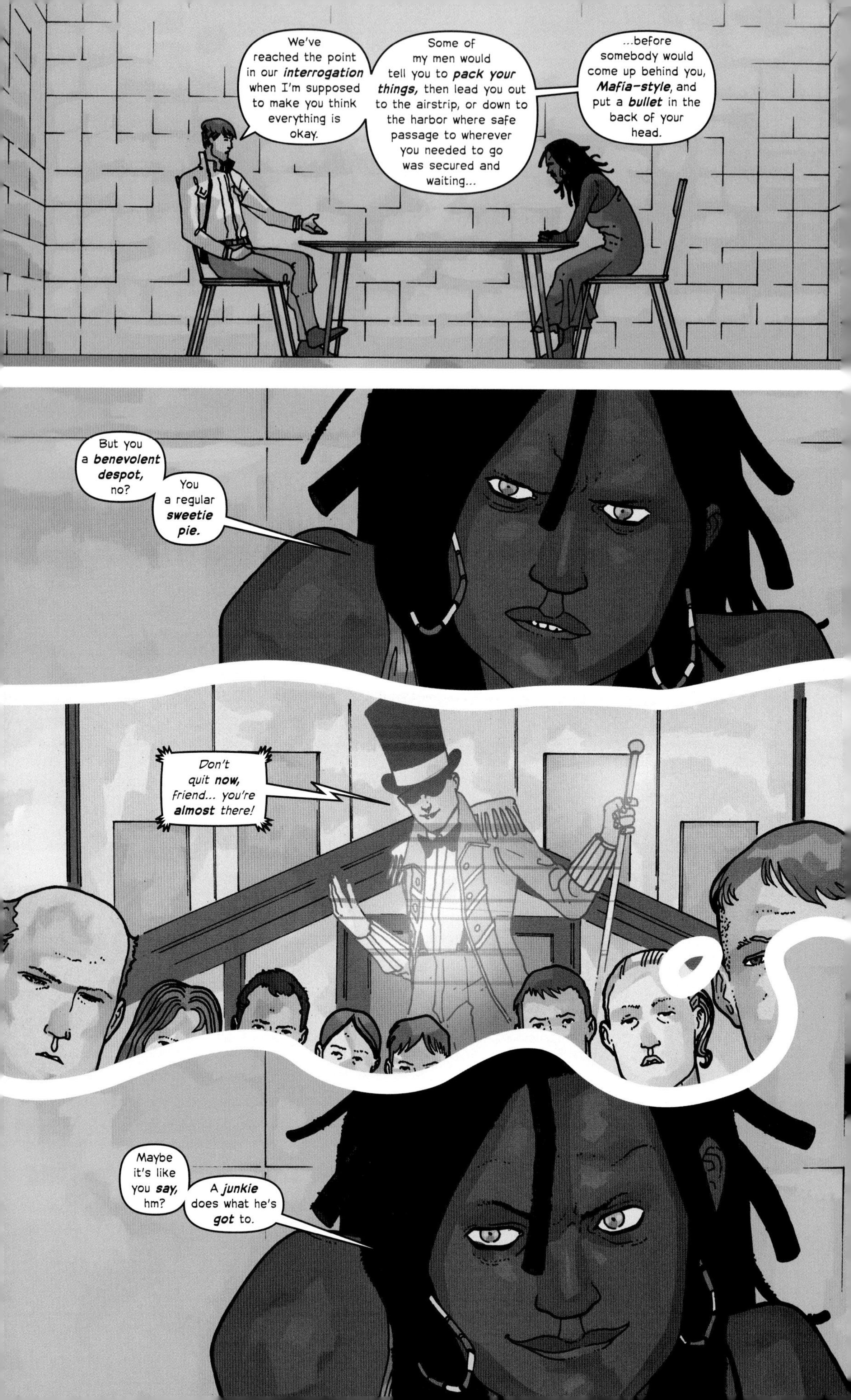

We've reached the point in our *interrogation* when I'm supposed to make you think everything is okay.
Some of my men would tell you to ***pack your things,*** then lead you out to the airstrip, or down to the harbor where safe passage to wherever you needed to go was secured and waiting...
...before somebody would come up behind you, ***Mafia-style***, and put a ***bullet*** in the back of your head.
But you a ***benevolent despot,*** no?
You a regular ***sweetie pie.***
*Don't quit **now**, friend... you're **almost** there!*
Maybe it's like you ***say,*** hm?
A ***junkie*** does what he's ***got*** to.

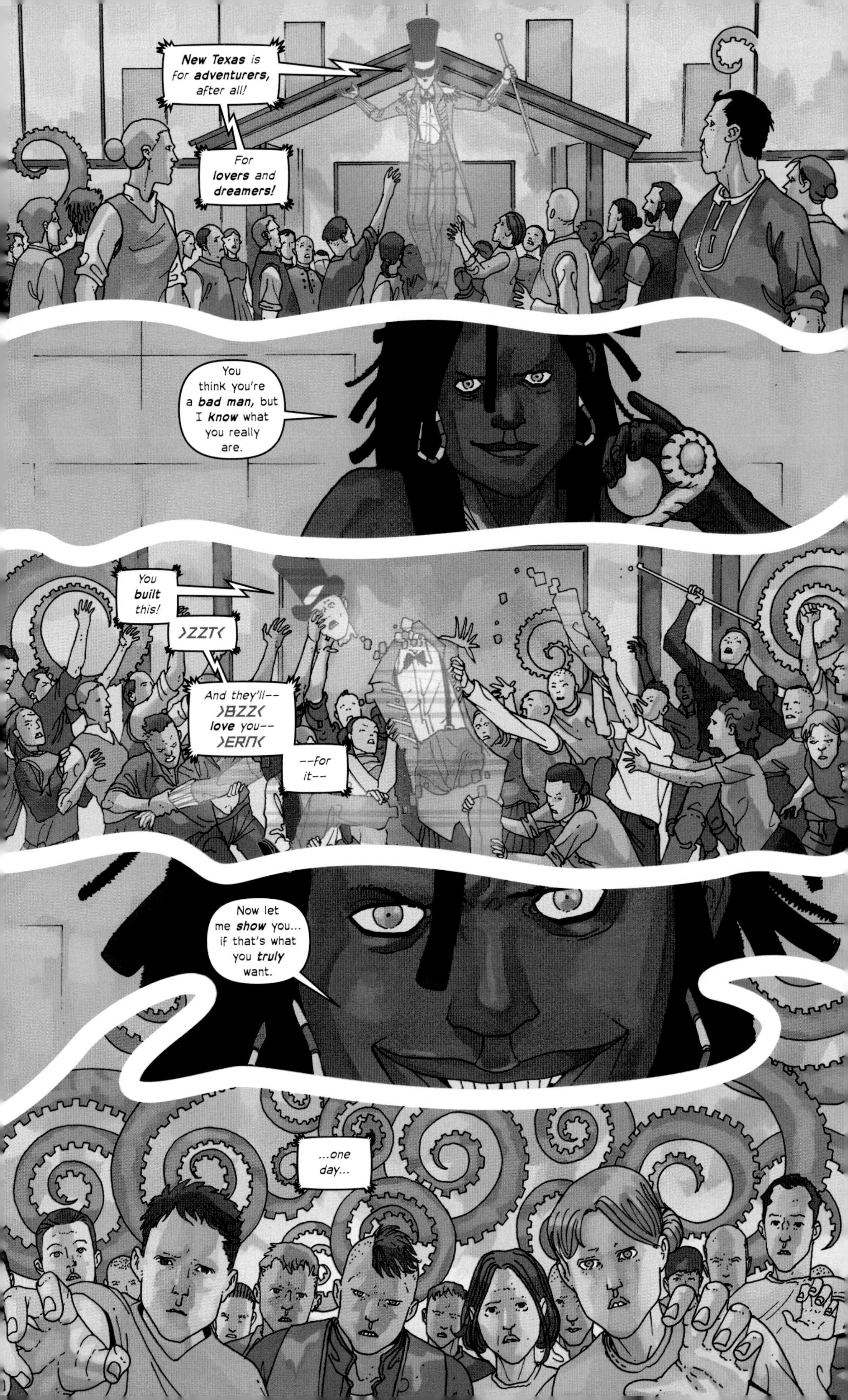
New Texas is for adventurers, after all!
For lovers and dreamers!
You think you're a bad man, but I know what you really are.
You built this!
>ZZT<
And they'll-- >BZZ< love you-- >ERK<
--for it--
Now let me show you... if that's what you truly want.
...one day...

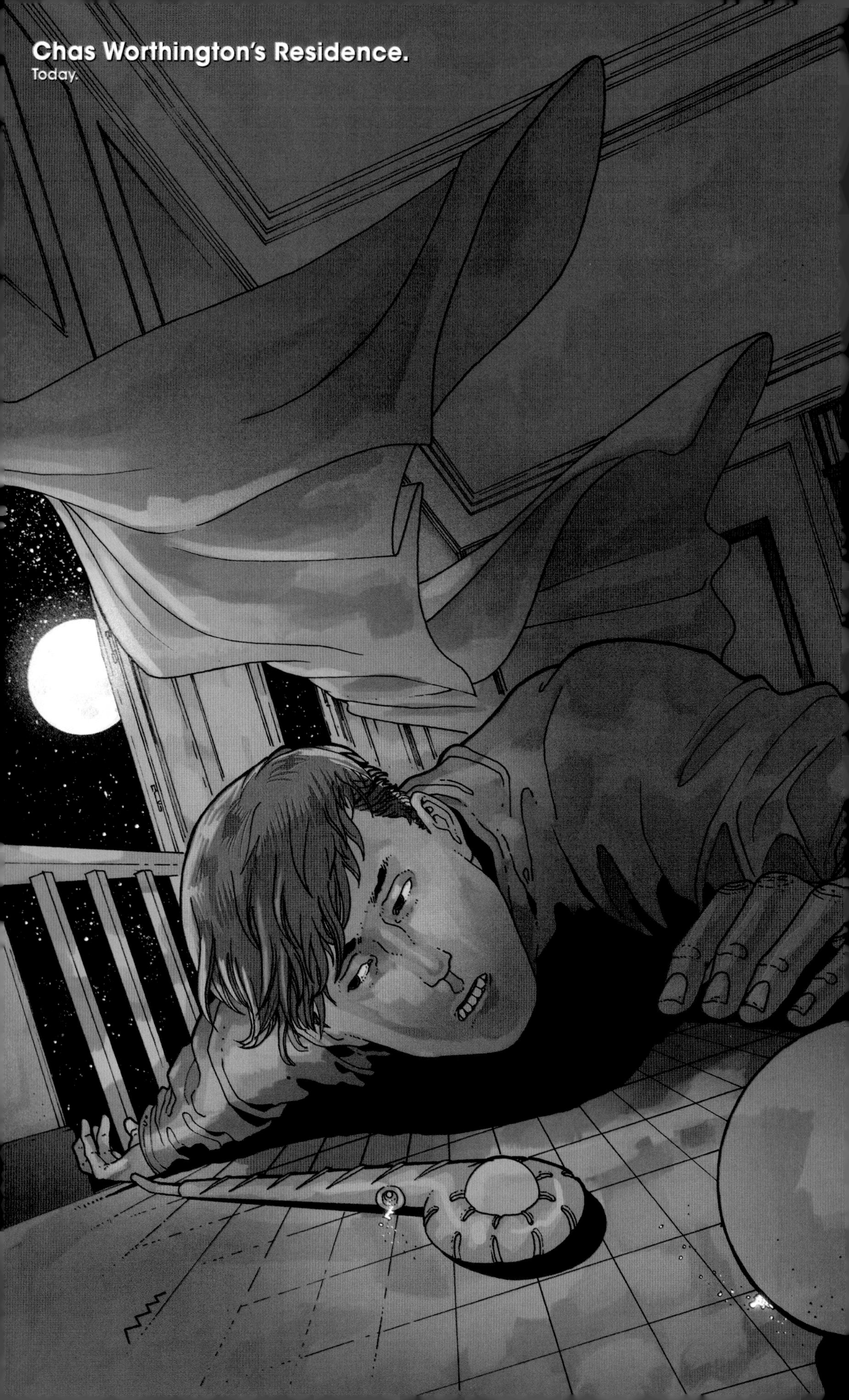
Chas Worthington's Residence.
Today.

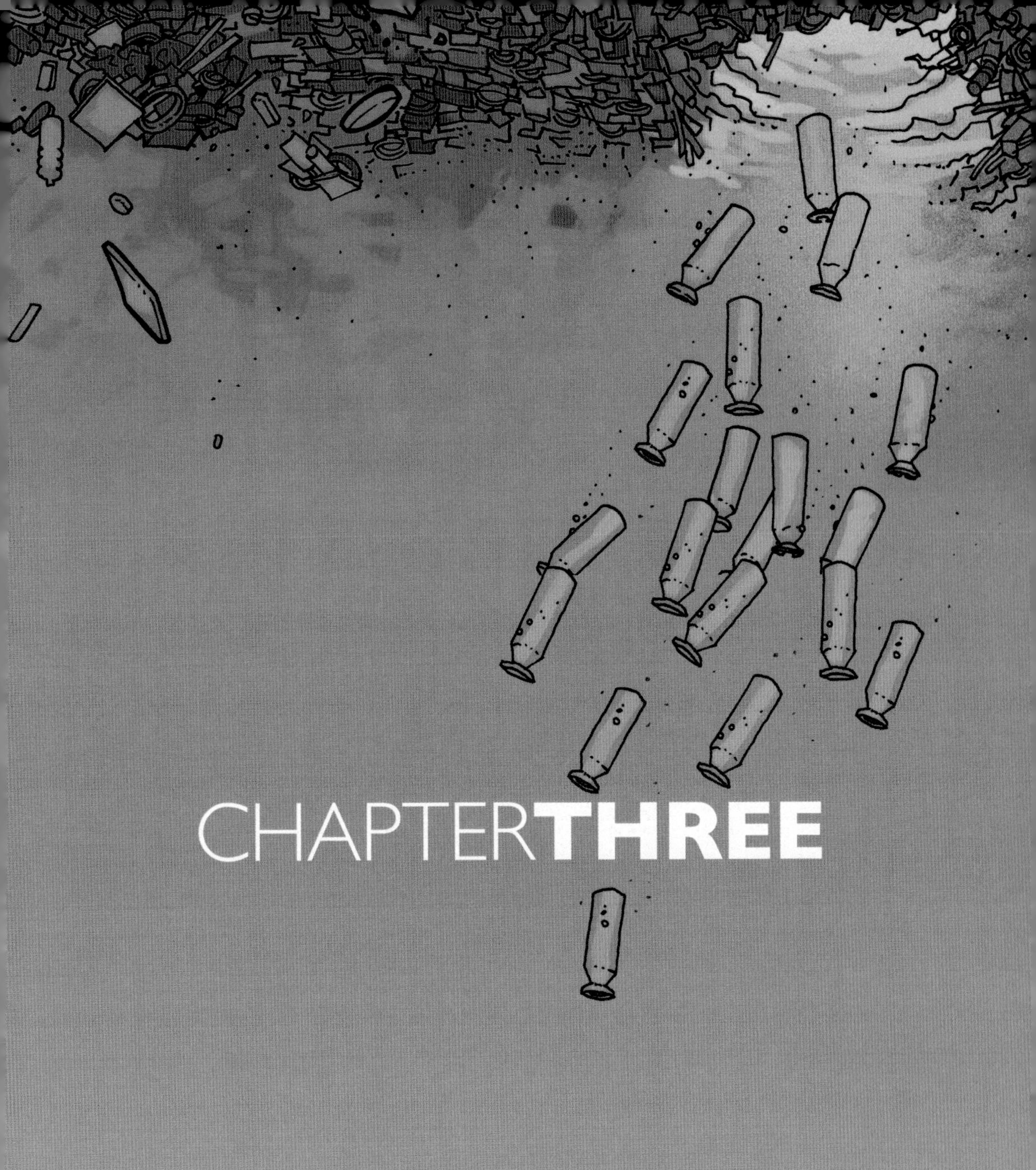

CHAPTER THREE

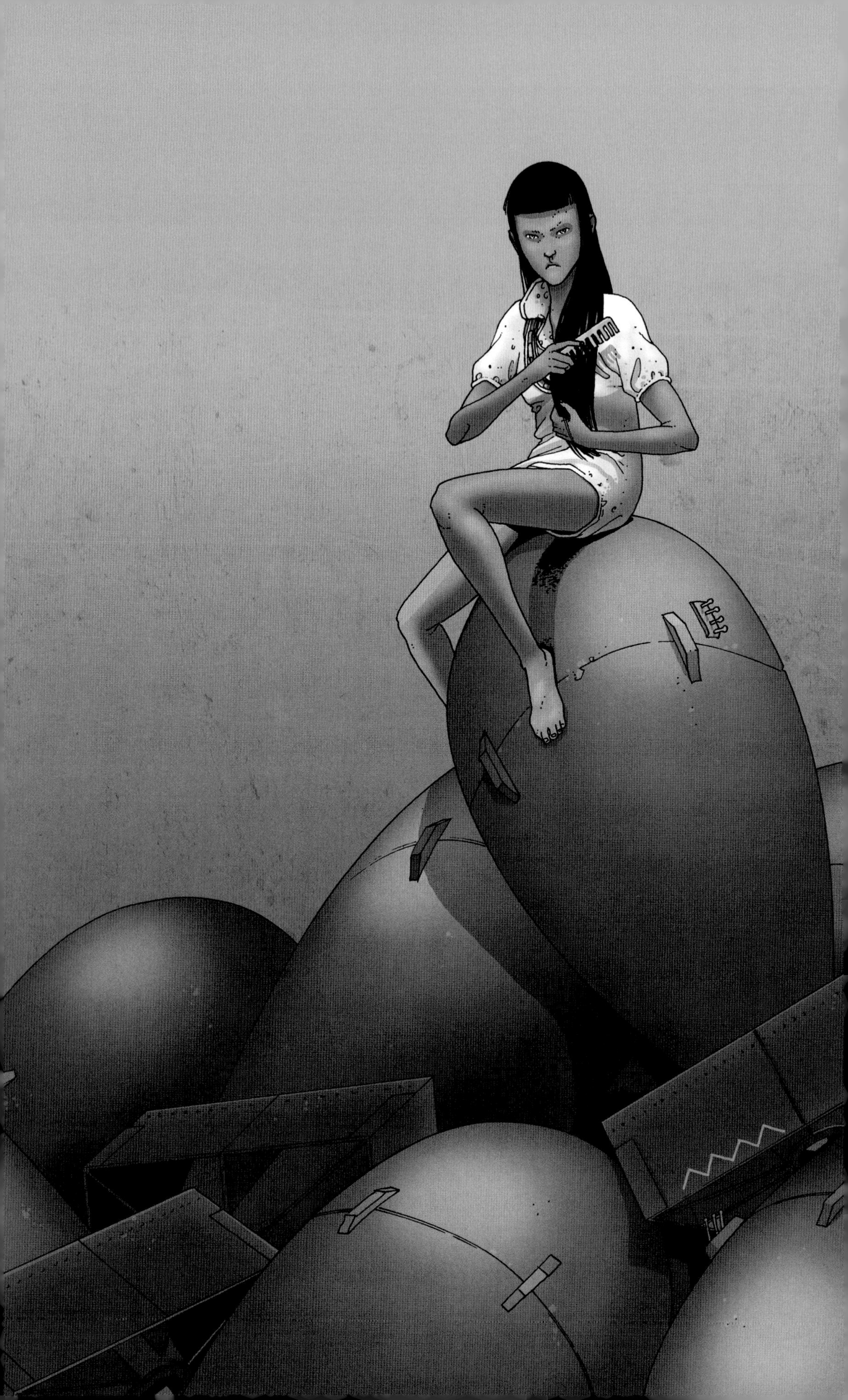

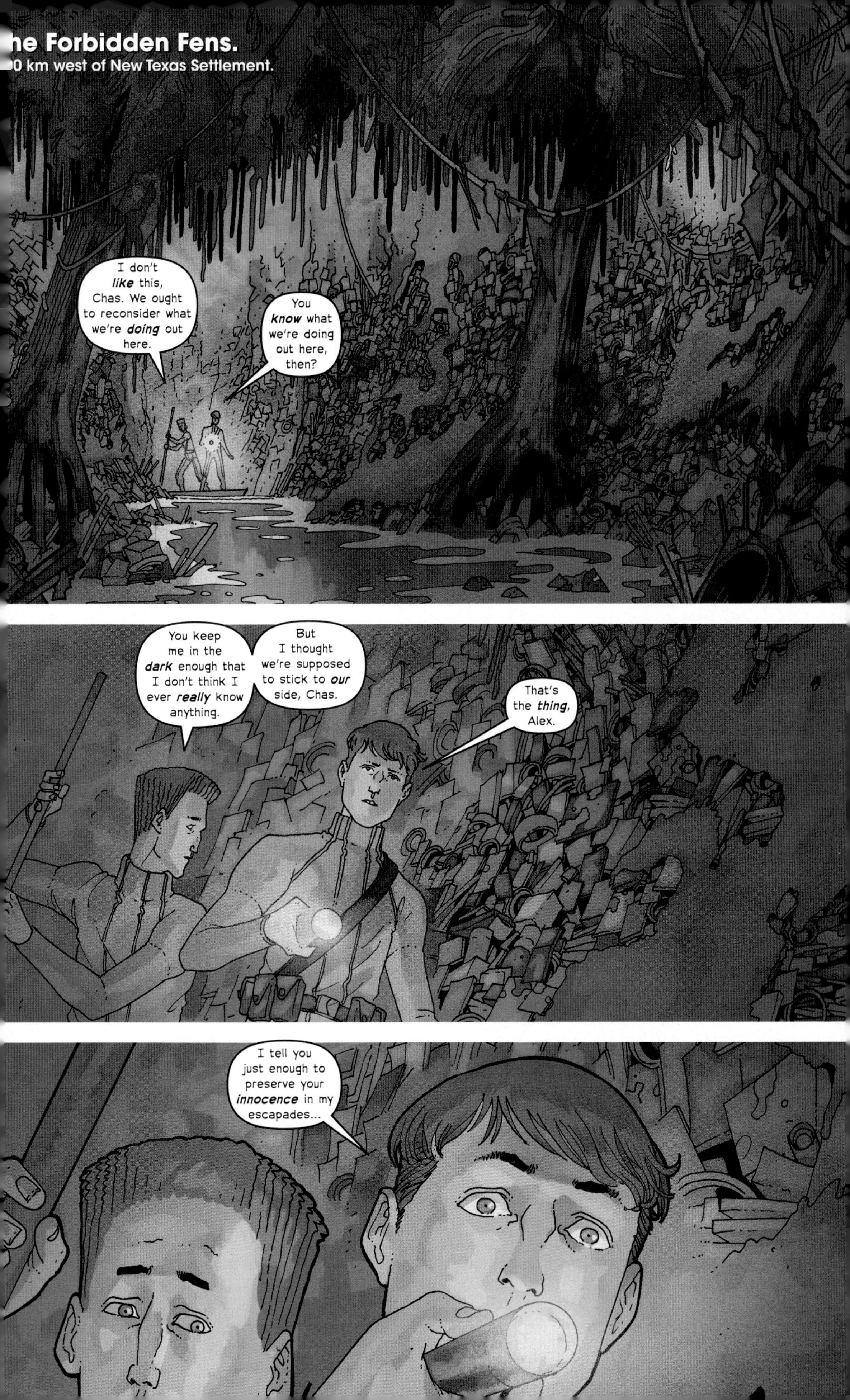
he Forbidden Fens.
0 km west of New Texas Settlement.
I don't *like* this, Chas. We ought to reconsider what we're *doing* out here.
You *know* what we're doing out here, then?
You keep me in the *dark* enough that I don't think I ever *really* know anything.
But I thought we're supposed to stick to *our* side, Chas.
That's the *thing*, Alex.
I tell you just enough to preserve your *innocence* in my escapades...

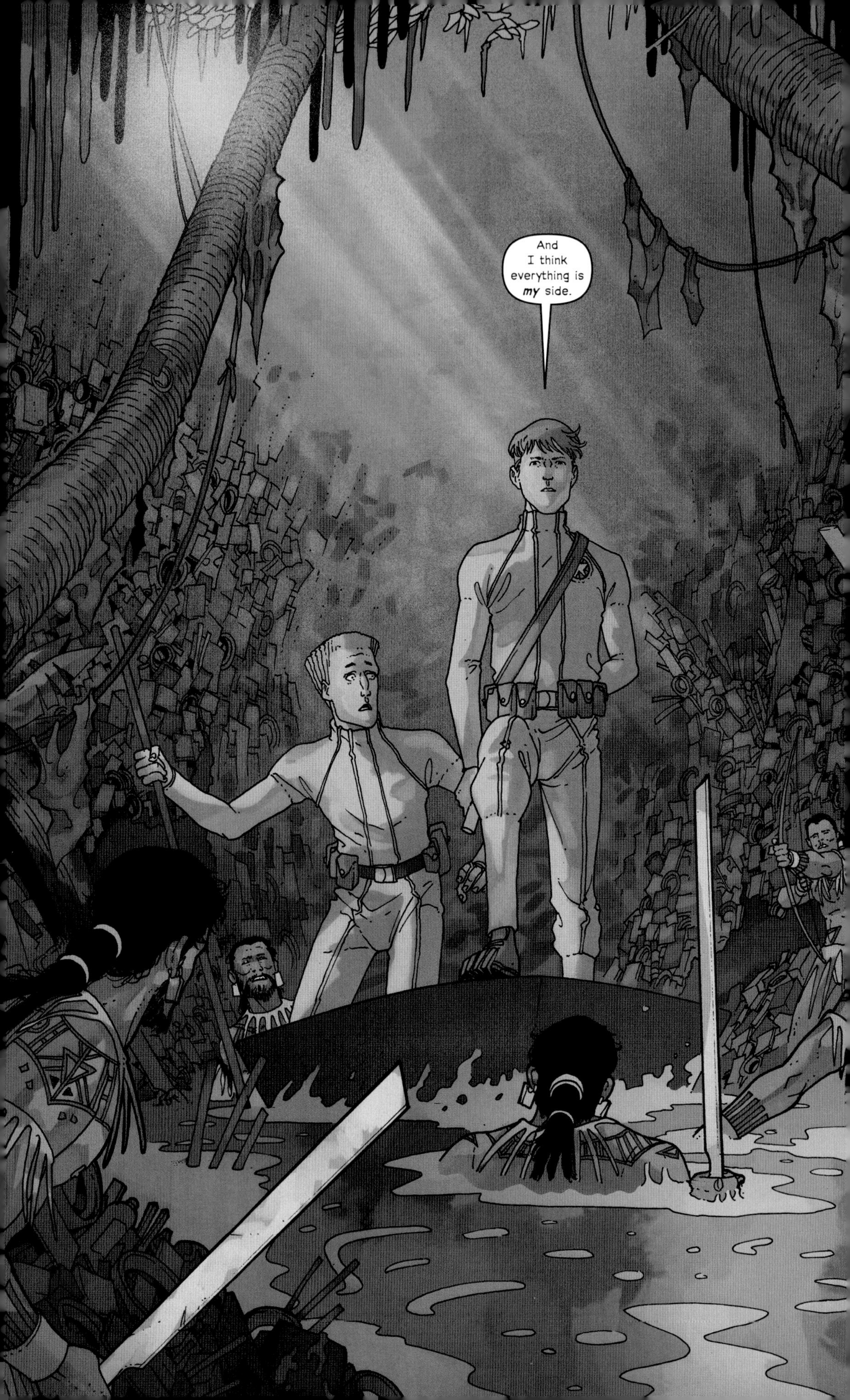
And I think everything is *my* side.

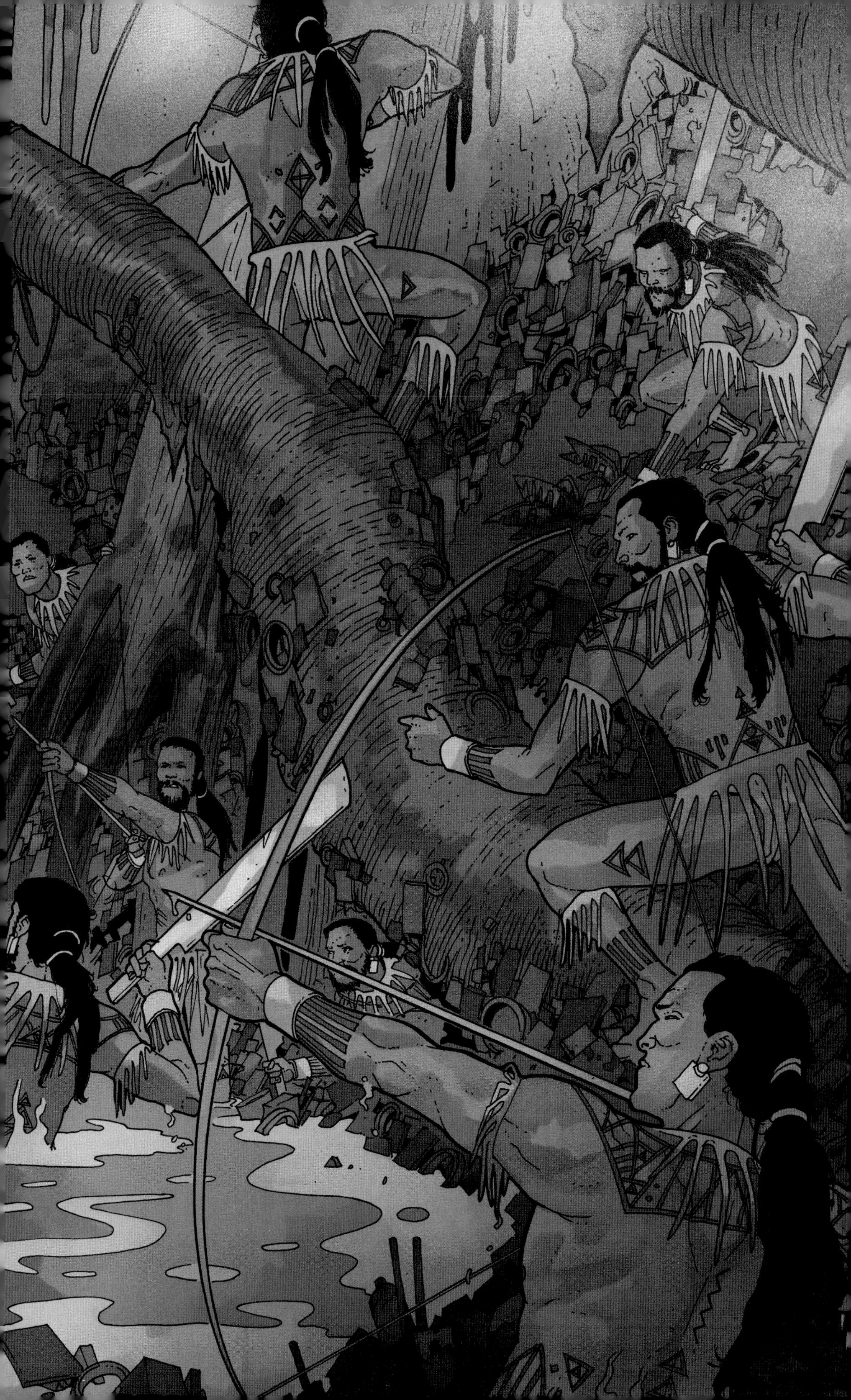

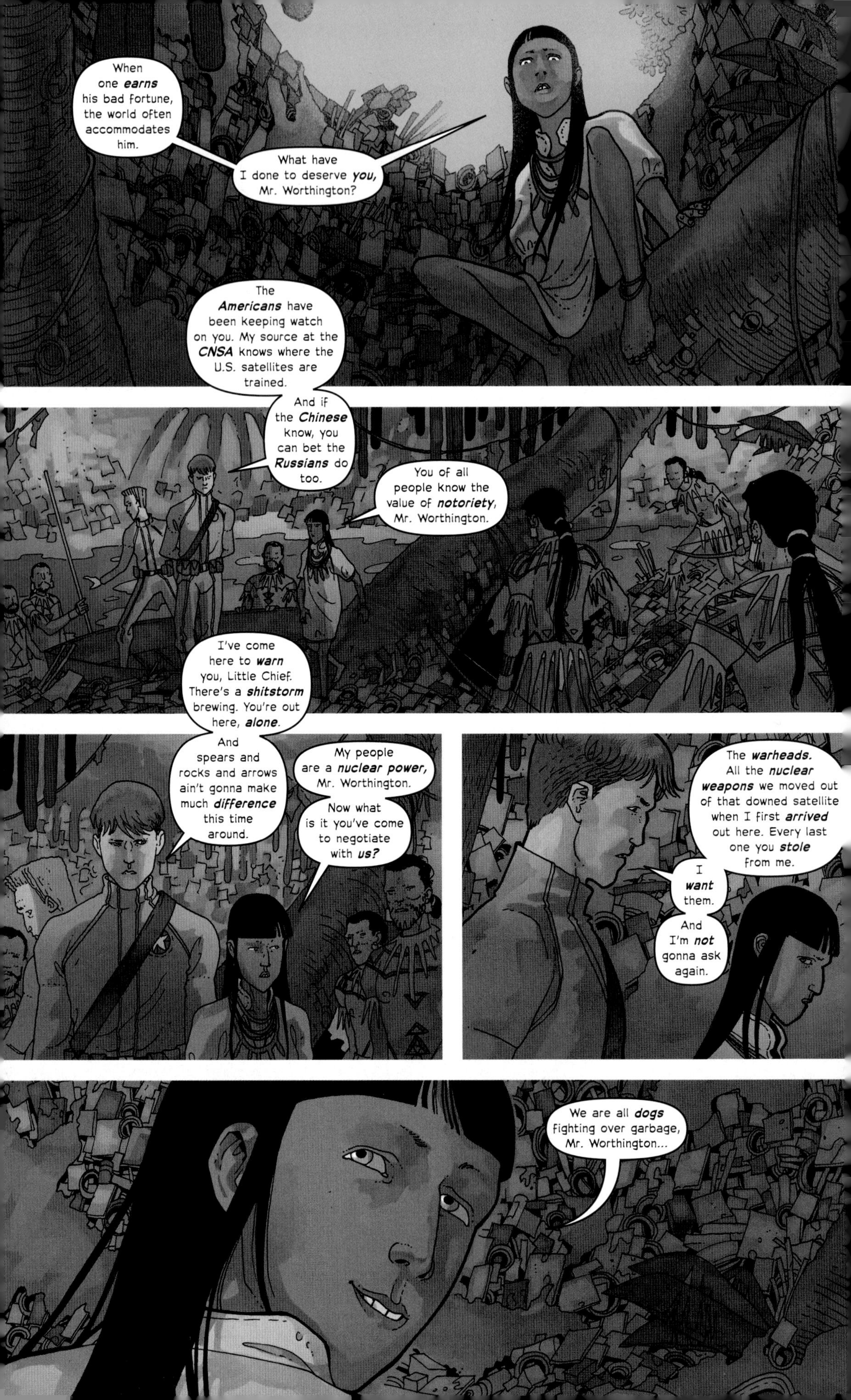
When one earns his bad fortune, the world often accommodates him.
What have I done to deserve you, Mr. Worthington?
The Americans have been keeping watch on you. My source at the CNSA knows where the U.S. satellites are trained.
And if the Chinese know, you can bet the Russians do too.
You of all people know the value of notoriety, Mr. Worthington.
I've come here to warn you, Little Chief. There's a shitstorm brewing. You're out here, alone.
And spears and rocks and arrows ain't gonna make much difference this time around.
My people are a nuclear power, Mr. Worthington.
Now what is it you've come to negotiate with us?
The warheads. All the nuclear weapons we moved out of that downed satellite when I first arrived out here. Every last one you stole from me.
I want them.
And I'm not gonna ask again.
We are all dogs fighting over garbage, Mr. Worthington...

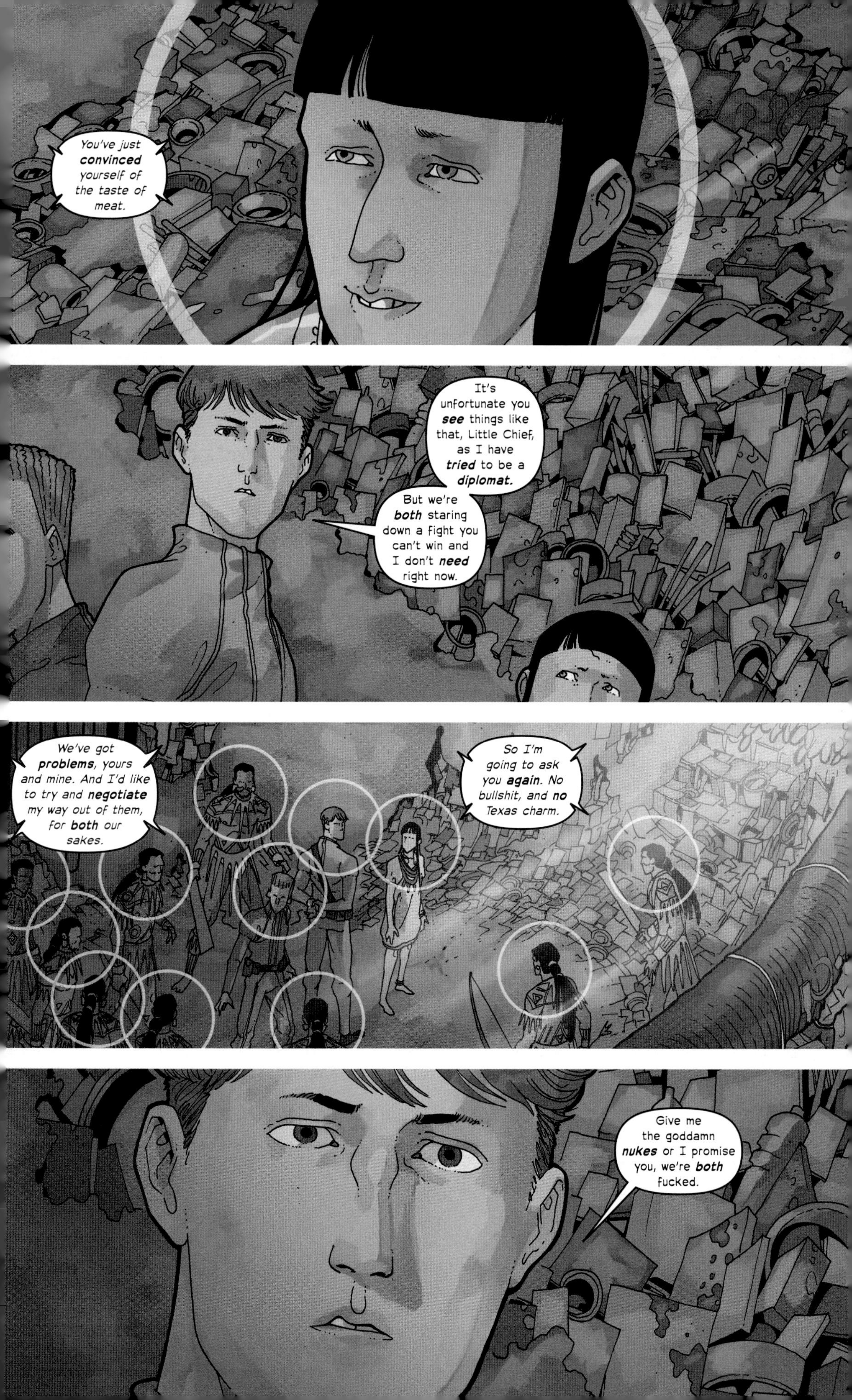
You've just convinced yourself of the taste of meat.
It's unfortunate you see things like that, Little Chief, as I have tried to be a diplomat.
But we're both staring down a fight you can't win and I don't need right now.
We've got problems, yours and mine. And I'd like to try and negotiate my way out of them, for both our sakes.
So I'm going to ask you again. No bullshit, and no Texas charm.
Give me the goddamn nukes or I promise you, we're both fucked.

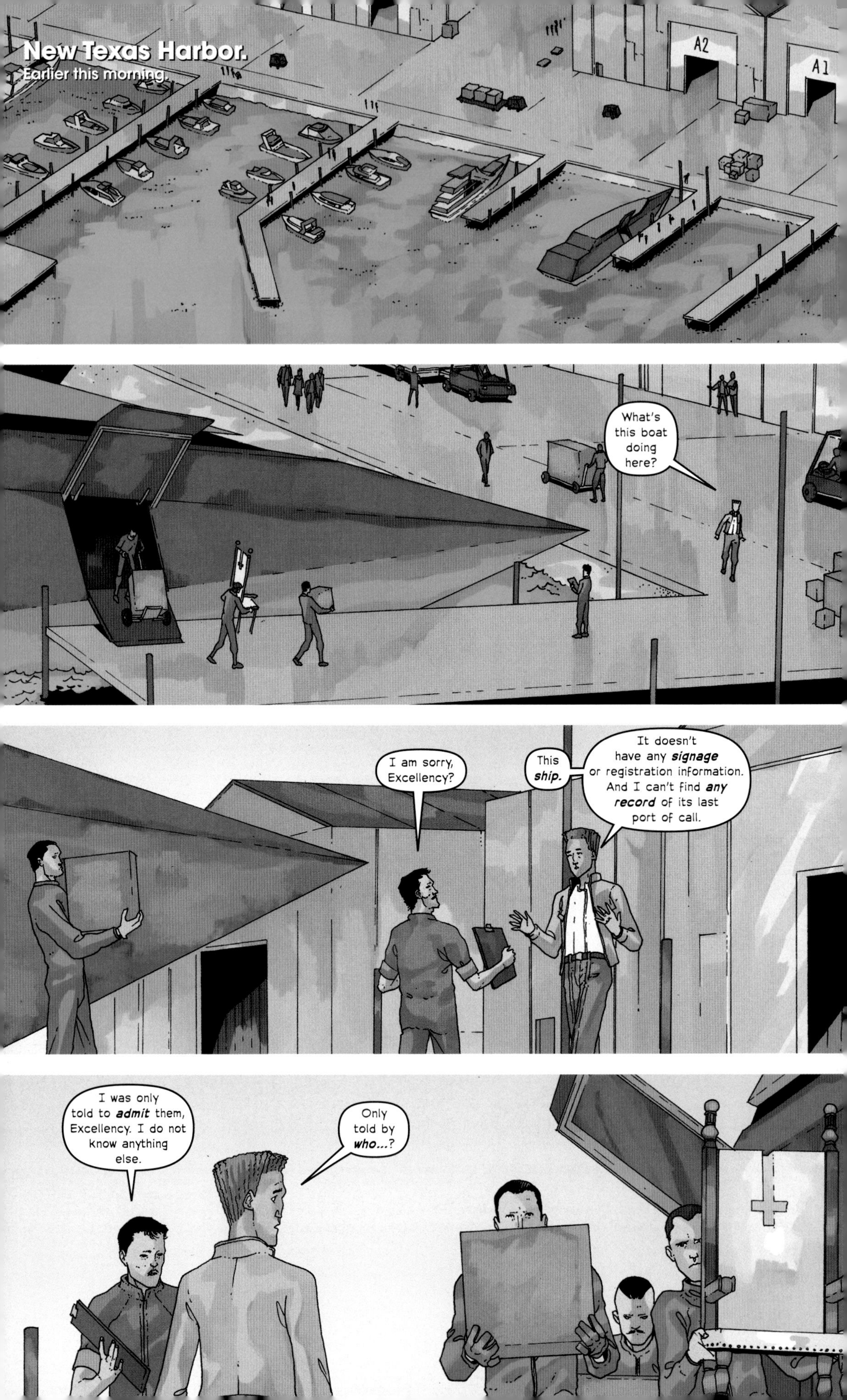
New Texas Harbor.
Earlier this morning.
A2
A1
What's this boat doing here?
I am sorry, Excellency?
This ship.
It doesn't have any signage or registration information. And I can't find any record of its last port of call.
I was only told to admit them, Excellency. I do not know anything else.
Only told by who...?

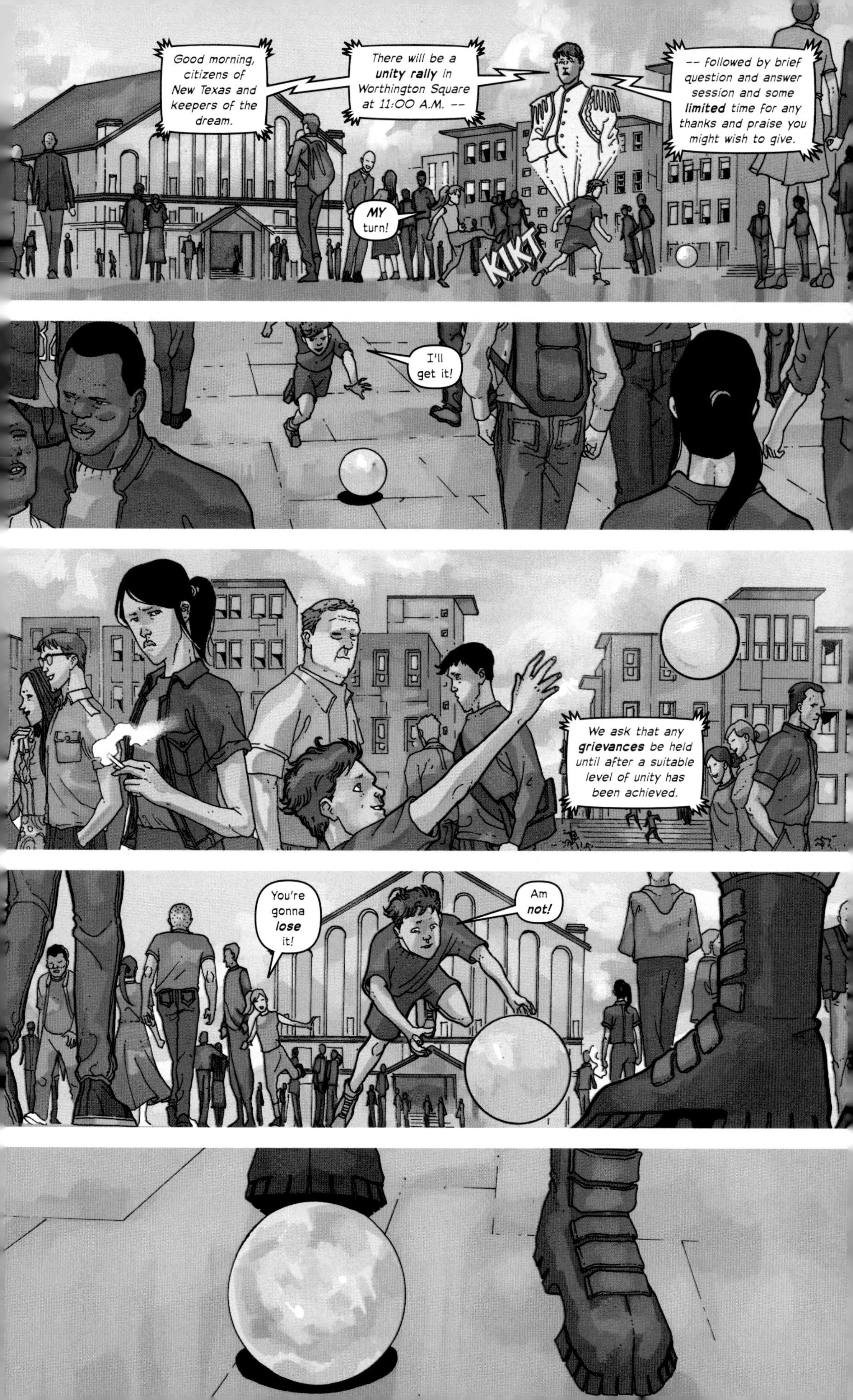
Good morning, citizens of New Texas and keepers of the dream.
There will be a **unity rally** in Worthington Square at 11:00 A.M. --
-- Followed by brief question and answer session and some **limited** time for any thanks and praise you might wish to give.
MY turn!
KIKT
I'll get it!
We ask that any **grievances** be held until after a suitable level of unity has been achieved.
You're gonna **lose** it!
Am **not!**

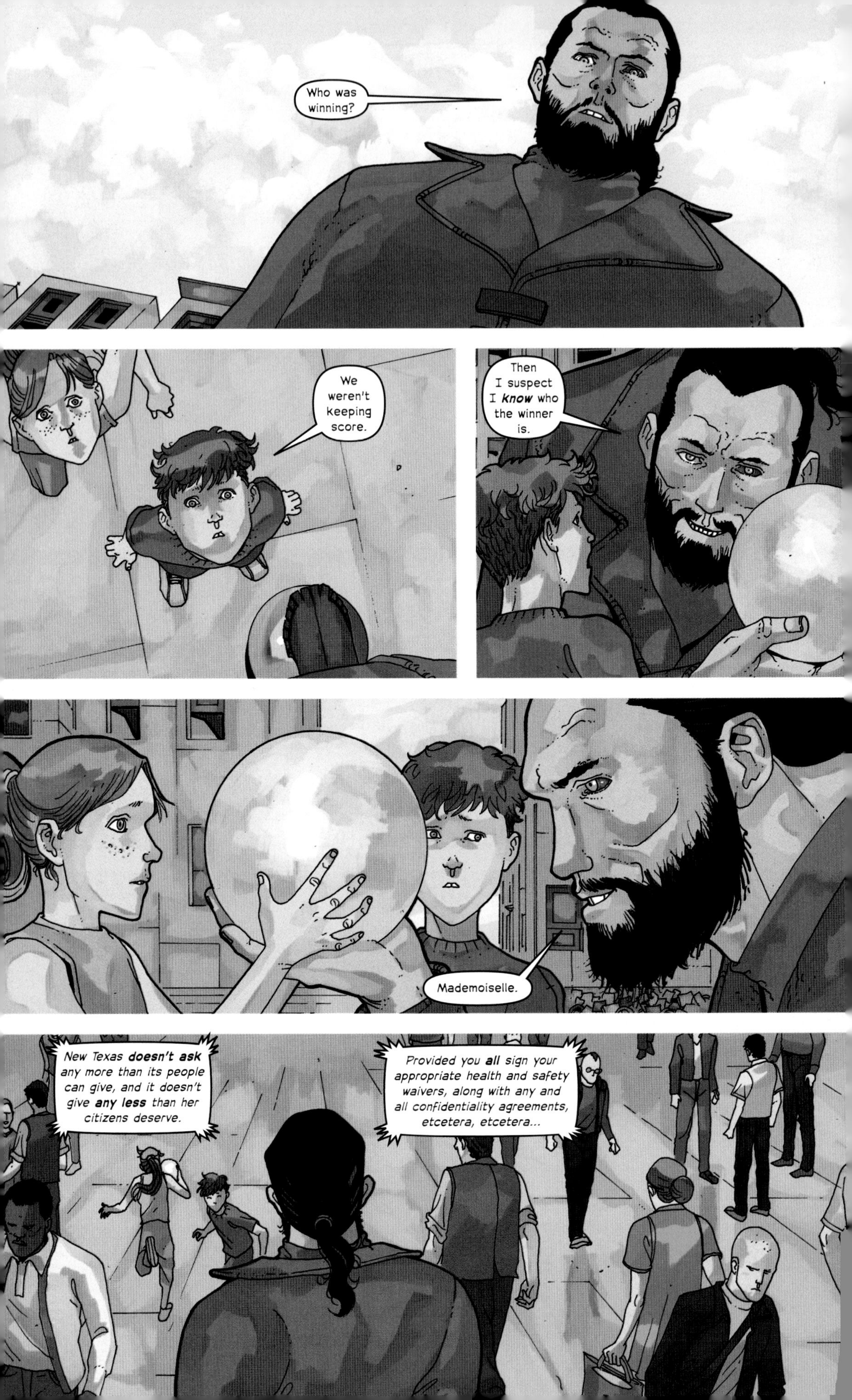
Who was winning?
We weren't keeping score.
Then I suspect I **know** who the winner is.
Mademoiselle.
*New Texas **doesn't ask** any more than its people can give, and it doesn't give **any less** than her citizens deserve.*
*Provided you **all** sign your appropriate health and safety waivers, along with any and all confidentiality agreements, etcetera, etcetera...*

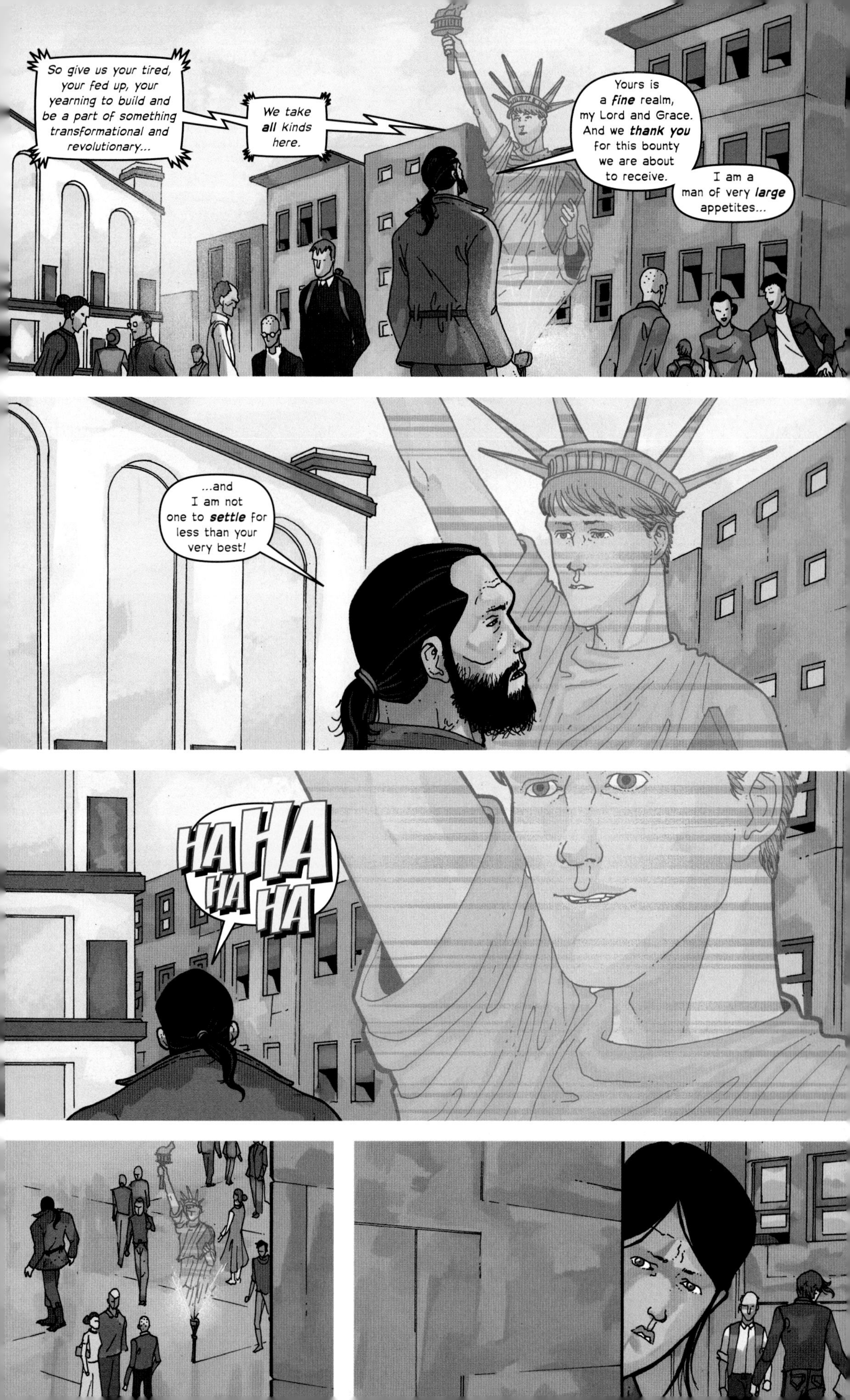
So give us your tired, your fed up, your yearning to build and be a part of something transformational and revolutionary...
We take all kinds here.
Yours is a fine realm, my Lord and Grace. And we thank you for this bounty we are about to receive.
I am a man of very large appetites...
...and I am not one to settle for less than your very best!
HA HA HA HA

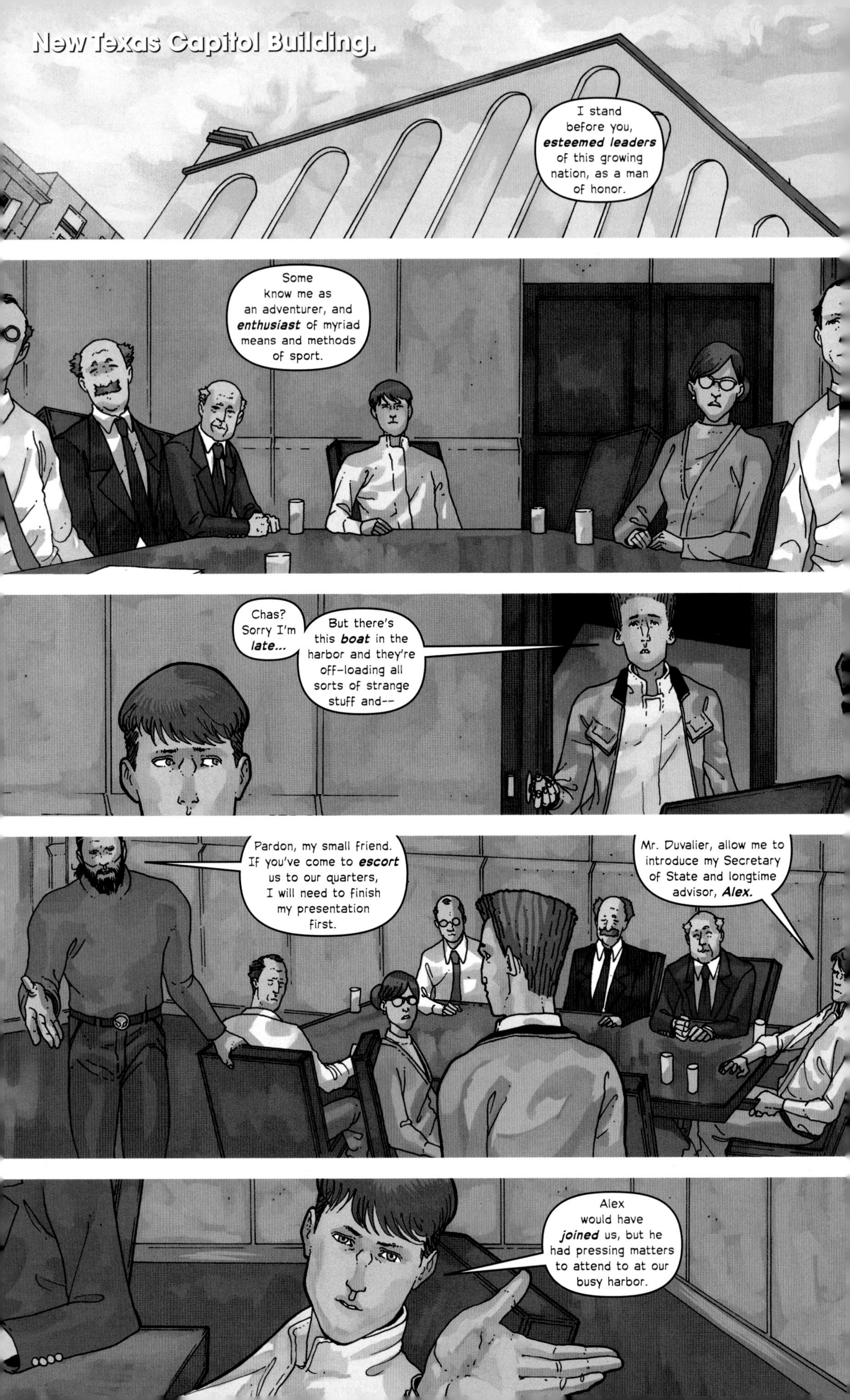
New Texas Capitol Building.
I stand before you, *esteemed leaders* of this growing nation, as a man of honor.
Some know me as an adventurer, and *enthusiast* of myriad means and methods of sport.
Chas? Sorry I'm *late...*
But there's this *boat* in the harbor and they're off-loading all sorts of strange stuff and--
Pardon, my small friend. If you've come to *escort* us to our quarters, I will need to finish my presentation first.
Mr. Duvalier, allow me to introduce my Secretary of State and longtime advisor, *Alex.*
Alex would have *joined* us, but he had pressing matters to attend to at our busy harbor.

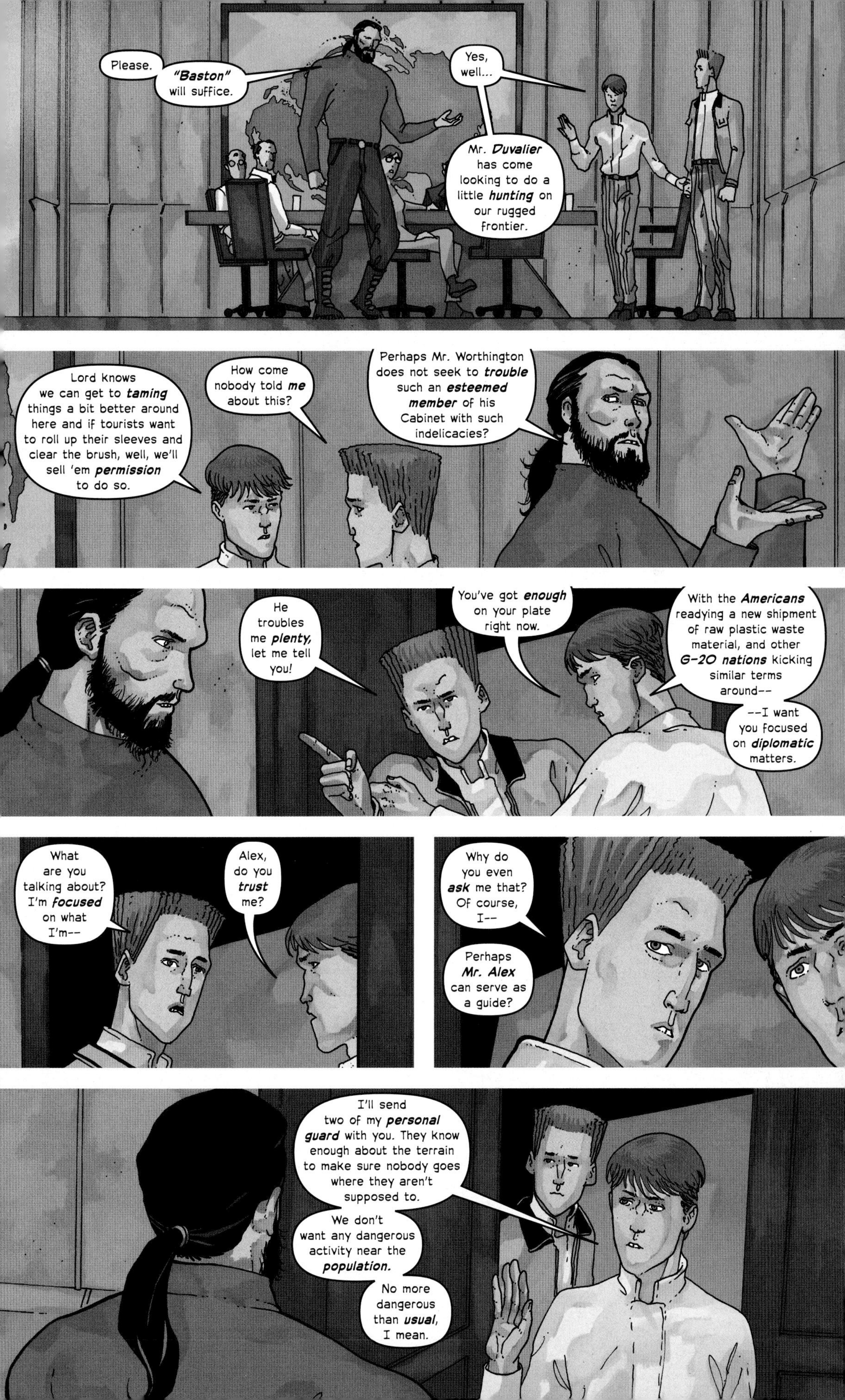
Please.
"Baston" will suffice.
Yes, well...
Mr. Duvalier has come looking to do a little hunting on our rugged frontier.
Lord knows we can get to taming things a bit better around here and if tourists want to roll up their sleeves and clear the brush, well, we'll sell 'em permission to do so.
How come nobody told me about this?
Perhaps Mr. Worthington does not seek to trouble such an esteemed member of his Cabinet with such indelicacies?
He troubles me plenty, let me tell you!
You've got enough on your plate right now.
With the Americans readying a new shipment of raw plastic waste material, and other G-20 nations kicking similar terms around--
--I want you focused on diplomatic matters.
What are you talking about? I'm focused on what I'm--
Alex, do you trust me?
Why do you even ask me that? Of course, I--
Perhaps Mr. Alex can serve as a guide?
I'll send two of my personal guard with you. They know enough about the terrain to make sure nobody goes where they aren't supposed to.
We don't want any dangerous activity near the population.
No more dangerous than usual, I mean.

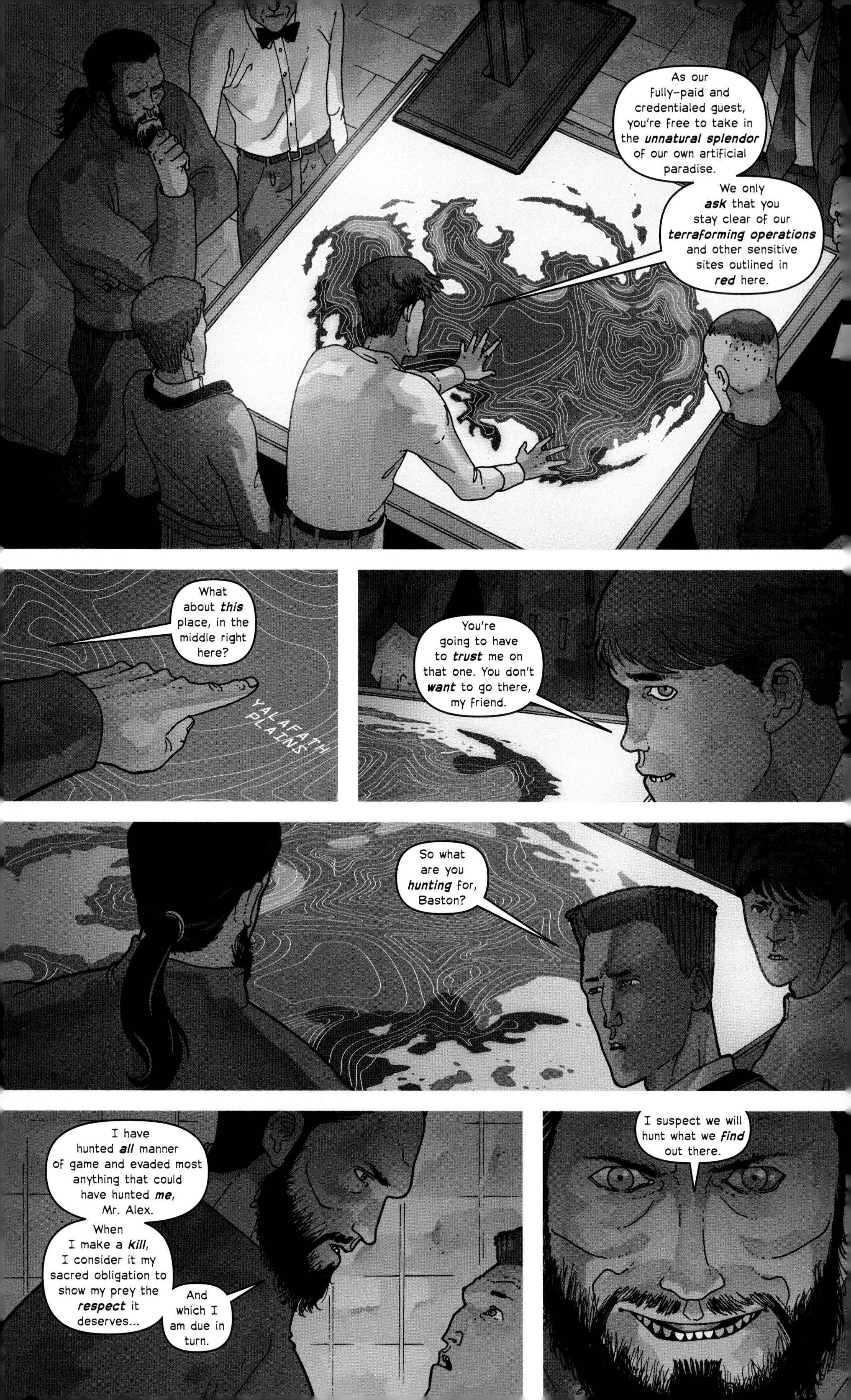
As our fully-paid and credentialed guest, you're free to take in the ***unnatural splendor*** of our own artificial paradise.
We only ***ask*** that you stay clear of our ***terraforming operations*** and other sensitive sites outlined in ***red*** here.
What about ***this*** place, in the middle right here?
YALAFATH PLAINS
You're going to have to ***trust*** me on that one. You don't ***want*** to go there, my friend.
So what are you ***hunting*** for, Baston?
I have hunted ***all*** manner of game and evaded most anything that could have hunted ***me***, Mr. Alex.
When I make a ***kill***, I consider it my sacred obligation to show my prey the ***respect*** it deserves...
And which I am due in turn.
I suspect we will hunt what we ***find*** out there.

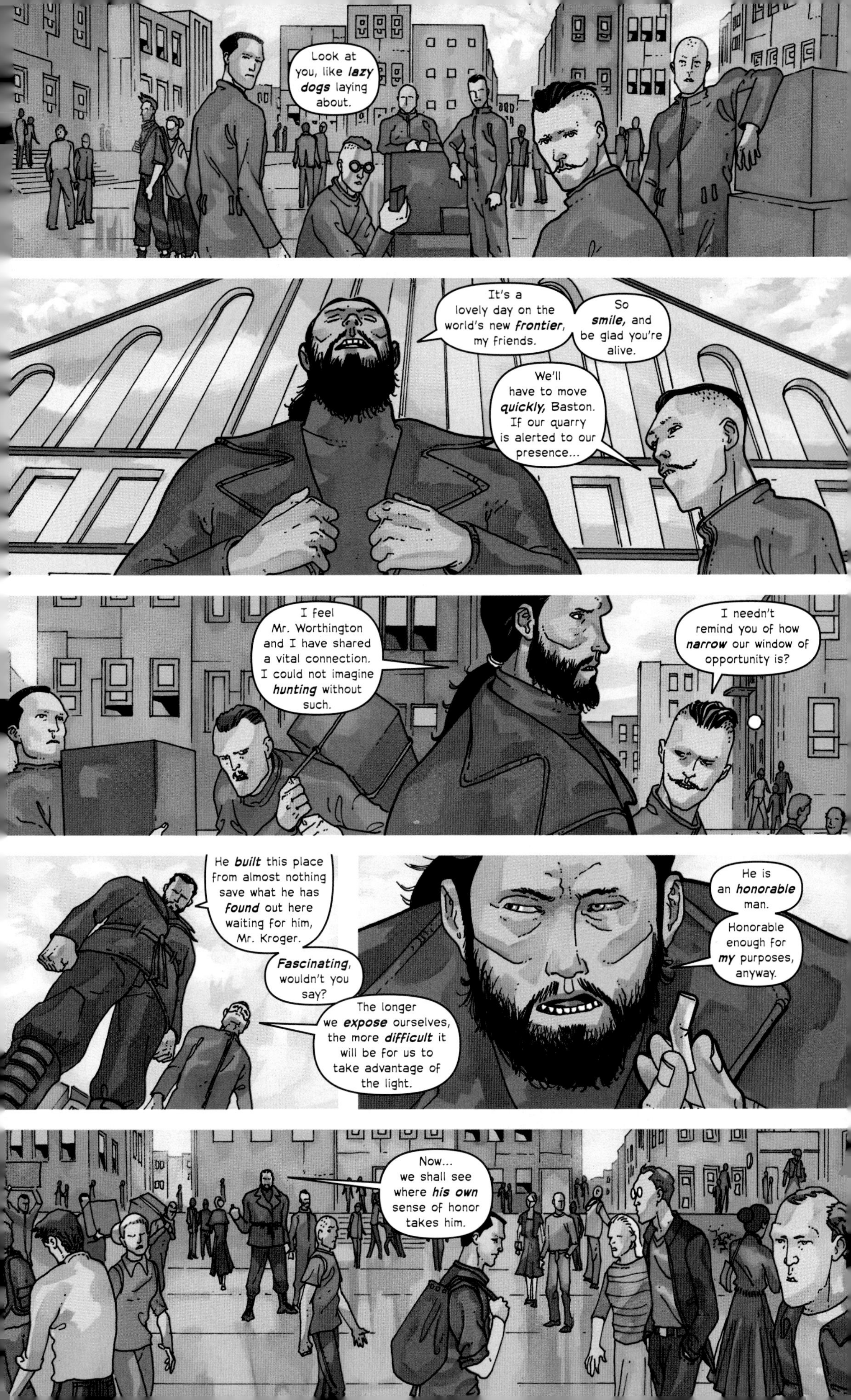
Look at you, like *lazy dogs* laying about.
It's a lovely day on the world's new *frontier*, my friends.
So *smile,* and be glad you're alive.
We'll have to move *quickly,* Baston. If our quarry is alerted to our presence...
I feel Mr. Worthington and I have shared a vital connection. I could not imagine *hunting* without such.
I needn't remind you of how *narrow* our window of opportunity is?
He *built* this place from almost nothing save what he has *found* out here waiting for him, Mr. Kroger.
Fascinating, wouldn't you say?
The longer we *expose* ourselves, the more *difficult* it will be for us to take advantage of the light.
He is an *honorable* man.
Honorable enough for *my* purposes, anyway.
Now... we shall see where *his own* sense of honor takes him.

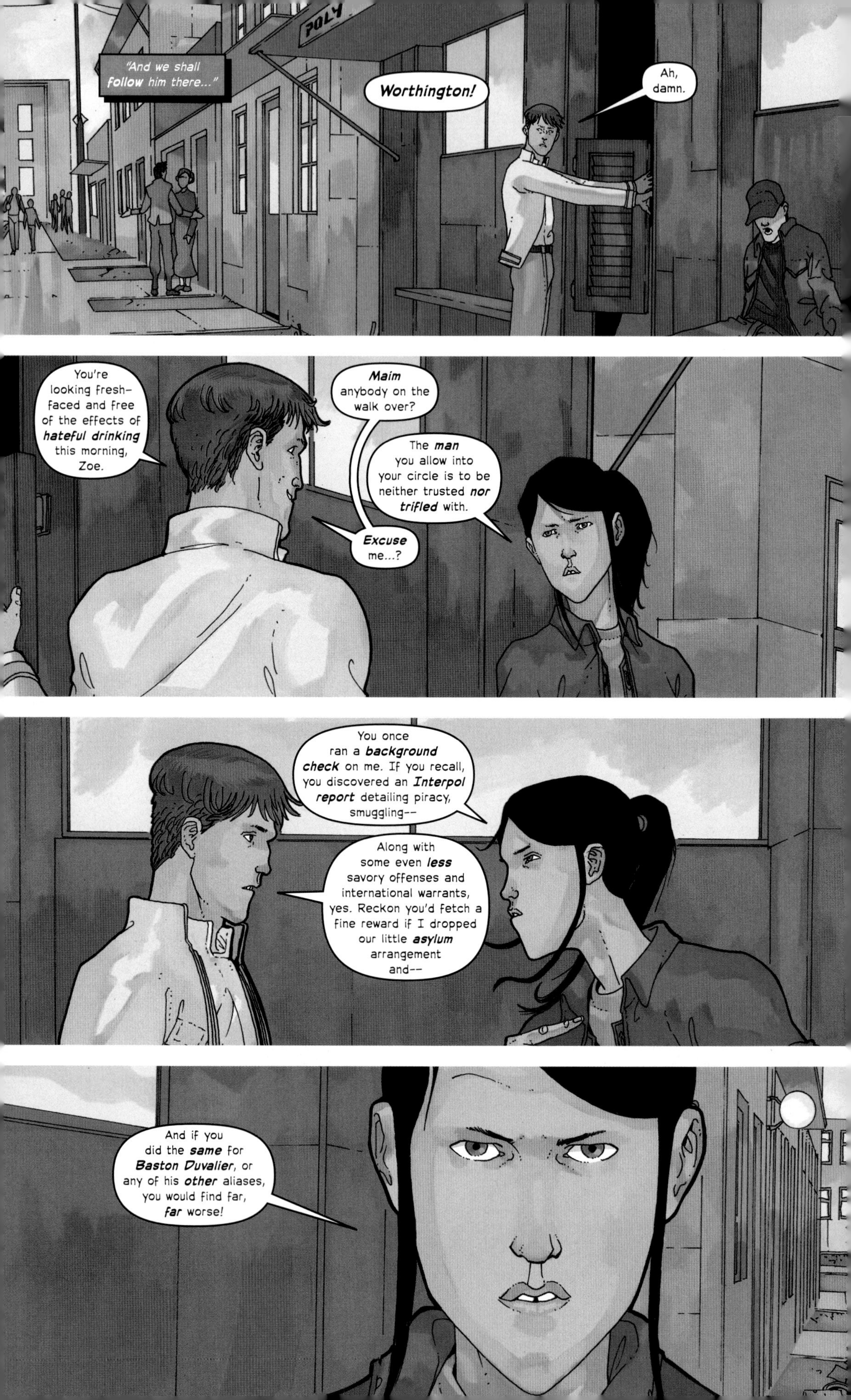
"And we shall follow him there..."
POLY
Worthington!
Ah, damn.
You're looking fresh-faced and free of the effects of hateful drinking this morning, Zoe.
Maim anybody on the walk over?
The man you allow into your circle is to be neither trusted nor trifled with.
Excuse me...?
You once ran a background check on me. If you recall, you discovered an Interpol report detailing piracy, smuggling--
Along with some even less savory offenses and international warrants, yes. Reckon you'd fetch a fine reward if I dropped our little asylum arrangement and--
And if you did the same for Baston Duvalier, or any of his other aliases, you would find far, far worse!

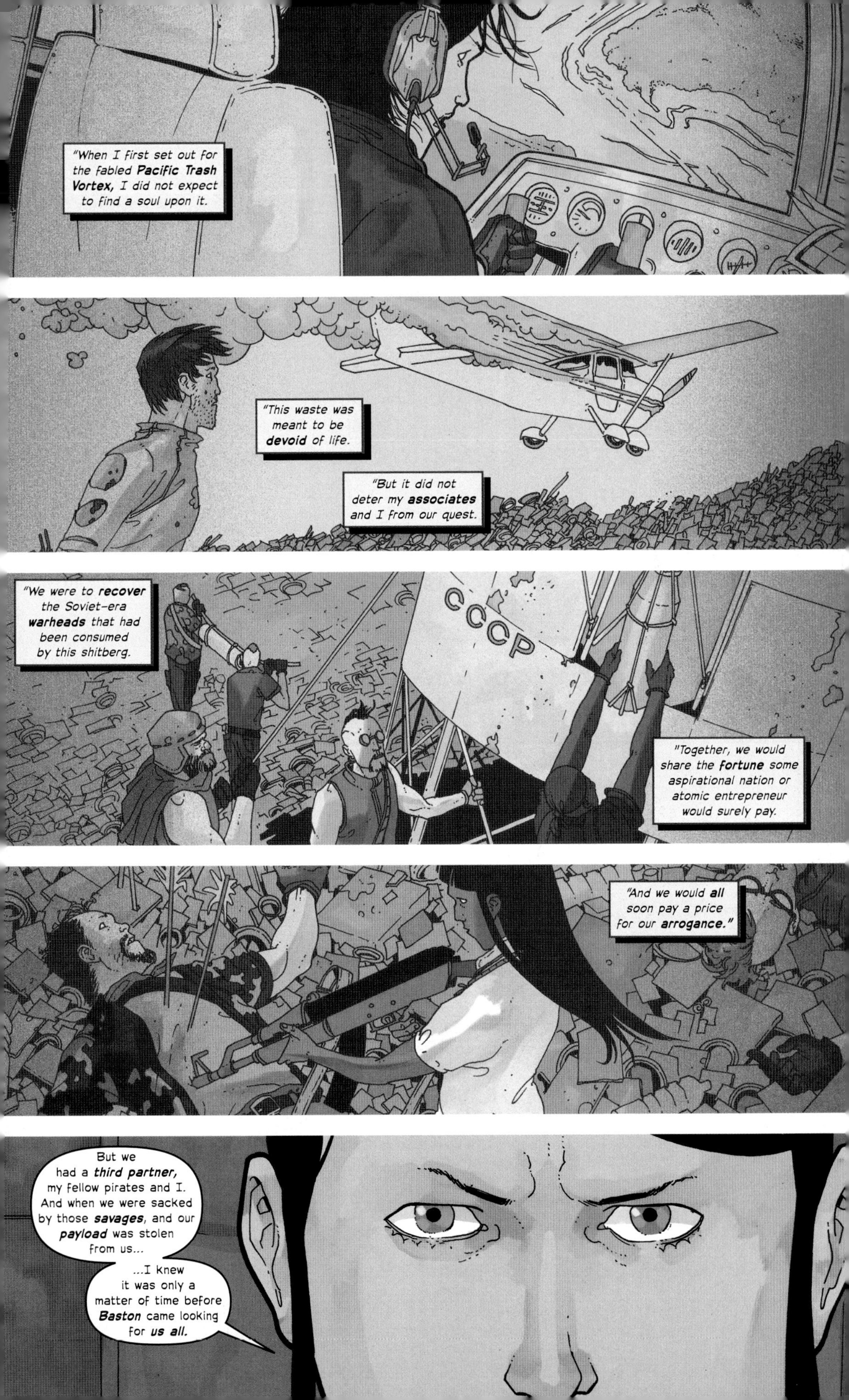
"When I first set out for the fabled **Pacific Trash Vortex**, I did not expect to find a soul upon it.
"This waste was meant to be **devoid** of life.
"But it did not deter my **associates** and I from our quest.
"We were to **recover** the Soviet-era **warheads** that had been consumed by this shitberg.
CCCP
"Together, we would share the **fortune** some aspirational nation or atomic entrepreneur would surely pay.
"And we would **all** soon pay a price for our **arrogance**."
But we had a ***third partner***, my fellow pirates and I. And when we were sacked by those ***savages***, and our ***payload*** was stolen from us...
...I knew it was only a matter of time before ***Baston*** came looking for ***us all.***

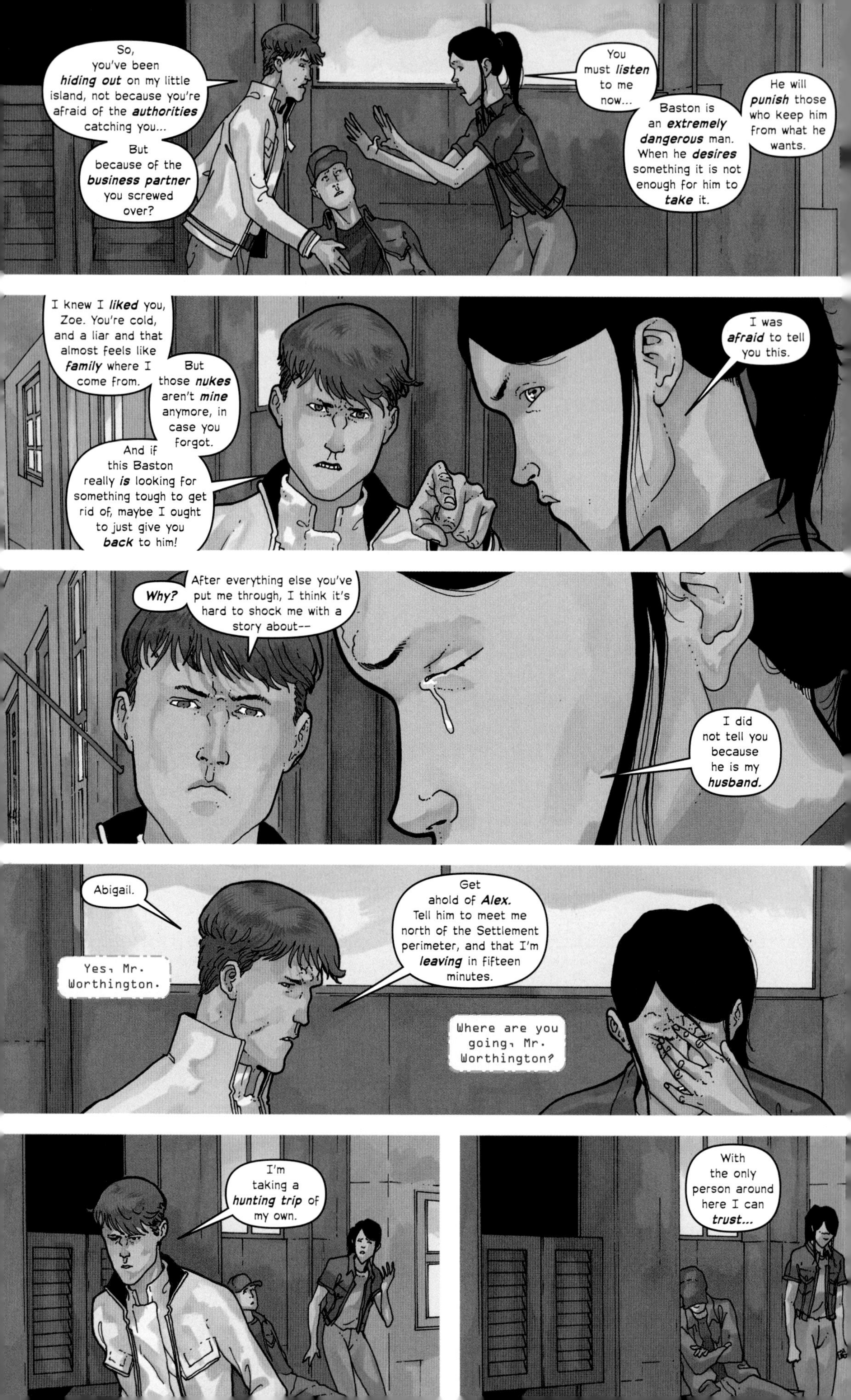
So, you've been hiding out on my little island, not because you're afraid of the authorities catching you...
But because of the business partner you screwed over?
You must listen to me now...
Baston is an extremely dangerous man. When he desires something it is not enough for him to take it.
He will punish those who keep him from what he wants.
I knew I liked you, Zoe. You're cold, and a liar and that almost feels like family where I come from.
But those nukes aren't mine anymore, in case you forgot.
And if this Baston really is looking for something tough to get rid of, maybe I ought to just give you back to him!
I was afraid to tell you this.
Why?
After everything else you've put me through, I think it's hard to shock me with a story about--
I did not tell you because he is my husband.
Abigail.
Yes, Mr. Worthington.
Get ahold of Alex. Tell him to meet me north of the Settlement perimeter, and that I'm leaving in fifteen minutes.
Where are you going, Mr. Worthington?
I'm taking a hunting trip of my own.
With the only person around here I can trust...

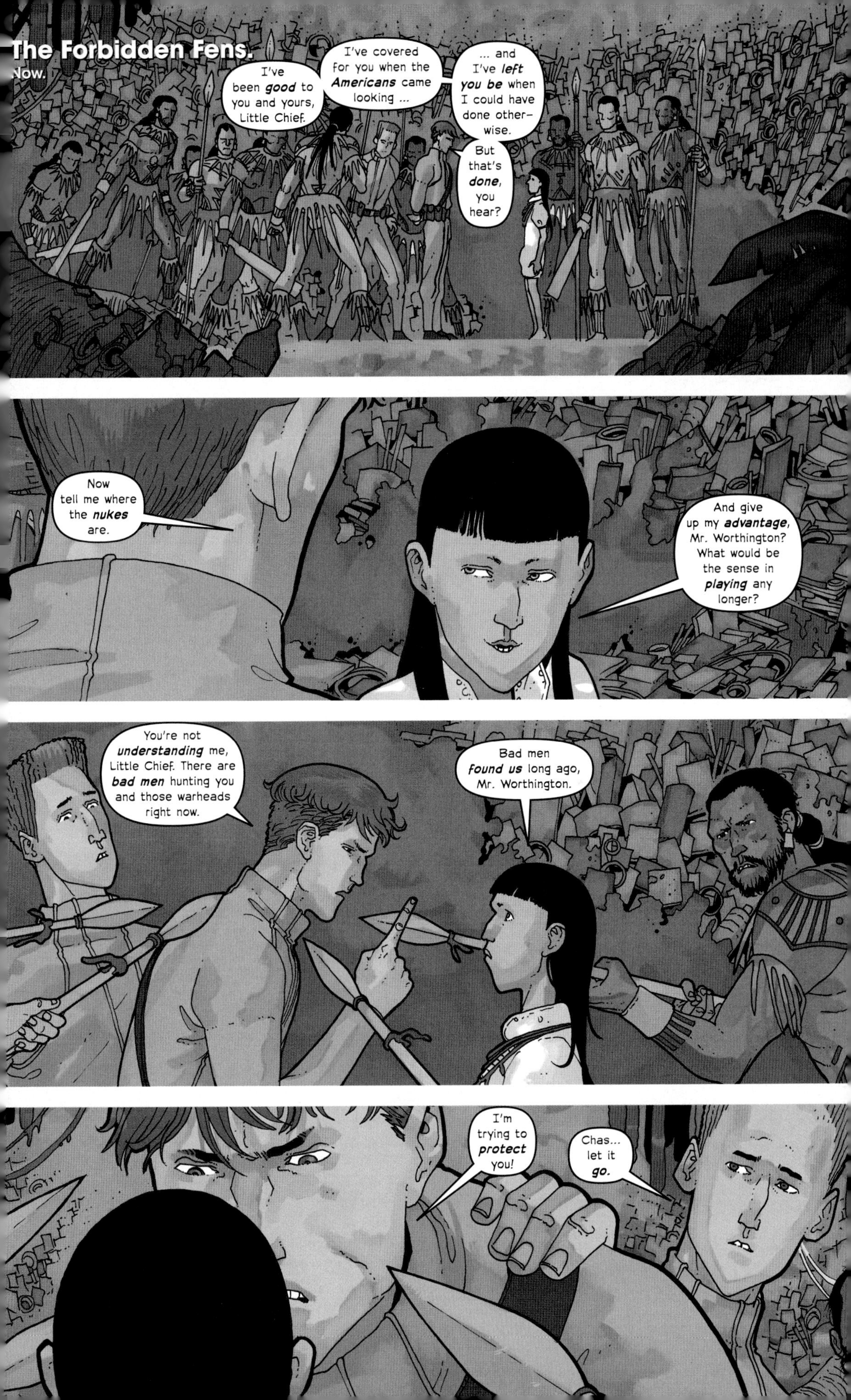

The Forbidden Fens.
Now.
I've been *good* to you and yours, Little Chief.
I've covered for you when the *Americans* came looking ...
... and I've *left you be* when I could have done other-wise.
But that's *done*, you hear?
Now tell me where the *nukes* are.
And give up my *advantage*, Mr. Worthington? What would be the sense in *playing* any longer?
You're not *understanding* me, Little Chief. There are *bad men* hunting you and those warheads right now.
Bad men *found us* long ago, Mr. Worthington.
I'm trying to *protect* you!
Chas... let it *go.*

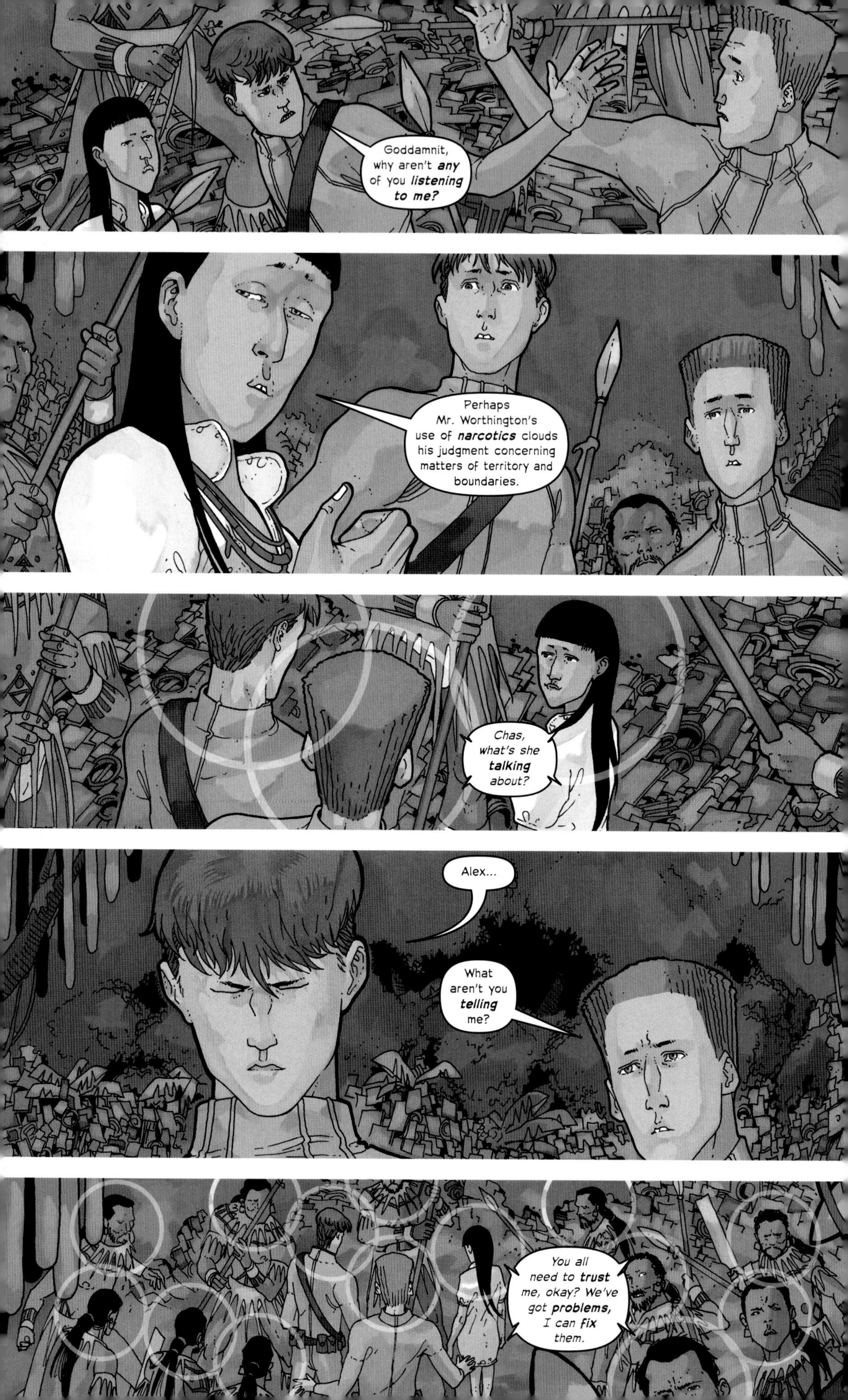
Goddamnit, why aren't *any* of you *listening to me?*
Perhaps Mr. Worthington's use of ***narcotics*** clouds his judgment concerning matters of territory and boundaries.
*Chas, what's she **talking** about?*
Alex...
What aren't you ***telling*** me?
*You all need to **trust** me, okay? We've got **problems,** I can **fix** them.*

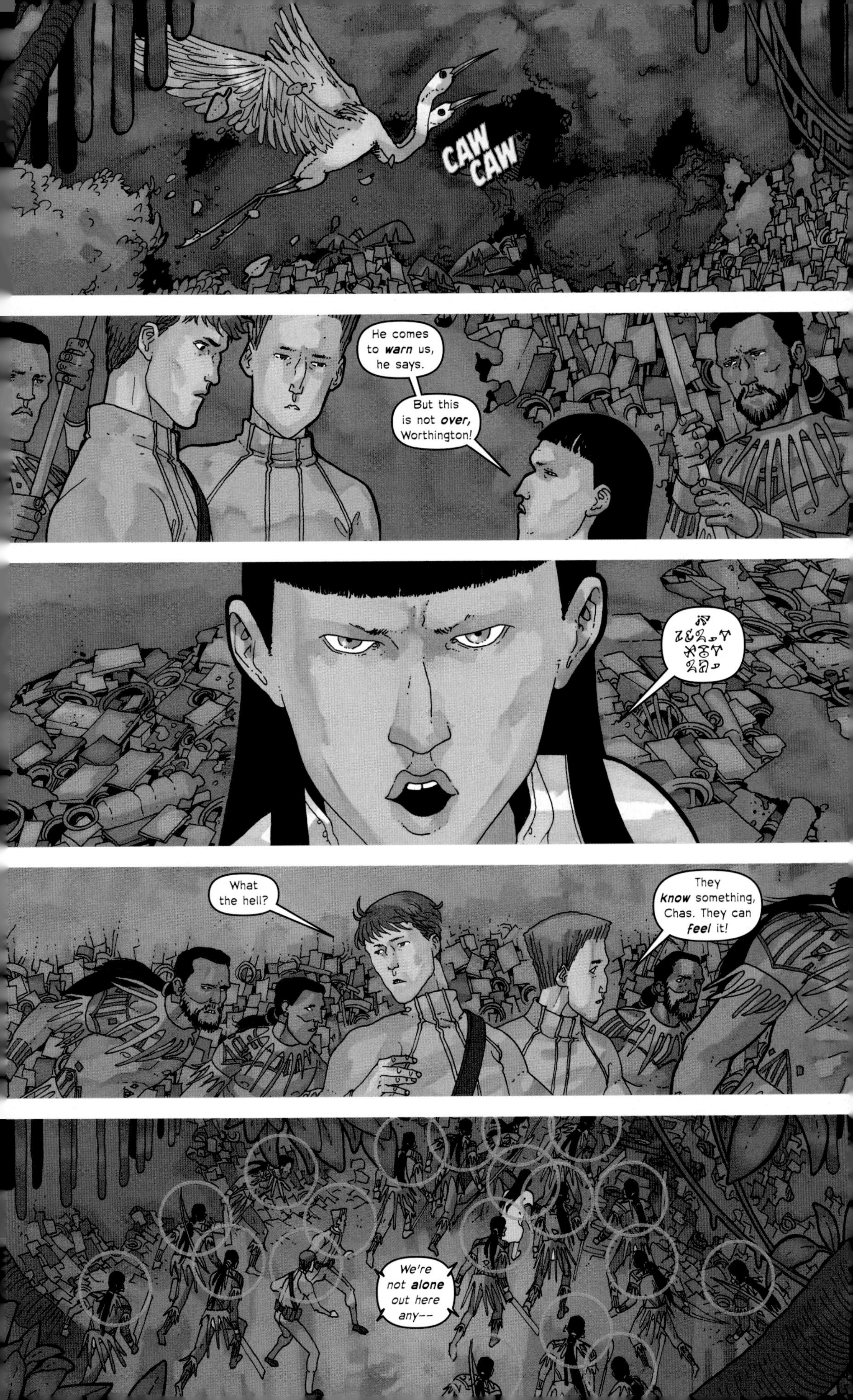
CAW CAW
He comes to *warn* us, he says.
But this is not *over,* Worthington!
What the hell?
They *know* something, Chas. They can *feel* it!
We're not *alone* out here any--

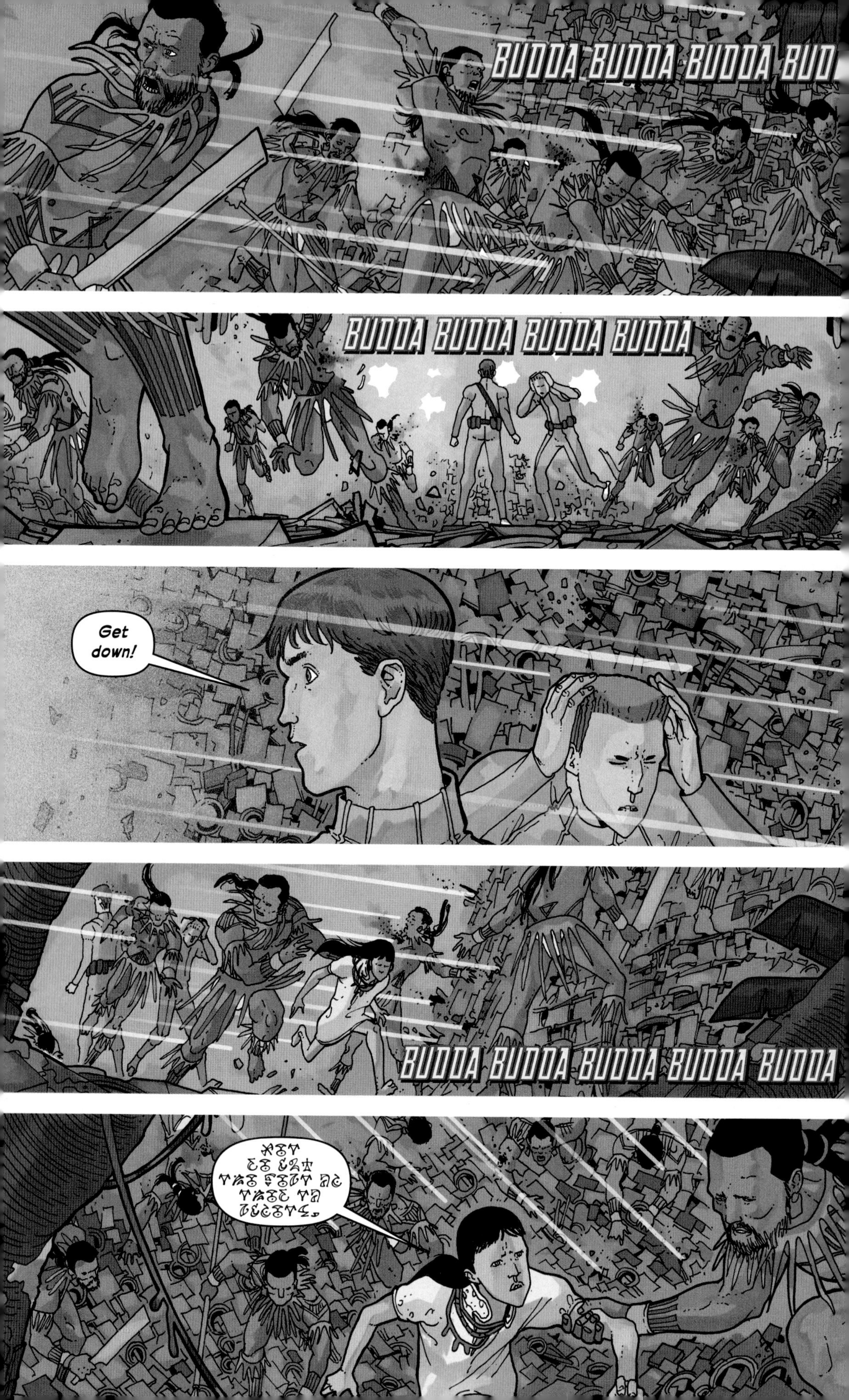
BUDDA BUDDA BUDDA BUD
BUDDA BUDDA BUDDA BUDDA
Get down!
BUDDA BUDDA BUDDA BUDDA BUDDA

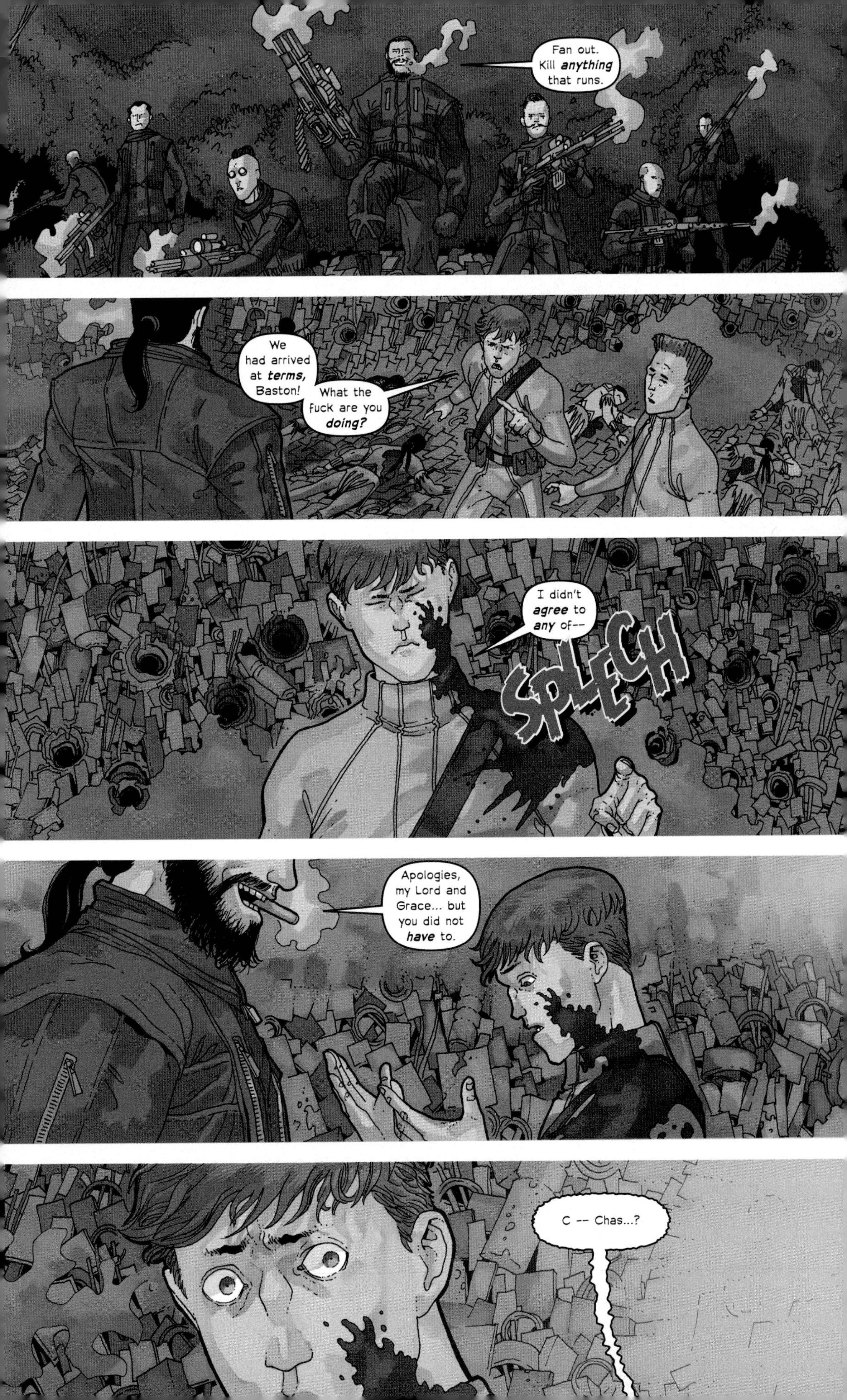
Fan out. Kill anything that runs.
We had arrived at terms, Baston!
What the fuck are you doing?
I didn't agree to any of--
SPLECH
Apologies, my Lord and Grace... but you did not have to.
C -- Chas...?

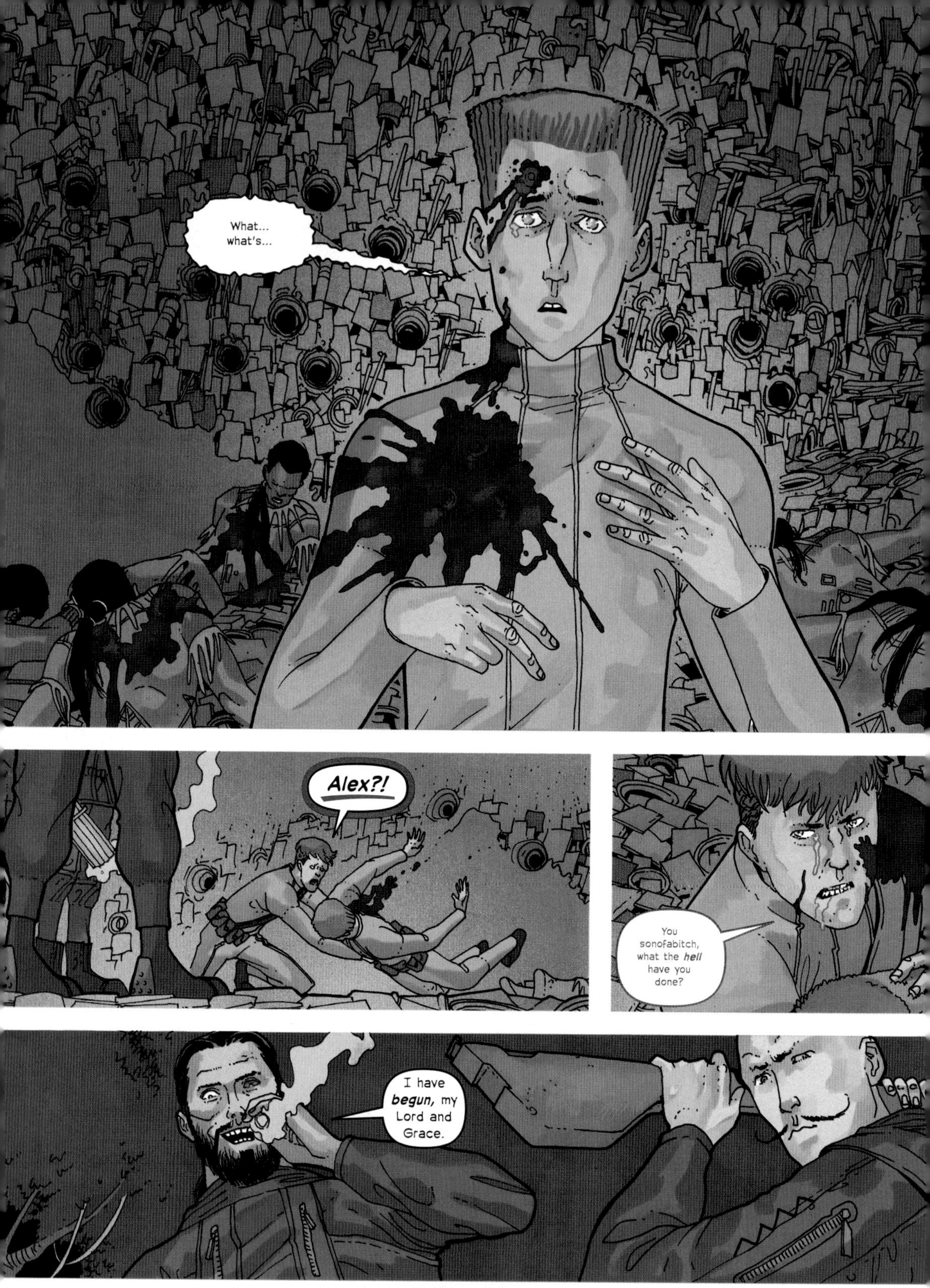
What... what's...
Alex?!
You sonofabitch, what the *hell* have you done?
I have *begun*, my Lord and Grace.

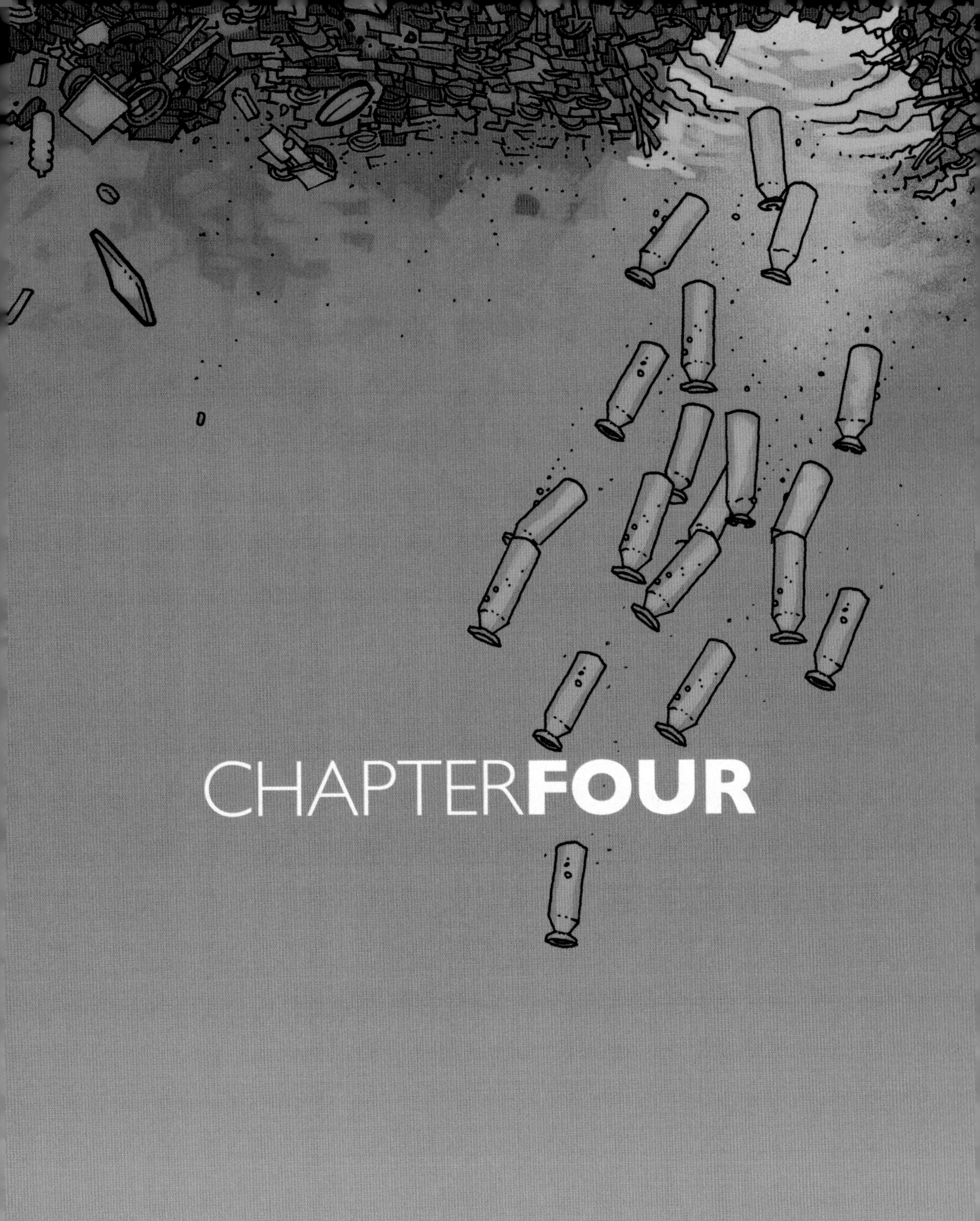

CHAPTER FOUR

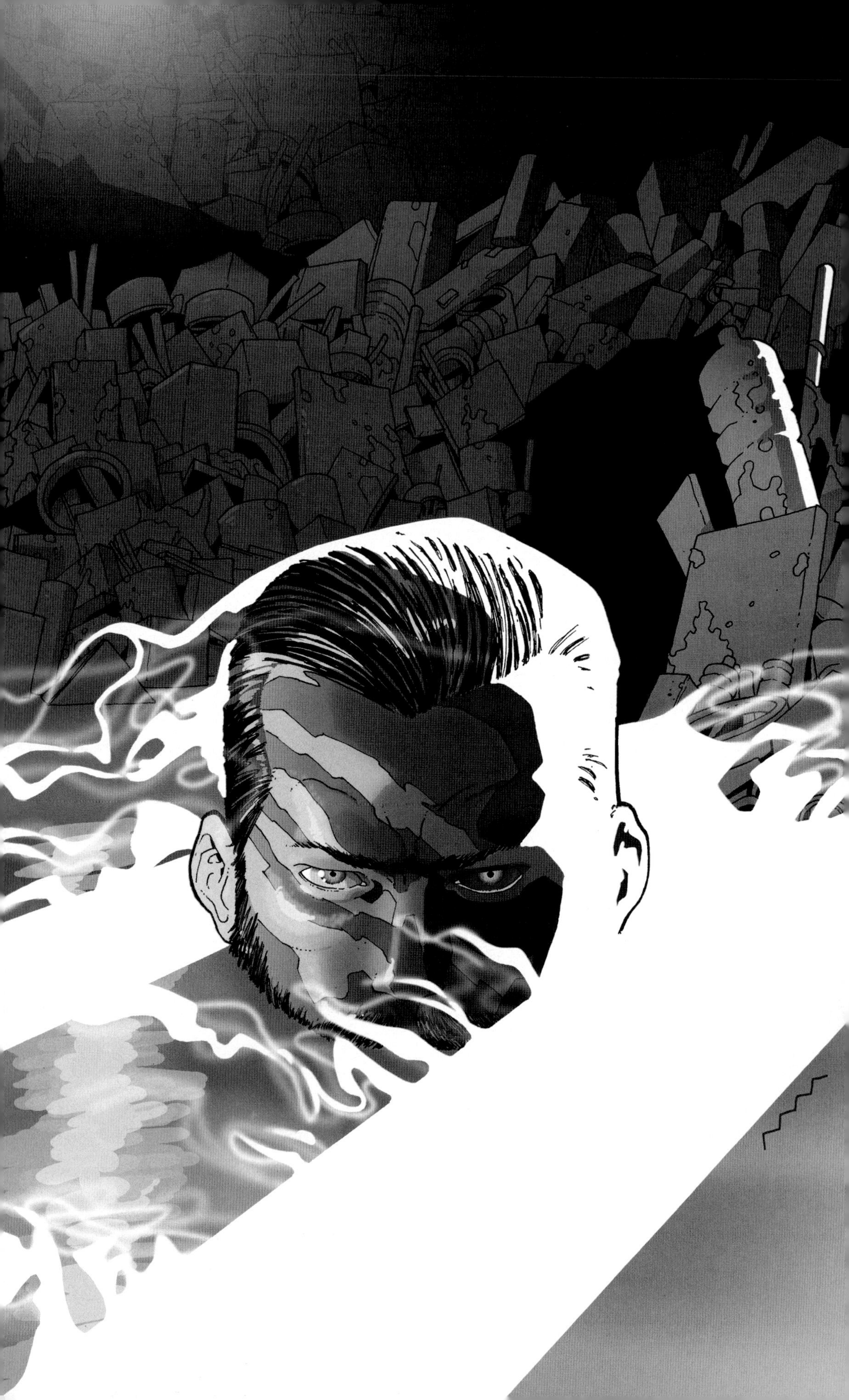

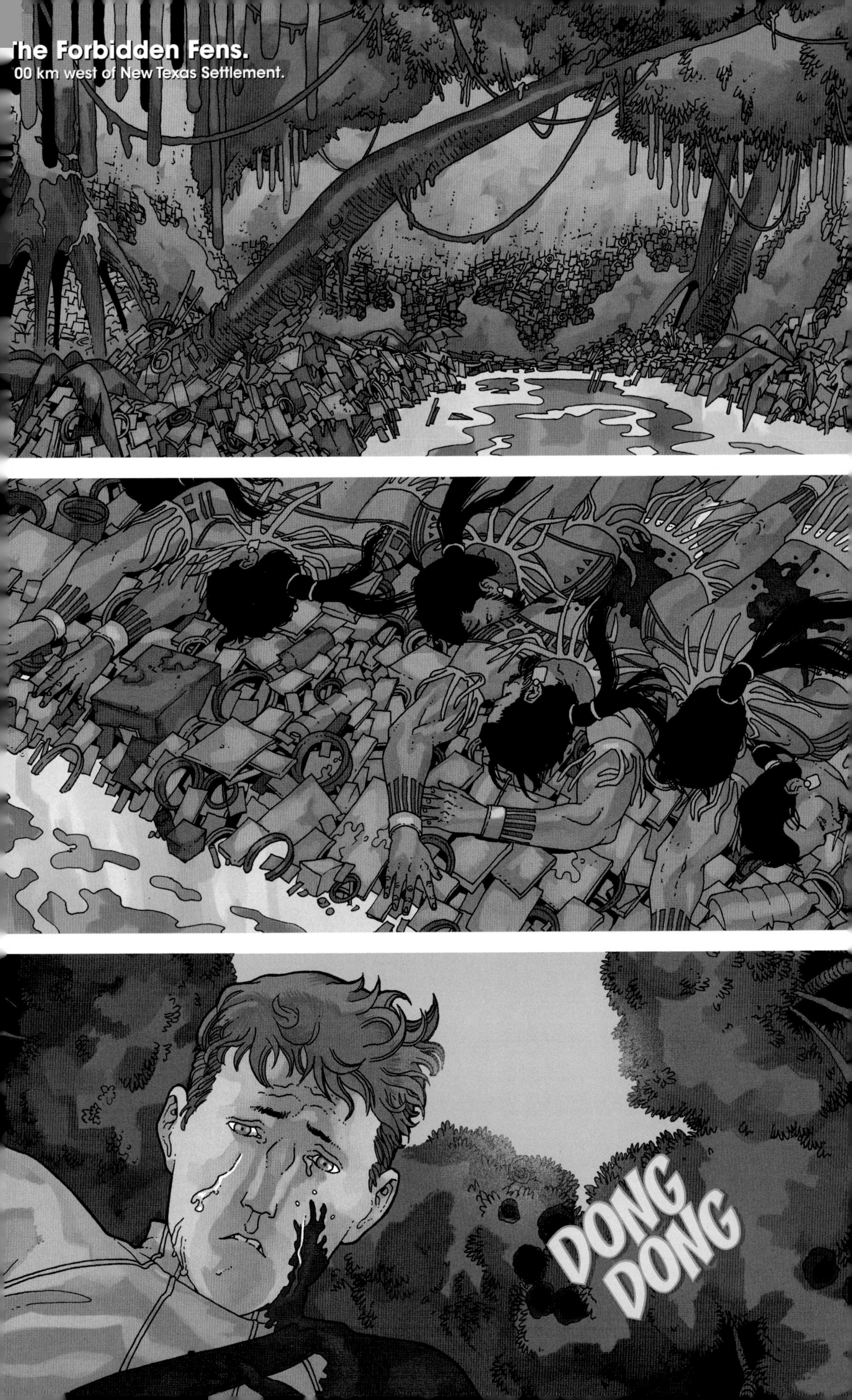
he Forbidden Fens.
00 km west of New Texas Settlement.
DONG
DONG

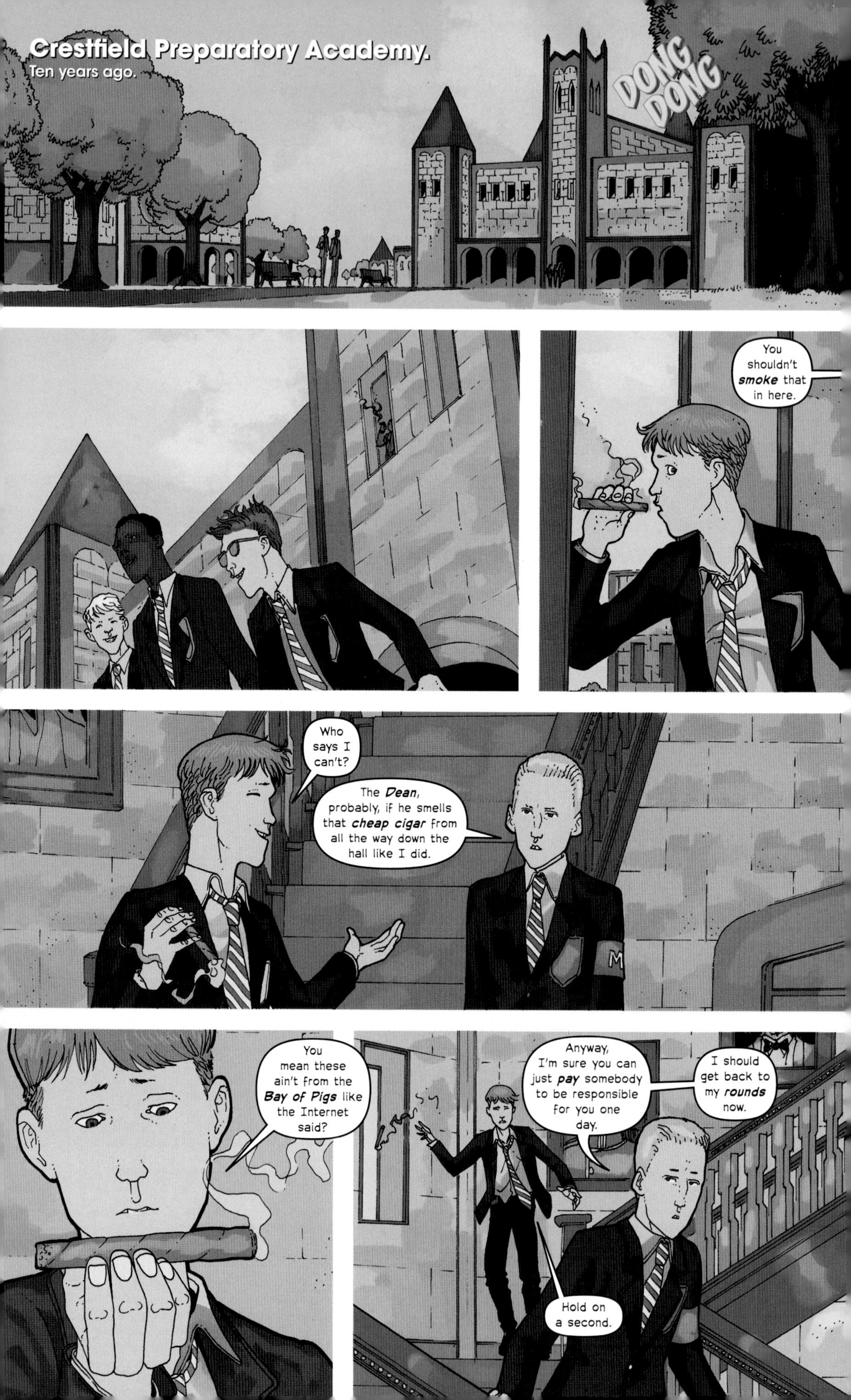
Crestfield Preparatory Academy.
Ten years ago.
DONG DONG
You shouldn't smoke that in here.
Who says I can't?
The Dean, probably, if he smells that cheap cigar from all the way down the hall like I did.
M
You mean these ain't from the Bay of Pigs like the Internet said?
Anyway, I'm sure you can just pay somebody to be responsible for you one day.
I should get back to my rounds now.
Hold on a second.

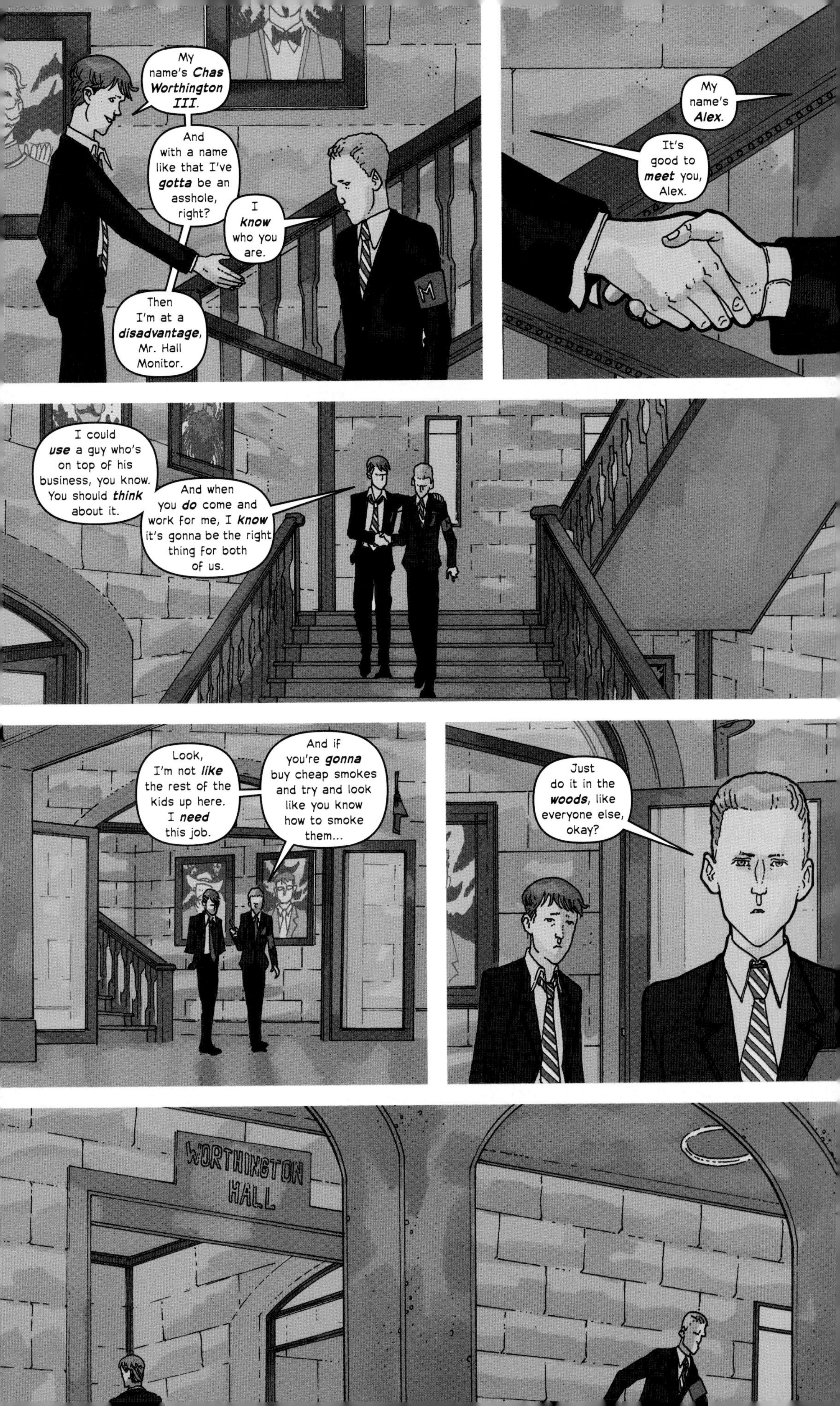

My name's Chas Worthington III.
And with a name like that I've gotta be an asshole, right?
I know who you are.
Then I'm at a disadvantage, Mr. Hall Monitor.
My name's Alex.
It's good to meet you, Alex.
I could use a guy who's on top of his business, you know. You should think about it.
And when you do come and work for me, I know it's gonna be the right thing for both of us.
Look, I'm not like the rest of the kids up here. I need this job.
And if you're gonna buy cheap smokes and try and look like you know how to smoke them...
Just do it in the woods, like everyone else, okay?
WORTHINGTON HALL

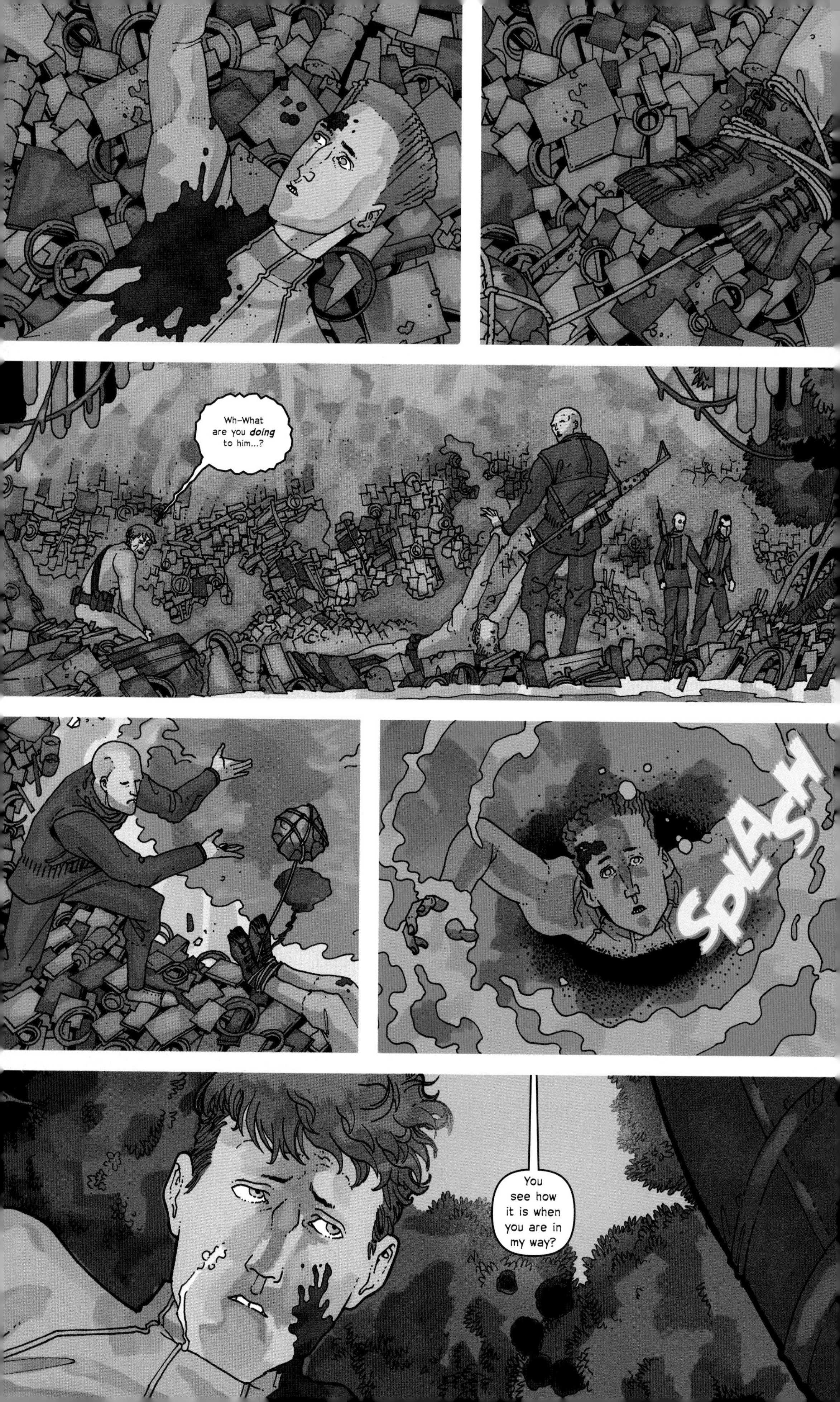
Wh-What are you *doing* to him...?
SPLASH
You see how it is when you are in my way?

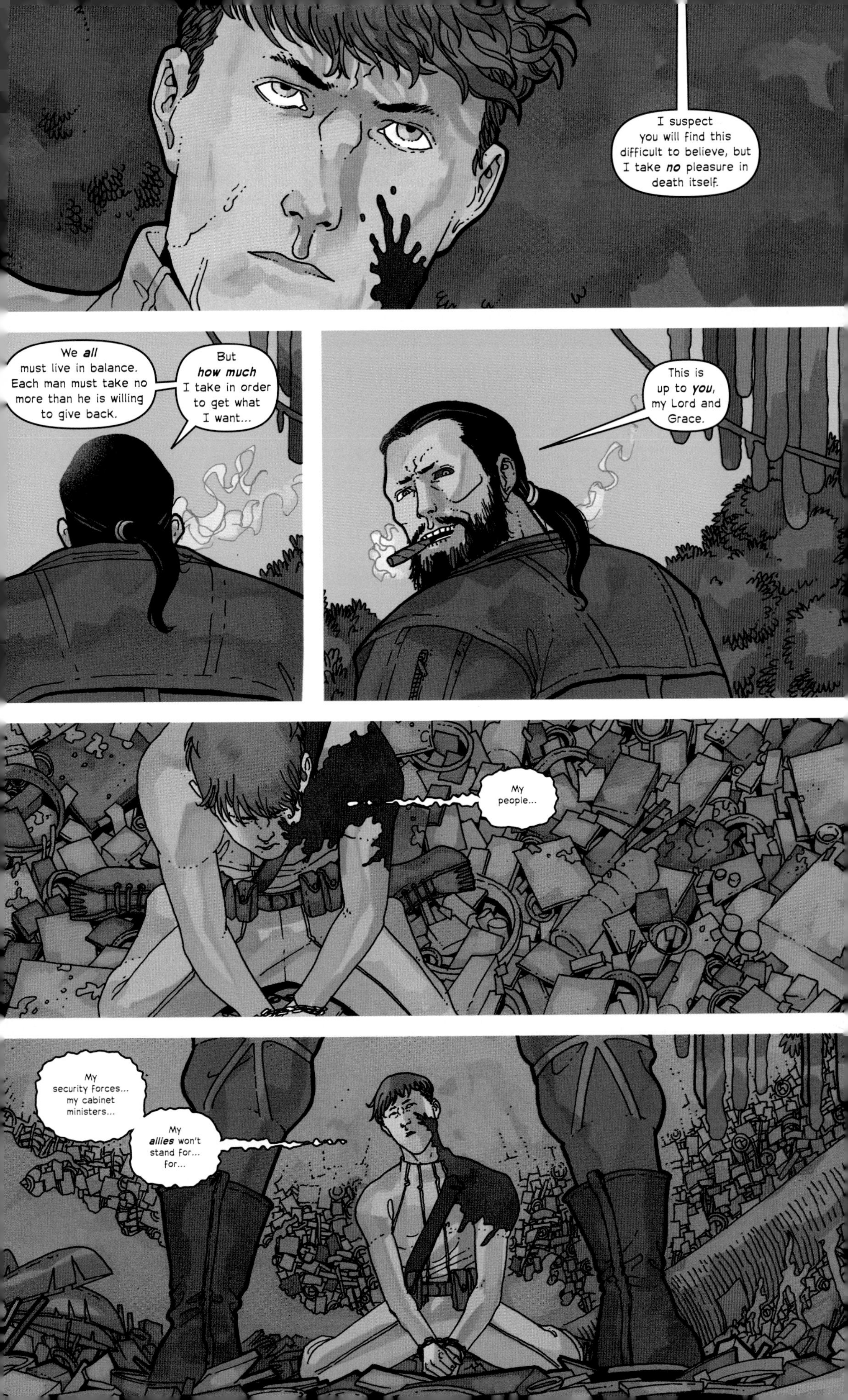
I suspect you will find this difficult to believe, but I take *no* pleasure in death itself.
We *all* must live in balance. Each man must take no more than he is willing to give back.
But *how much* I take in order to get what I want...
This is up to *you*, my Lord and Grace.
My people...
My security forces... my cabinet ministers...
My *allies* won't stand for... for...

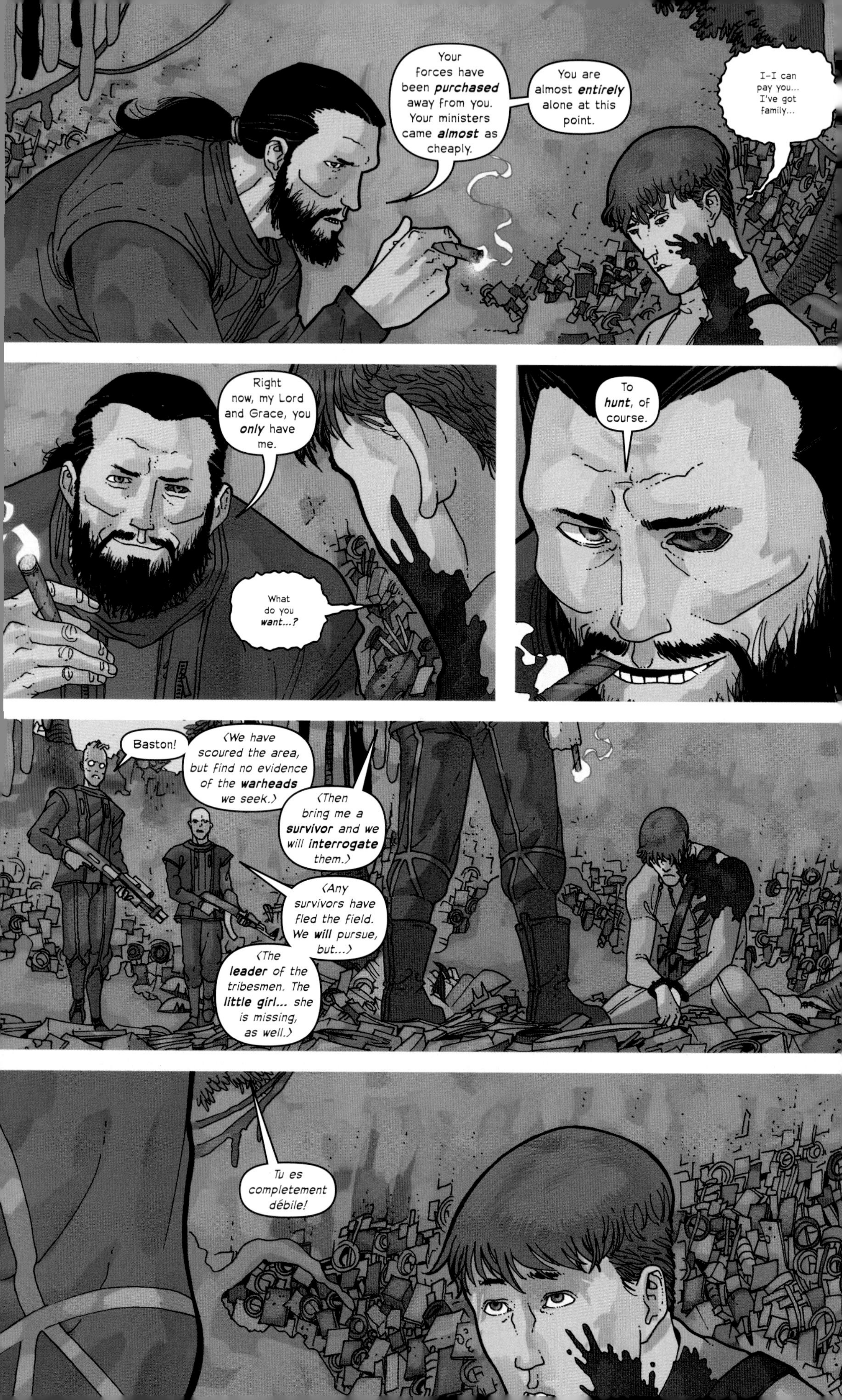
Your forces have been *purchased* away from you. Your ministers came *almost* as cheaply.
You are almost *entirely* alone at this point.
I–I can pay you... I've got family...
Right now, my Lord and Grace, you *only* have me.
What do you *want...?*
To *hunt*, of course.
Baston!
‹We have scoured the area, but find no evidence of the **warheads** we seek.›
‹Then bring me a **survivor** and we will **interrogate** them.›
‹Any survivors have fled the field. **We will** pursue, but...›
‹The **leader** of the tribesmen. The **little girl...** she is missing, as well.›
Tu es completement débile!

It would seem *our* hunt must wait until the appropriate level of tension has been achieved.

Take Mr. Worthington *home* now, please.

We will continue our *dialogue* later.

HNNN

All right then, *let's* go.

What are *you* looking at, eh?

Get a *move* on!

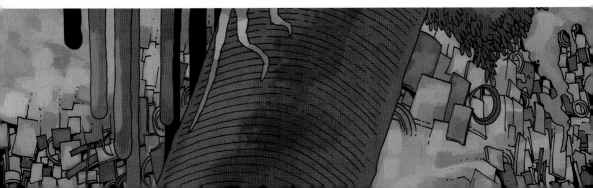

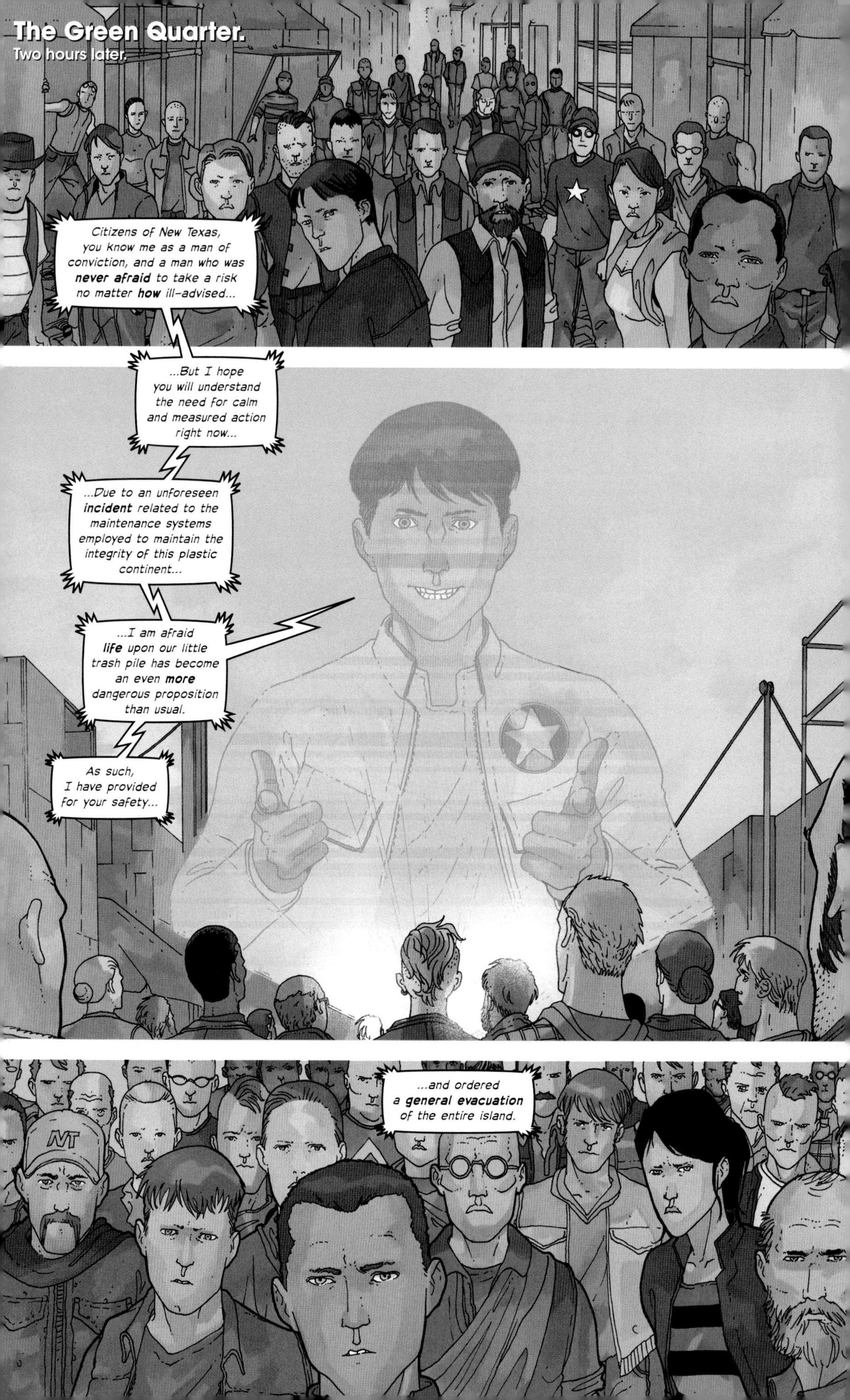
The Green Quarter.
Two hours later.
Citizens of New Texas, you know me as a man of conviction, and a man who was **never afraid** to take a risk no matter **how** ill-advised...
...But I hope you will understand the need for calm and measured action right now...
...Due to an unforeseen **incident** related to the maintenance systems employed to maintain the integrity of this plastic continent...
...I am afraid **life** upon our little trash pile has become an even **more** dangerous proposition than usual.
As such, I have provided for your safety...
...and ordered a **general evacuation** of the entire island.
NT

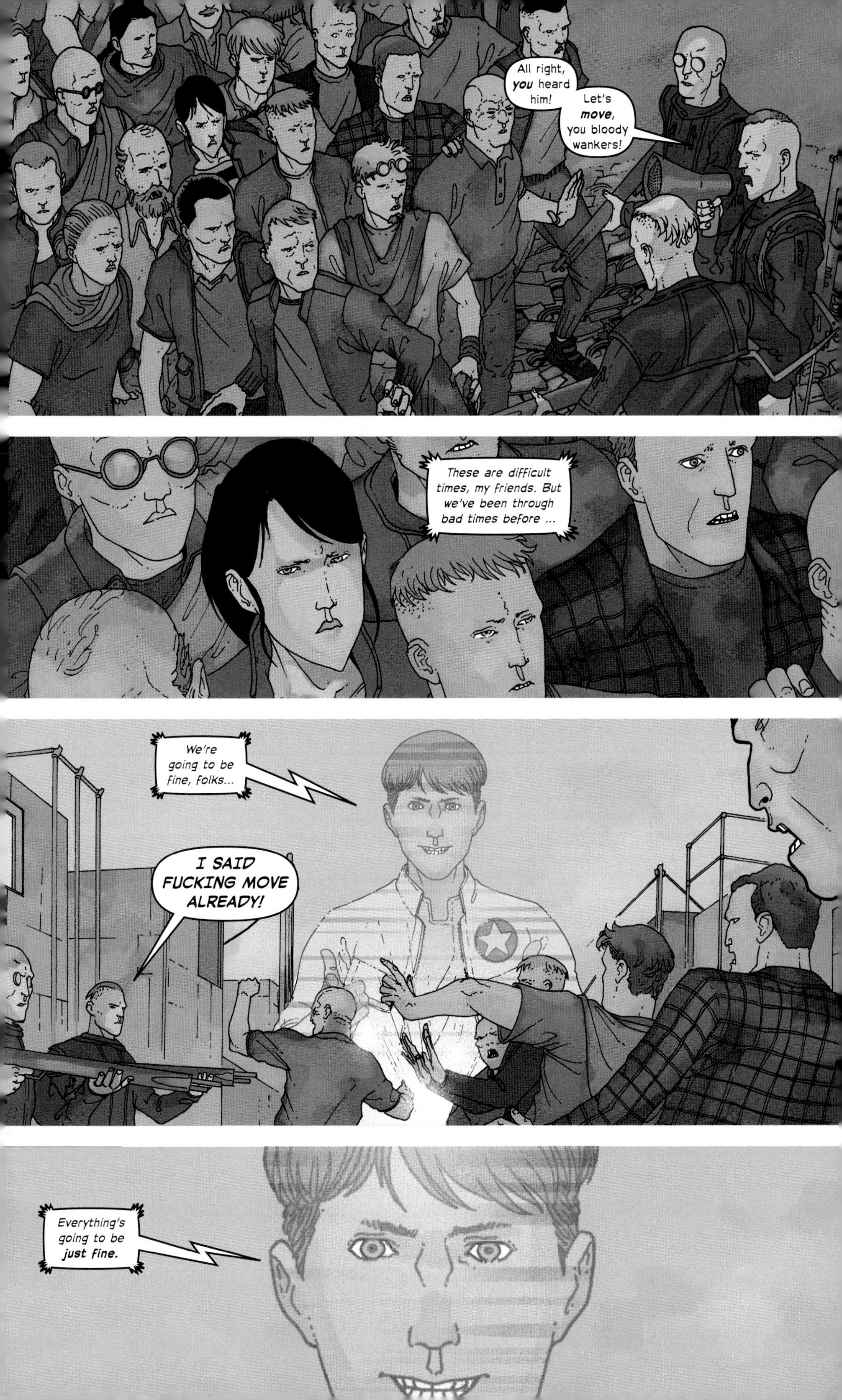
All right, *you* heard him!
Let's *move*, you bloody wankers!
These are difficult times, my friends. But we've been through bad times before ...
We're going to be fine, folks...
I SAID FUCKING MOVE ALREADY!
Everything's going to be *just fine.*

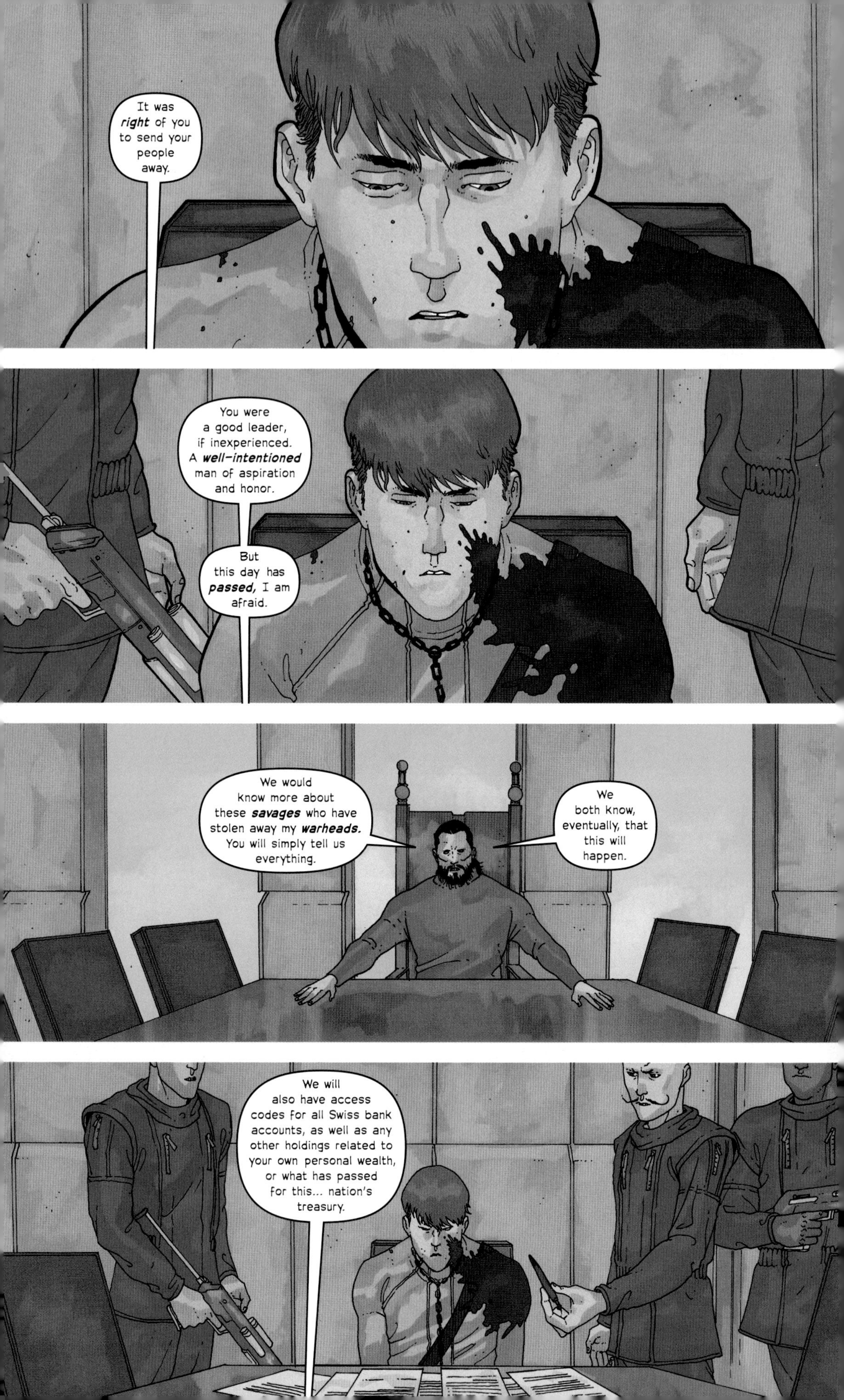

It was *right* of you to send your people away.
You were a good leader, if inexperienced. A *well-intentioned* man of aspiration and honor.
But this day has *passed,* I am afraid.
We would know more about these *savages* who have stolen away my *warheads.* You will simply tell us everything.
We both know, eventually, that this will happen.
We will also have access codes for all Swiss bank accounts, as well as any other holdings related to your own personal wealth, or what has passed for this... nation's treasury.

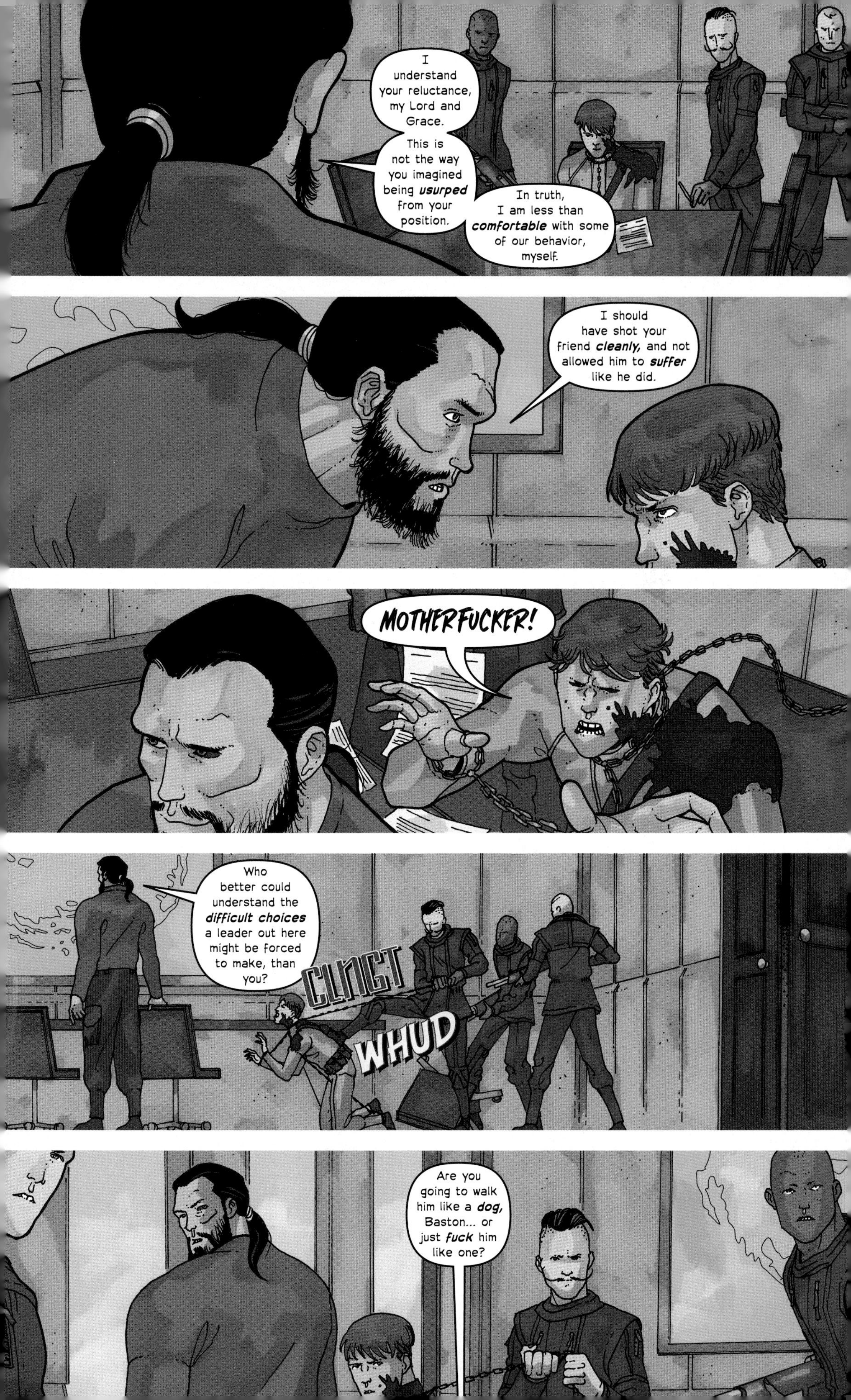
I understand your reluctance, my Lord and Grace.
This is not the way you imagined being *usurped* from your position.
In truth, I am less than *comfortable* with some of our behavior, myself.
I should have shot your friend *cleanly,* and not allowed him to *suffer* like he did.
MOTHERFUCKER!
Who better could understand the *difficult choices* a leader out here might be forced to make, than you?
CLNGT
WHUD
Are you going to walk him like a *dog,* Baston... or just *fuck* him like one?

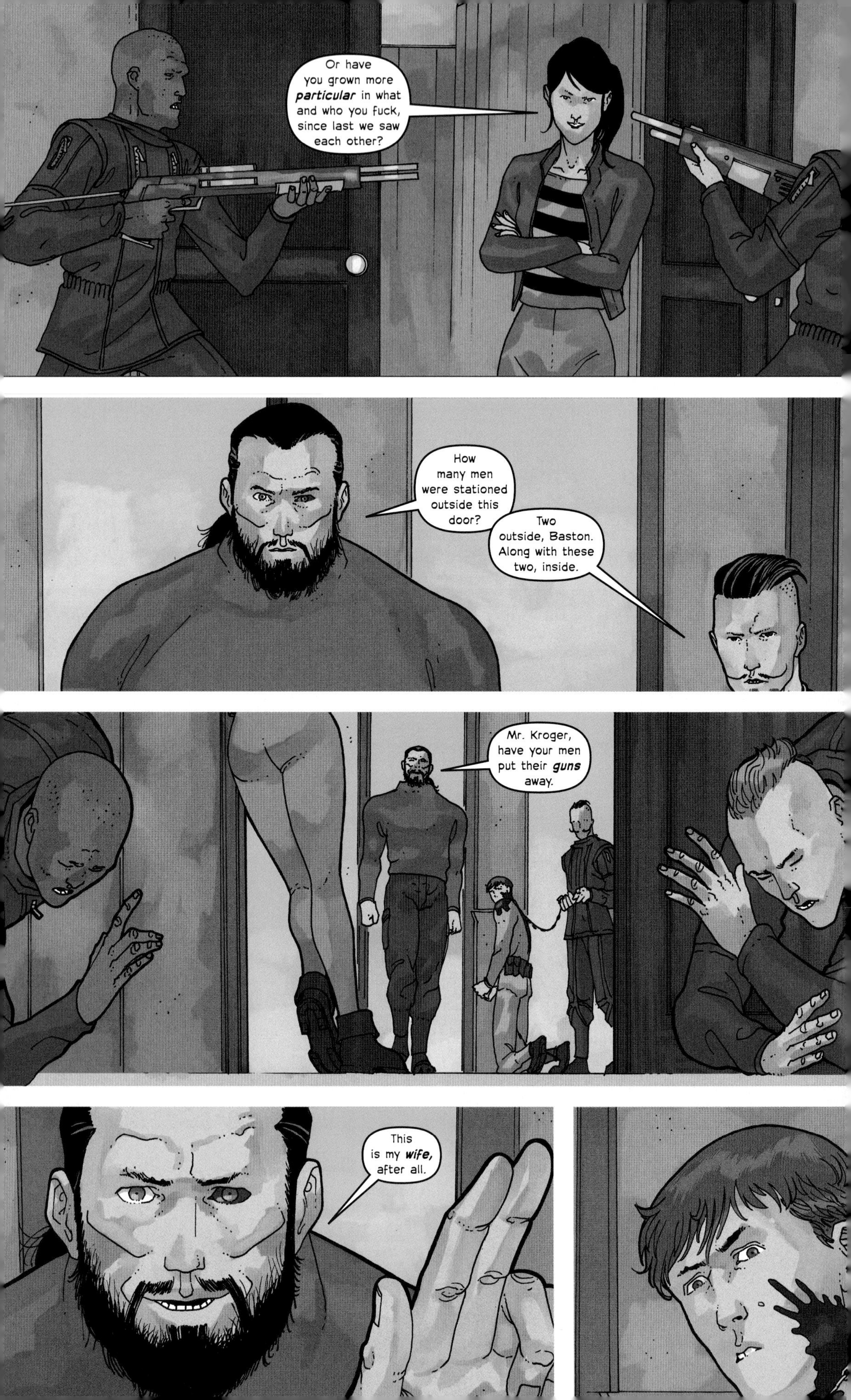
Or have you grown more *particular* in what and who you fuck, since last we saw each other?
How many men were stationed outside this door?
Two outside, Baston. Along with these two, inside.
Mr. Kroger, have your men put their *guns* away.
This is my *wife,* after all.

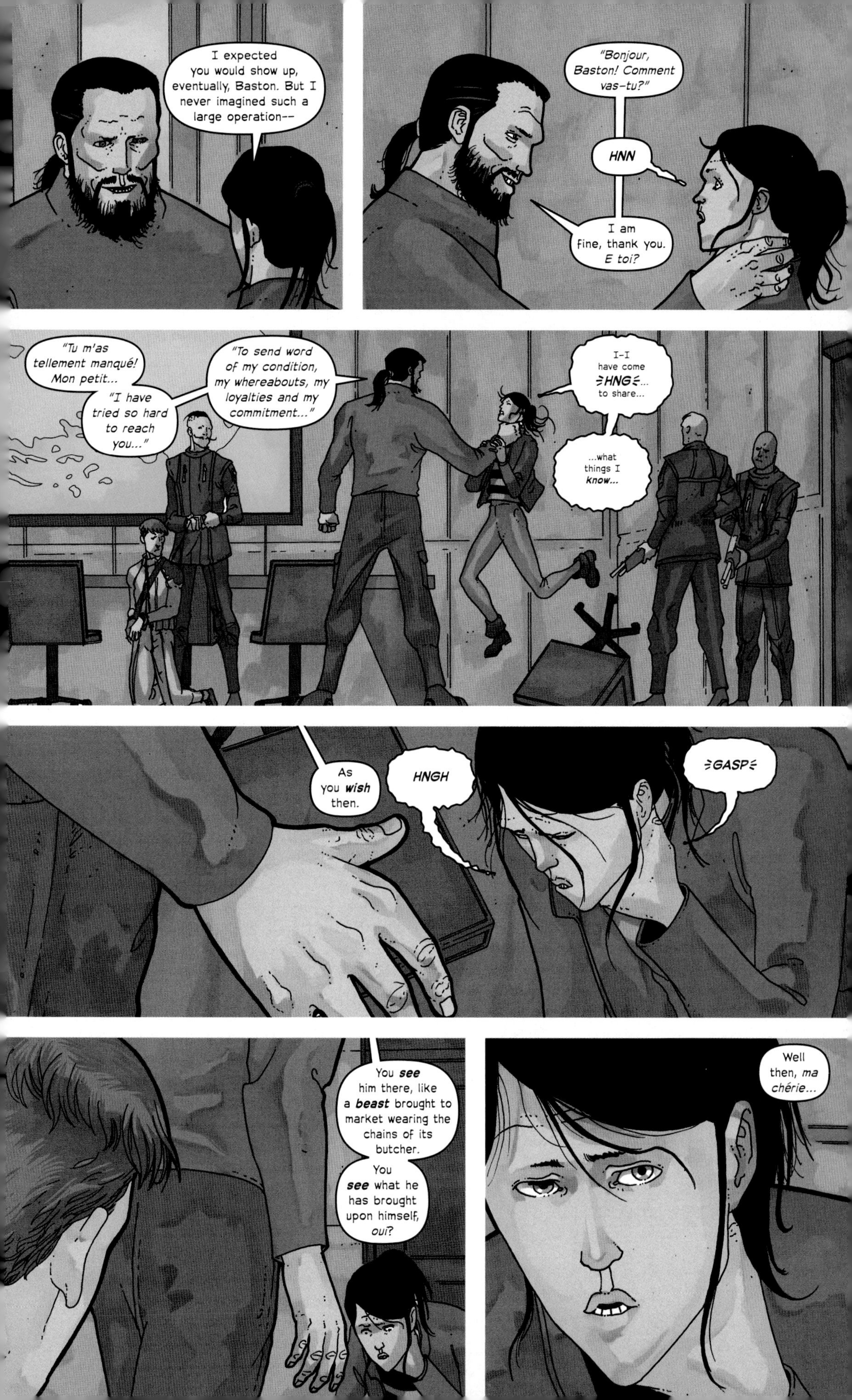
I expected you would show up, eventually, Baston. But I never imagined such a large operation--
"Bonjour, Baston! Comment vas-tu?"
HNN
I am fine, thank you. E toi?
"Tu m'as tellement manqué! Mon petit...
"I have tried so hard to reach you..."
"To send word of my condition, my whereabouts, my loyalties and my commitment..."
I-I have come
HNG...
to share...
...what things I know...
As you wish then.
HNGH
GASP
You see him there, like a beast brought to market wearing the chains of its butcher.
You see what he has brought upon himself, oui?
Well then, ma chérie...

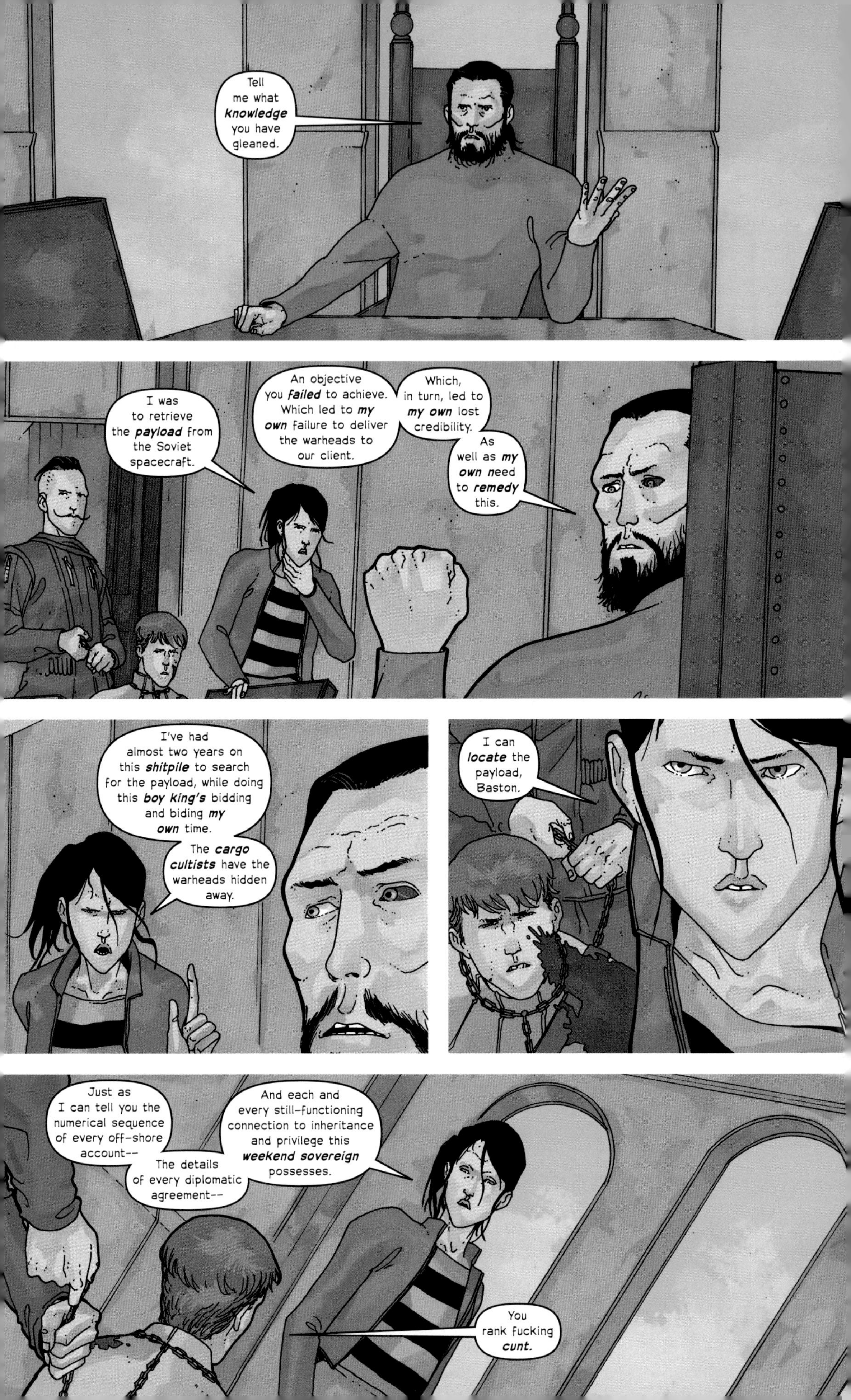
Tell me what knowledge you have gleaned.
I was to retrieve the payload from the Soviet spacecraft.
An objective you failed to achieve. Which led to my own failure to deliver the warheads to our client.
Which, in turn, led to my own lost credibility.
As well as my own need to remedy this.
I've had almost two years on this shitpile to search for the payload, while doing this boy king's bidding and biding my own time.
The cargo cultists have the warheads hidden away.
I can locate the payload, Baston.
Just as I can tell you the numerical sequence of every off-shore account--
The details of every diplomatic agreement--
And each and every still-functioning connection to inheritance and privilege this weekend sovereign possesses.
You rank fucking cunt.

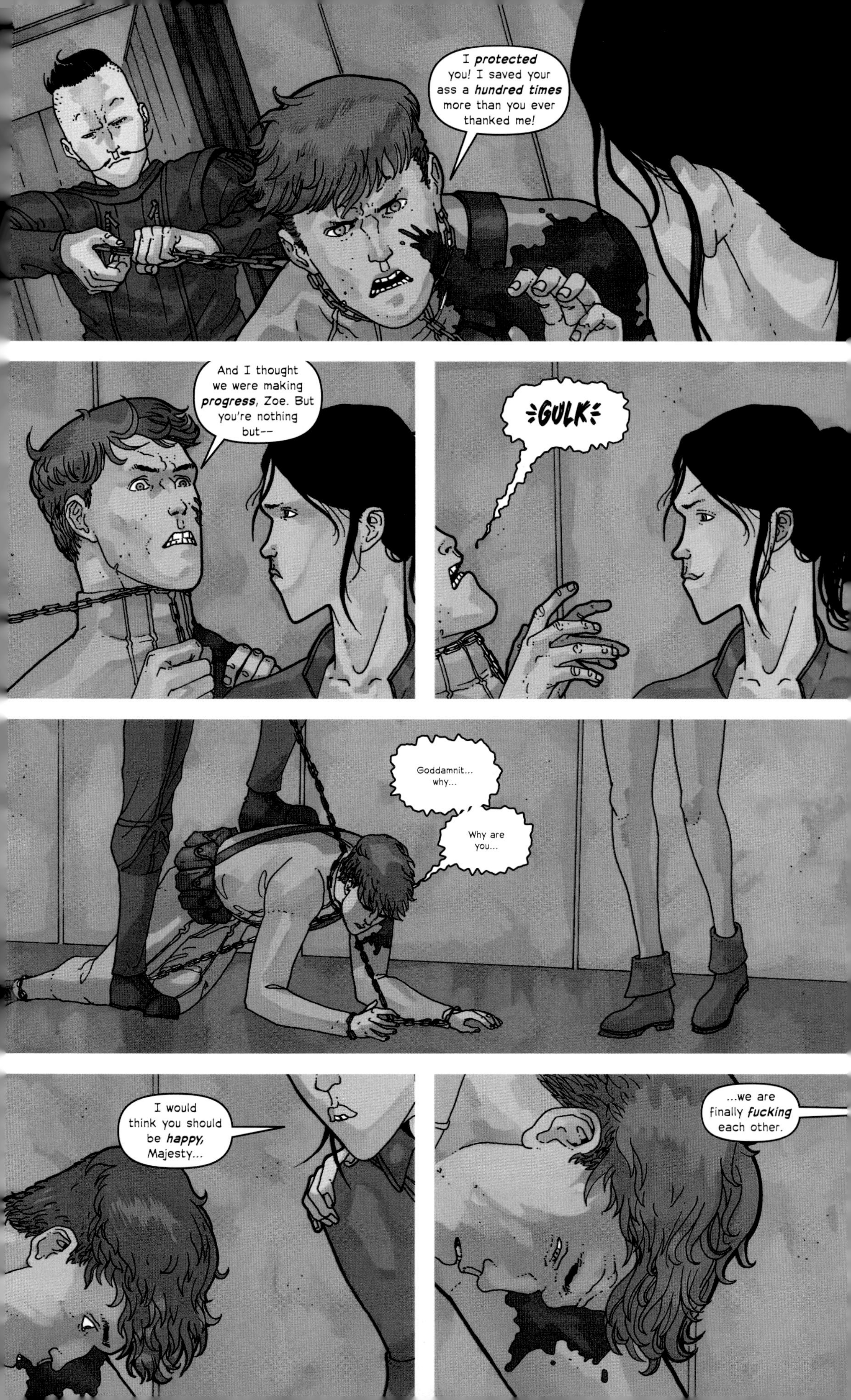
I protected you! I saved your ass a hundred times more than you ever thanked me!
And I thought we were making progress, Zoe. But you're nothing but--
GULK
Goddamnit... why...
Why are you...
I would think you should be happy, Majesty...
...we are finally fucking each other.

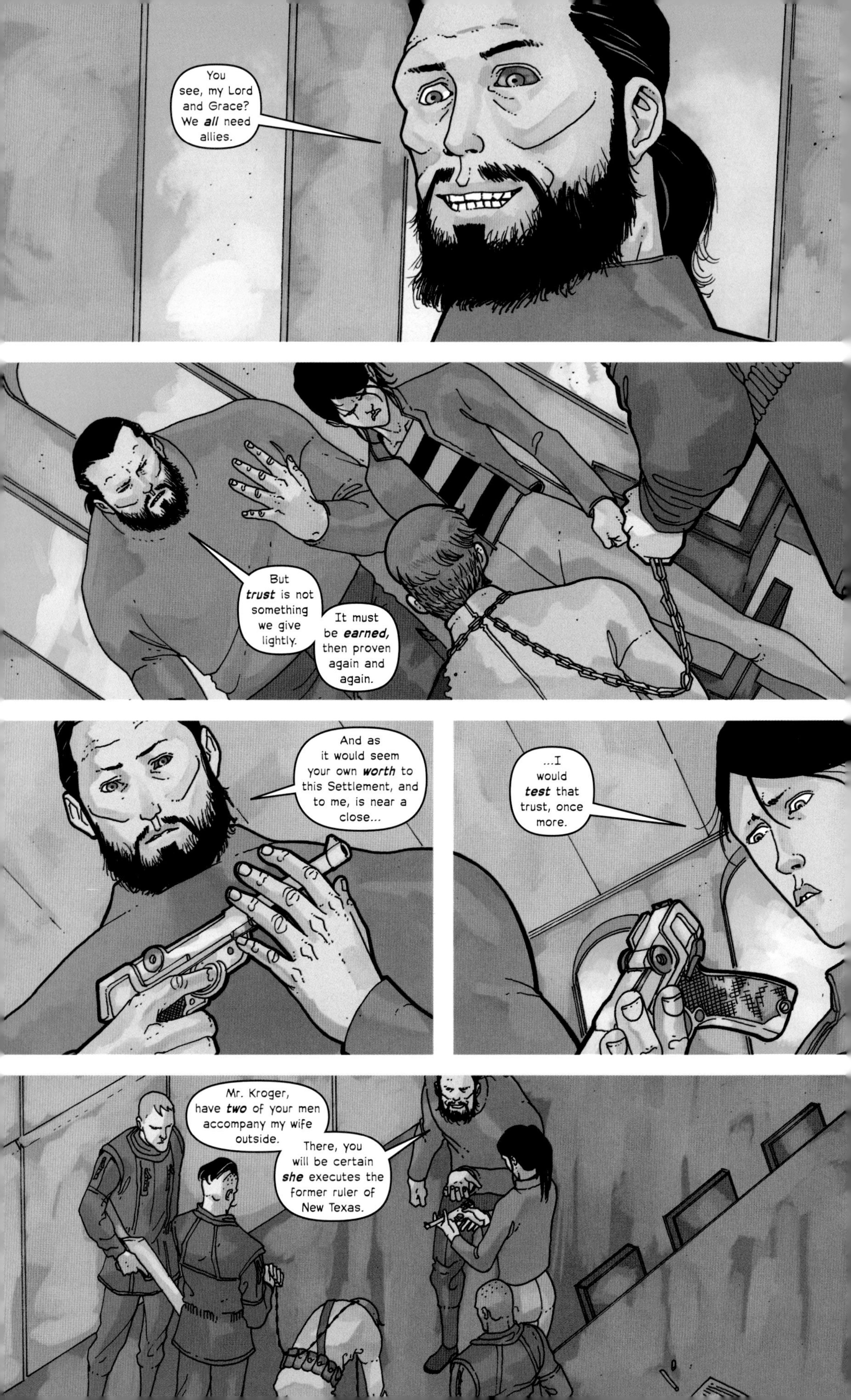
You see, my Lord and Grace? We *all* need allies.
But *trust* is not something we give lightly.
It must be *earned,* then proven again and again.
And as it would seem your own *worth* to this Settlement, and to me, is near a close...
...I would *test* that trust, once more.
Mr. Kroger, have *two* of your men accompany my wife outside.
There, you will be certain *she* executes the former ruler of New Texas.

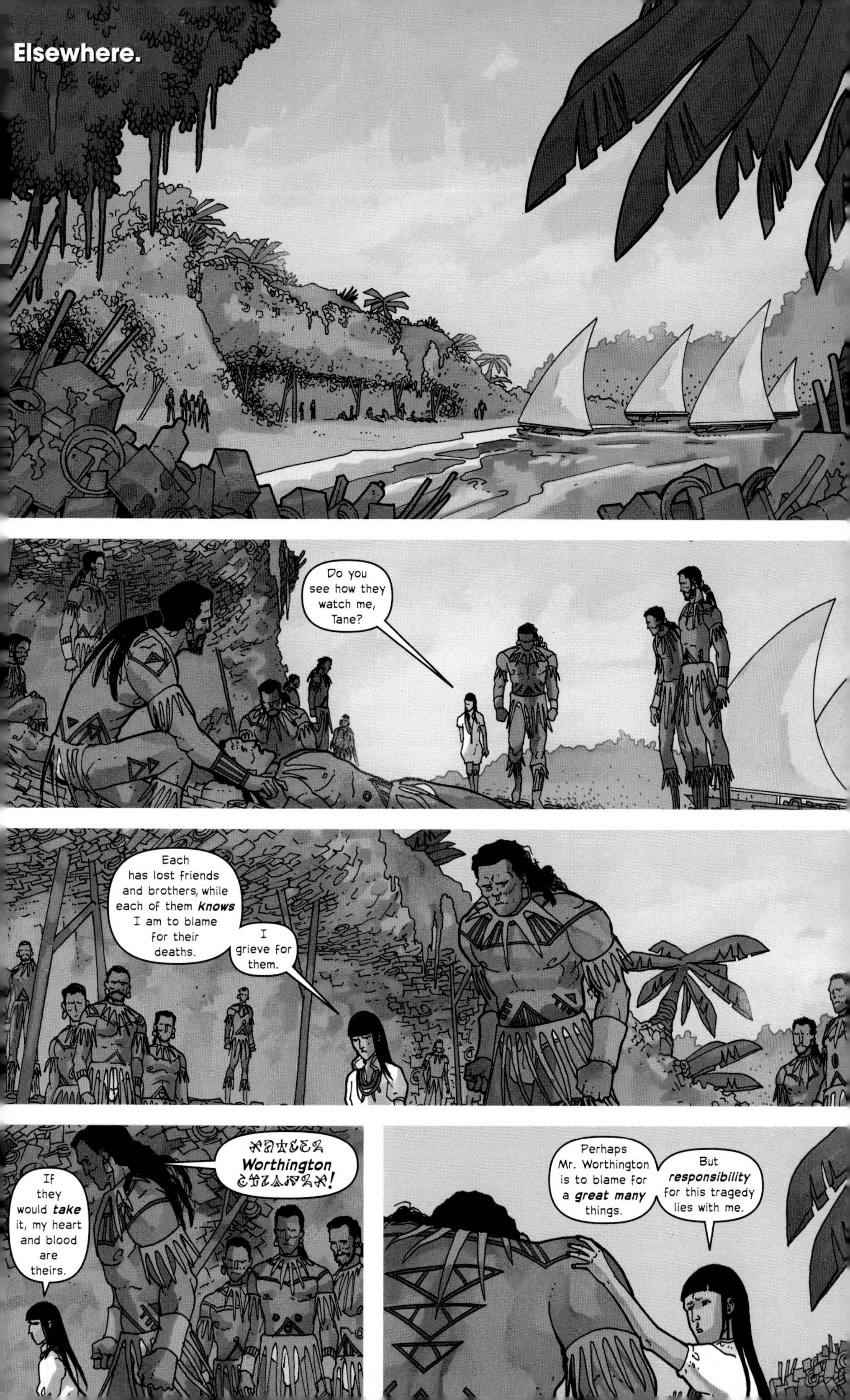
Elsewhere.
Do you see how they watch me, Tane?
Each has lost friends and brothers, while each of them *knows* I am to blame for their deaths.
I grieve for them.
If they would *take* it, my heart and blood are theirs.
Worthington
Perhaps Mr. Worthington is to blame for a *great many* things.
But *responsibility* for this tragedy lies with me.

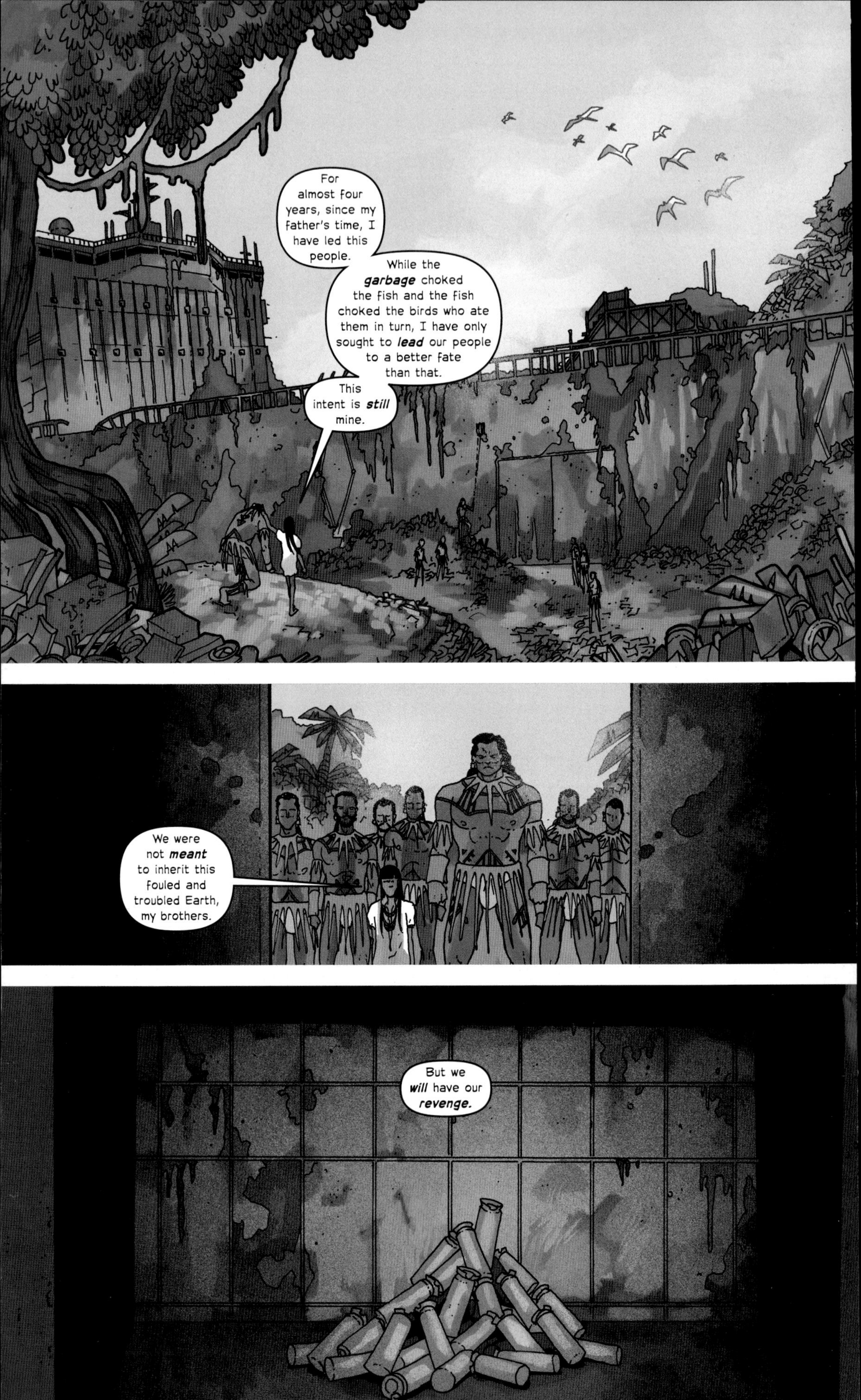
For almost four years, since my father's time, I have led this people.
While the *garbage* choked the fish and the fish choked the birds who ate them in turn, I have only sought to *lead* our people to a better fate than that.
This intent is *still* mine.
We were not *meant* to inherit this fouled and troubled Earth, my brothers.
But we *will* have our *revenge.*

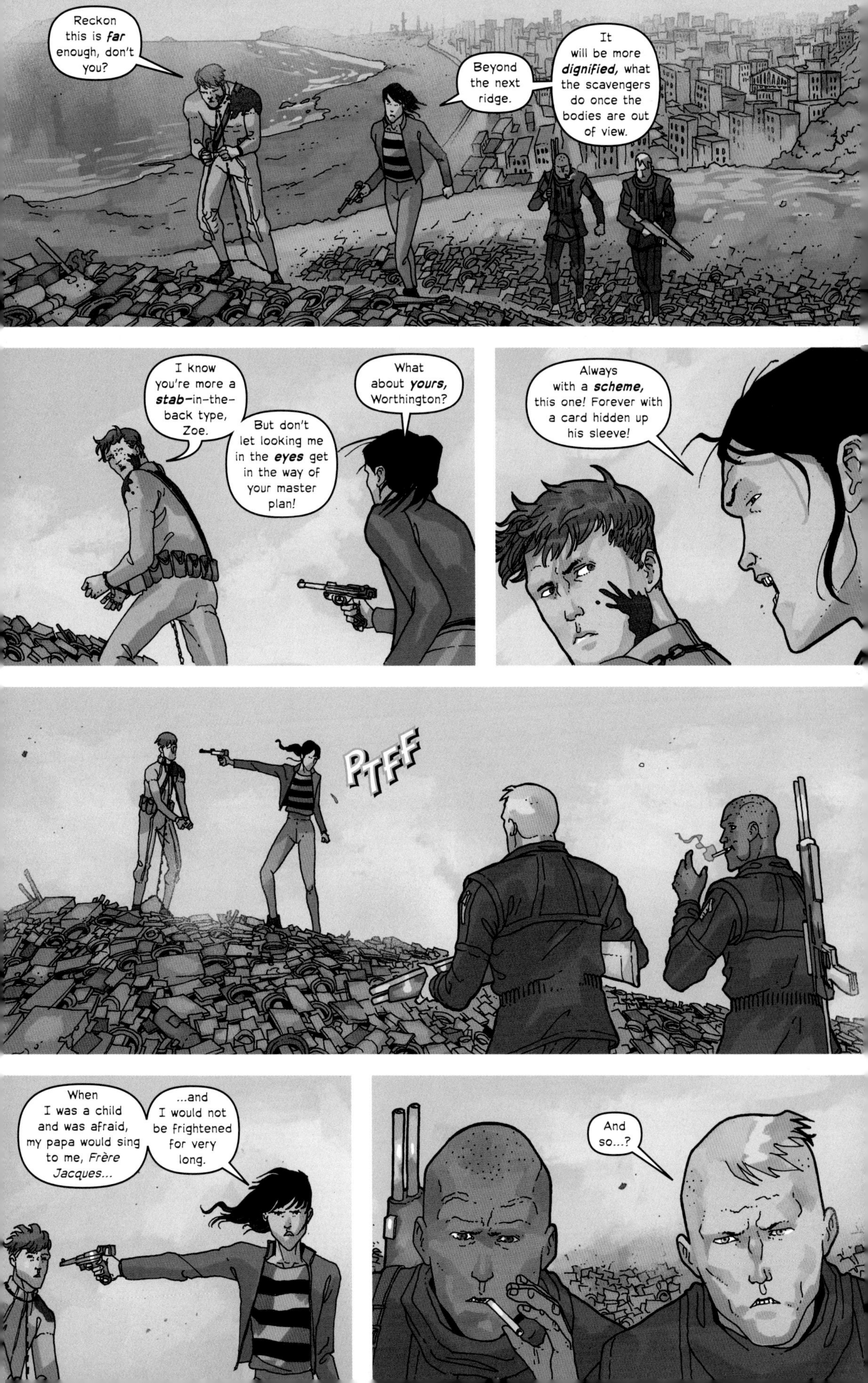
Reckon this is *far* enough, don't you?
Beyond the next ridge.
It will be more ***dignified,*** what the scavengers do once the bodies are out of view.
I know you're more a ***stab***-in-the-back type, Zoe.
But don't let looking me in the ***eyes*** get in the way of your master plan!
What about ***yours,*** Worthington?
Always with a ***scheme,*** this one! Forever with a card hidden up his sleeve!
PTFF
When I was a child and was afraid, my papa would sing to me, *Frère Jacques...*
...and I would not be frightened for very long.
And so...?

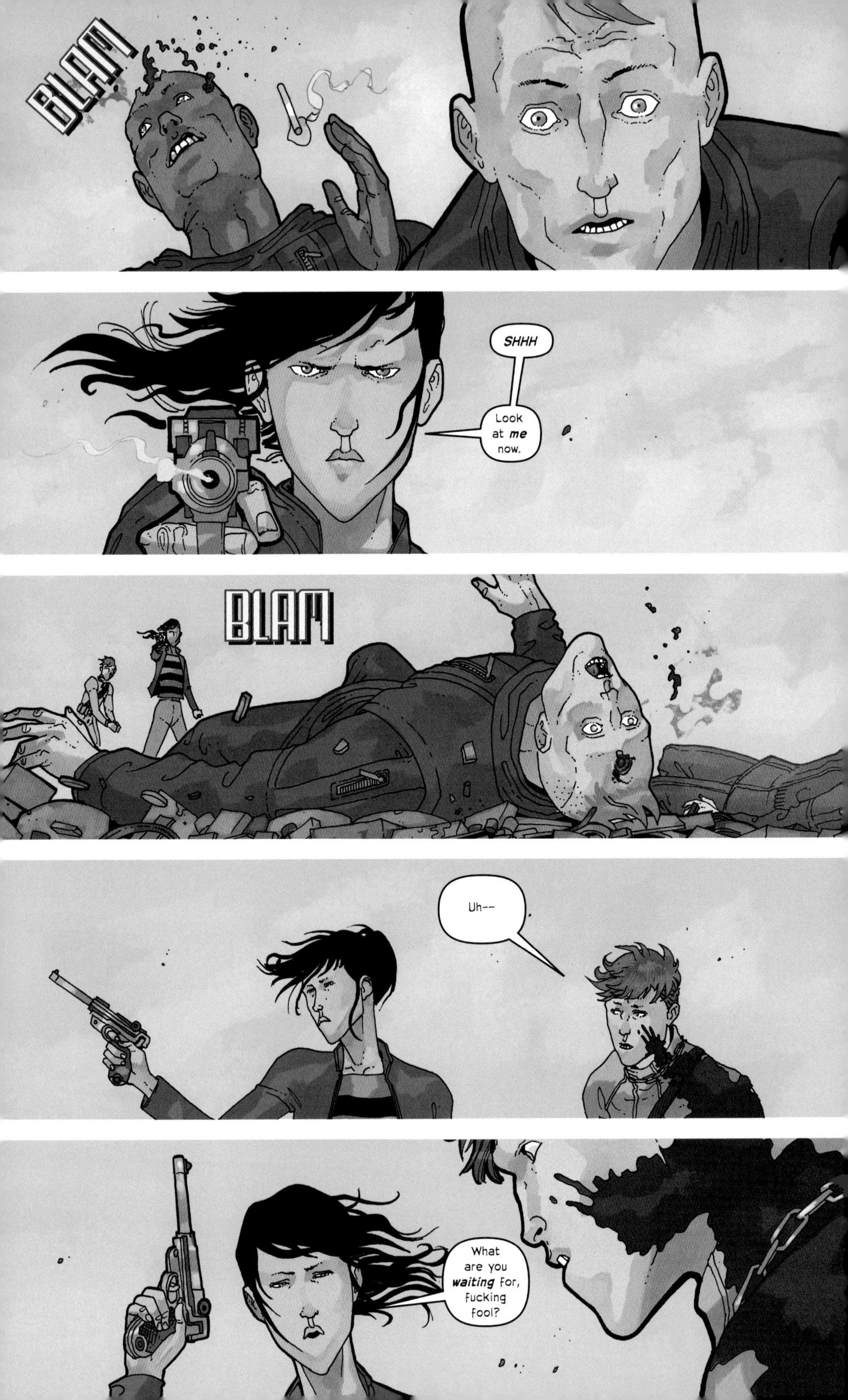
BLAM
SHHH
Look at *me* now.
BLAM
Uh--
What are you *waiting* for, fucking fool?

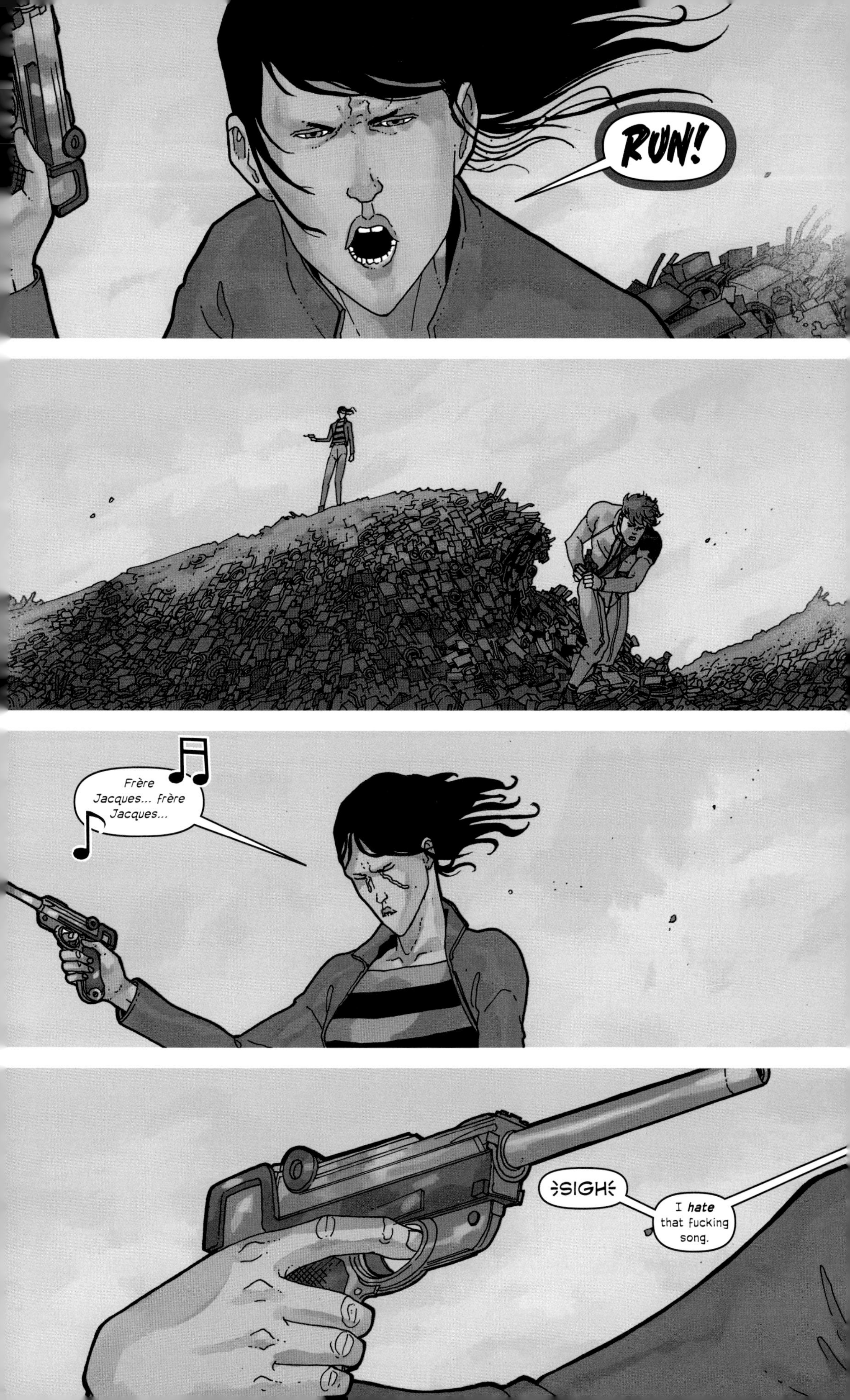
RUN!
Frère Jacques... frère Jacques...
SIGH
I hate that fucking song.

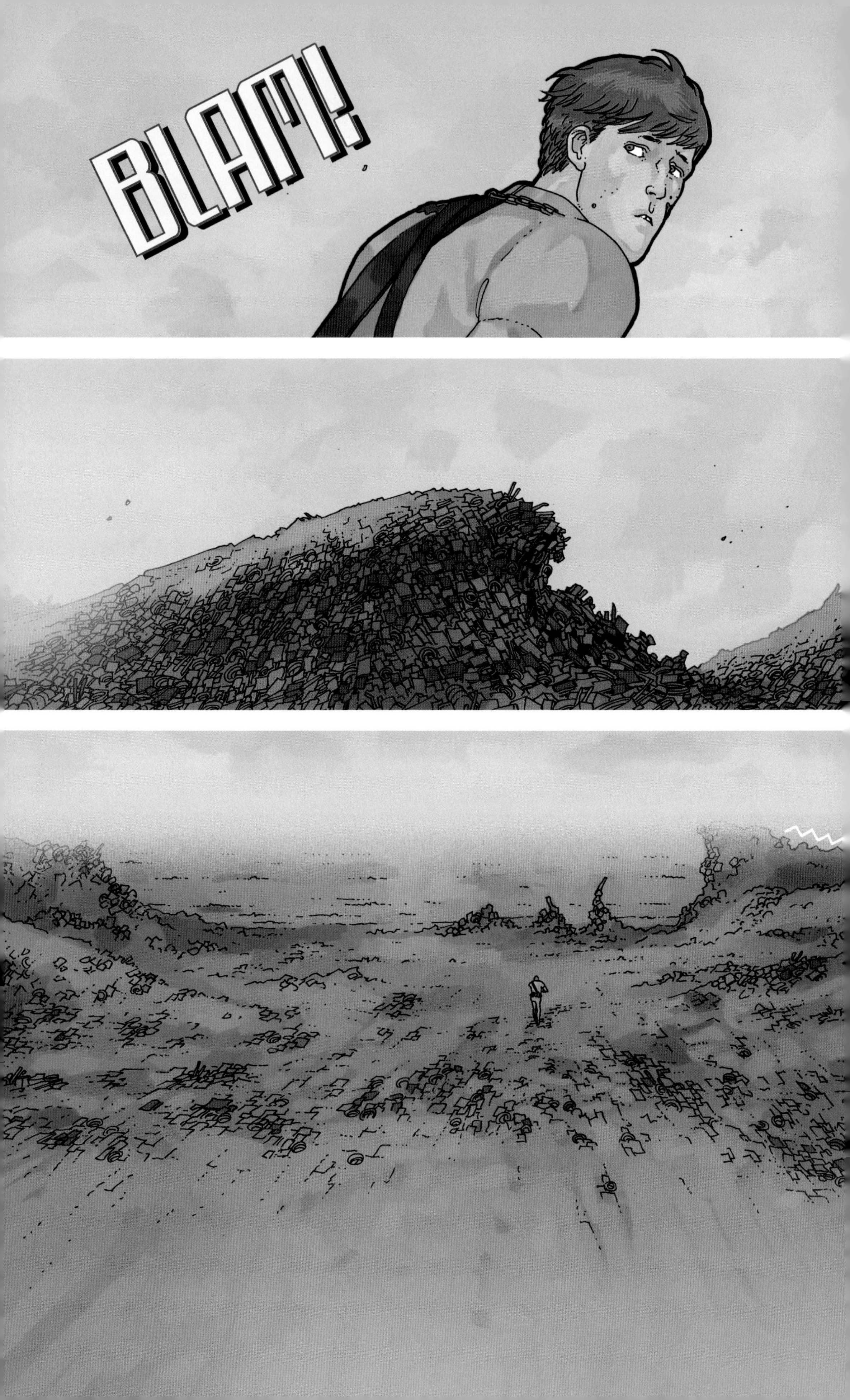
BLAM!

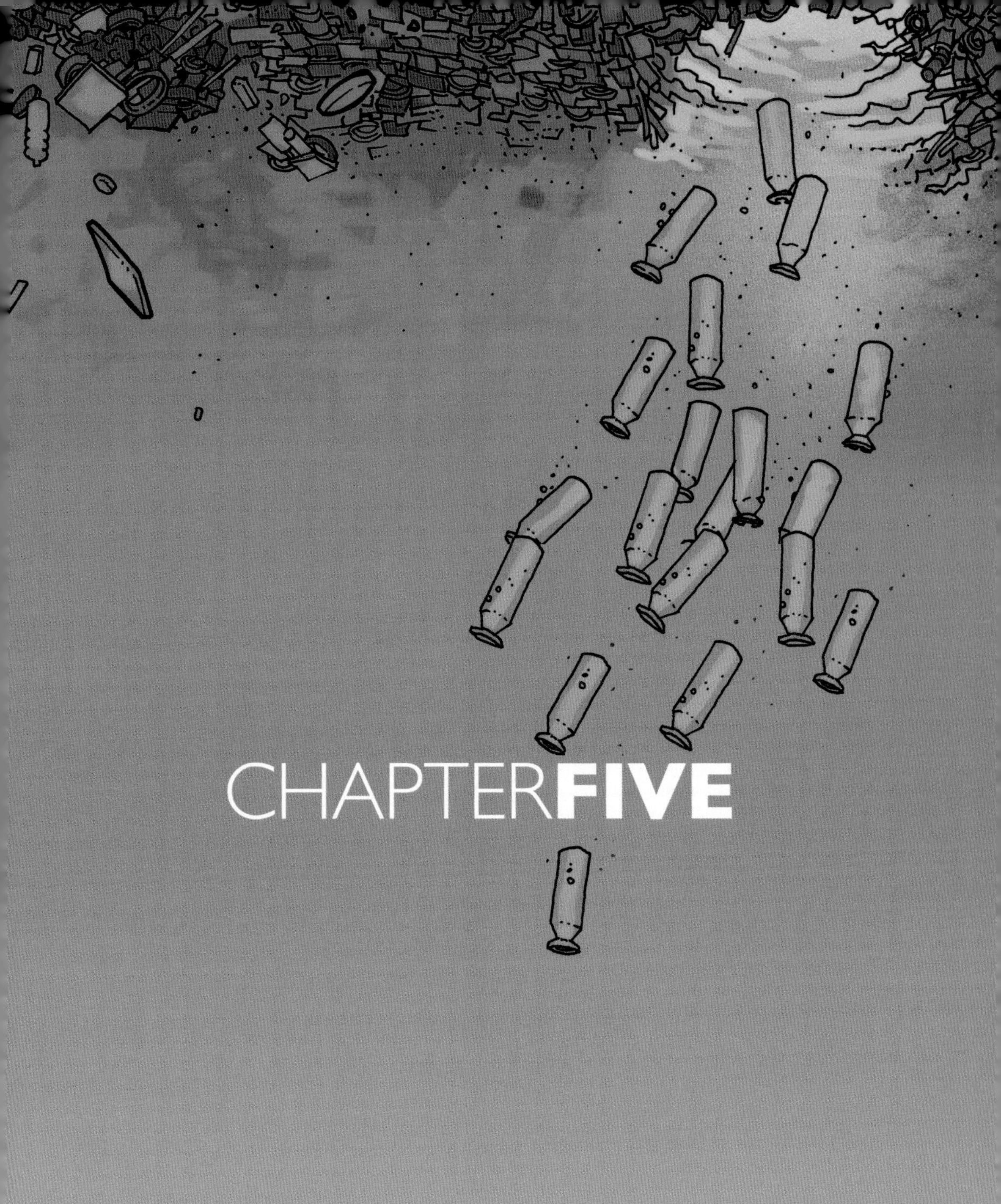

CHAPTER FIVE

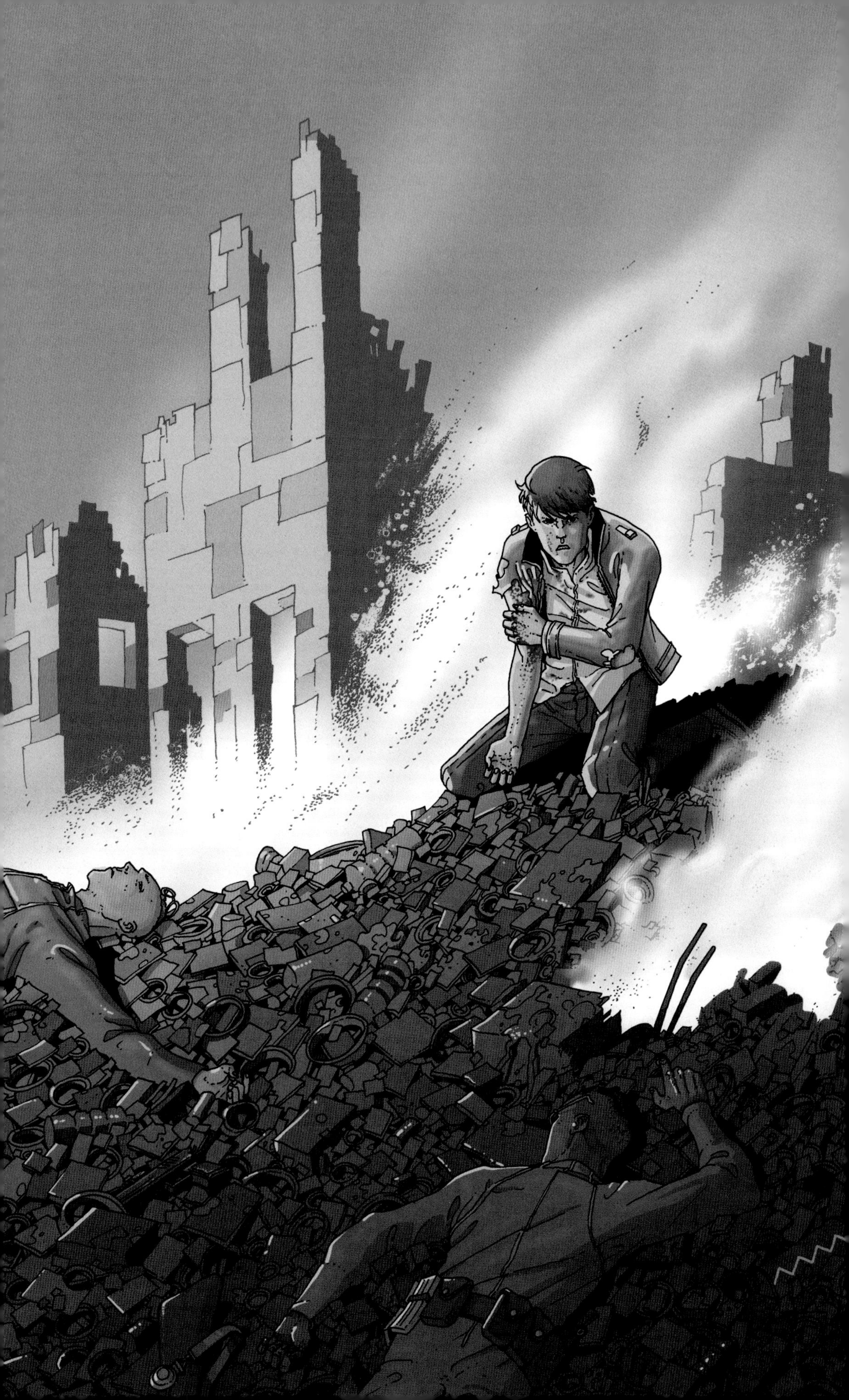

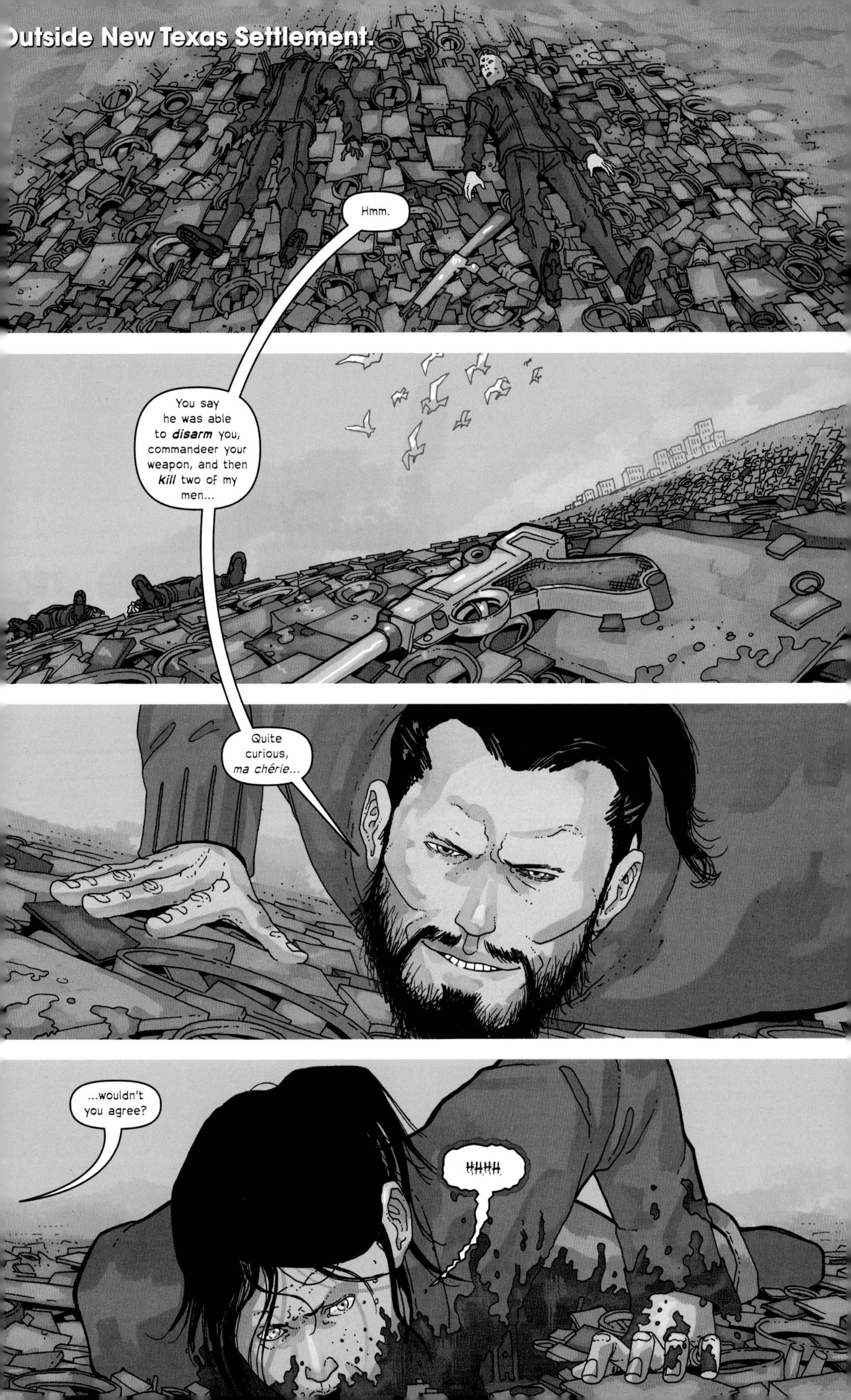
Outside New Texas Settlement.
Hmm.
You say he was able to *disarm* you, commandeer your weapon, and then *kill* two of my men...
Quite curious, *ma chérie*...
...wouldn't you agree?
HHHH.

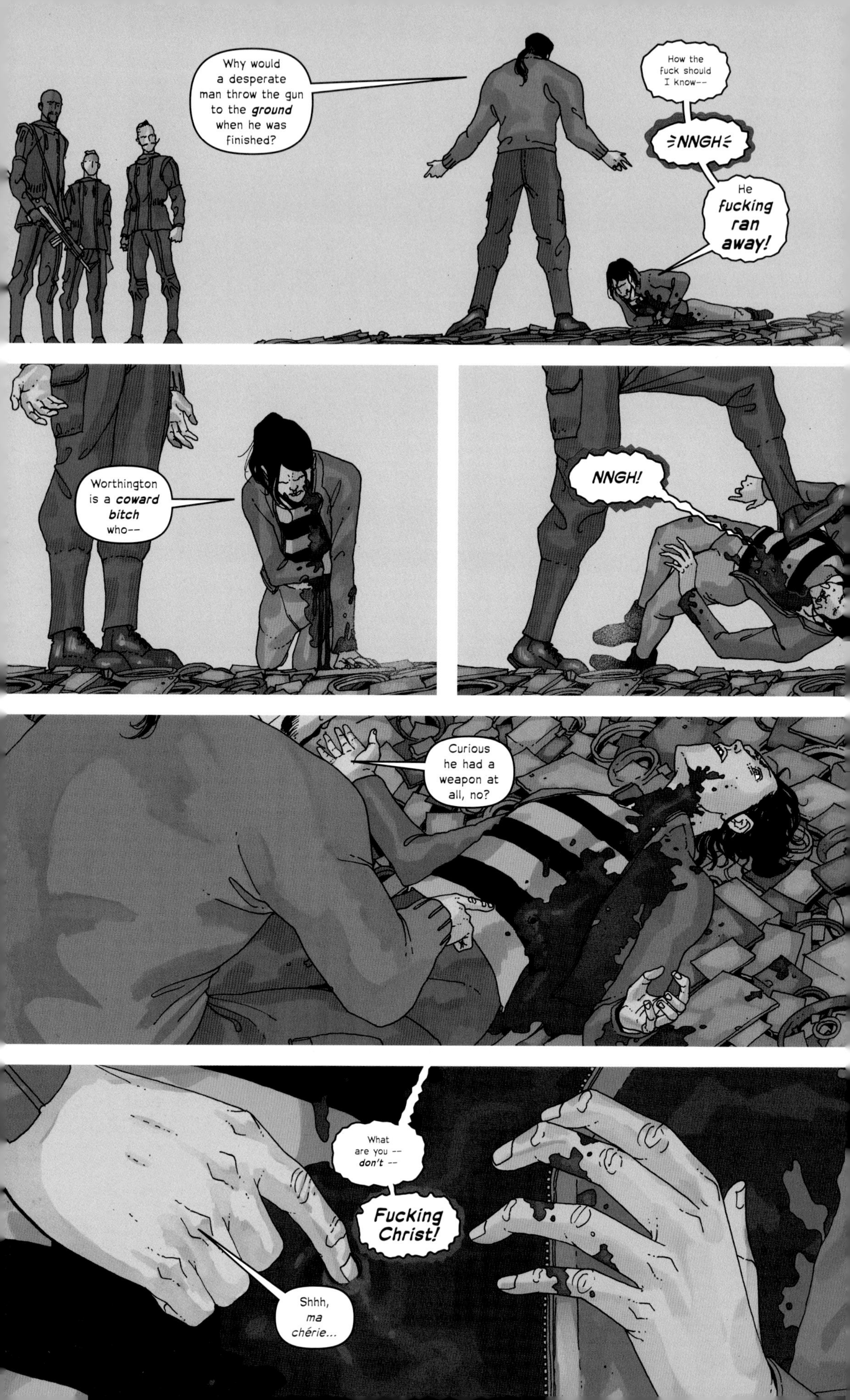

Why would a desperate man throw the gun to the *ground* when he was finished?
How the fuck should I know--
NNGH
He *fucking ran away!*
Worthington is a *coward bitch* who--
NNGH!
Curious he had a weapon at all, no?
What are you -- *don't* --
Fucking Christ!
Shhh, *ma chérie*...

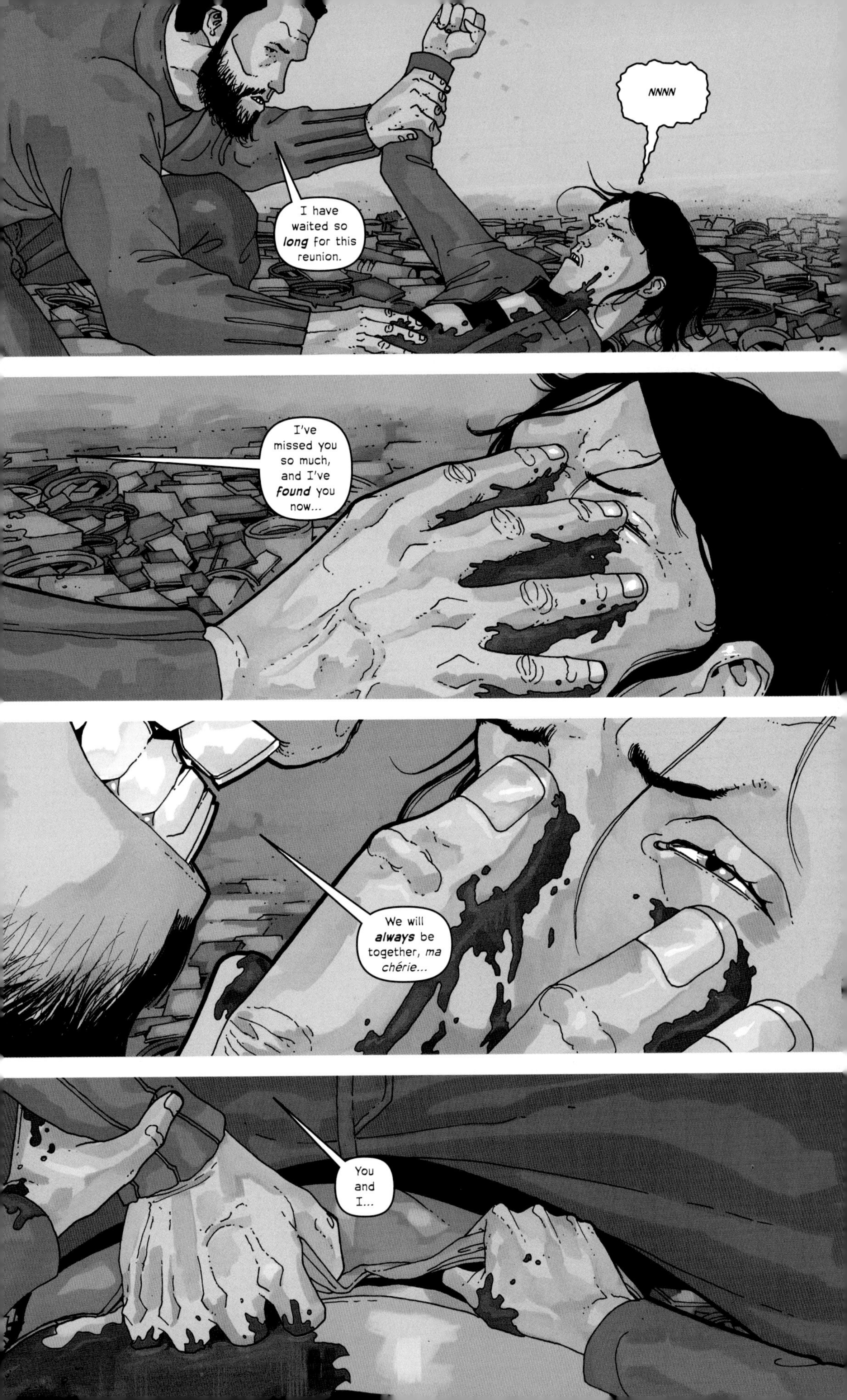
NNNN
I have waited so *long* for this reunion.
I've missed you so much, and I've *found* you now...
We will *always* be together, *ma chérie*...
You and I...

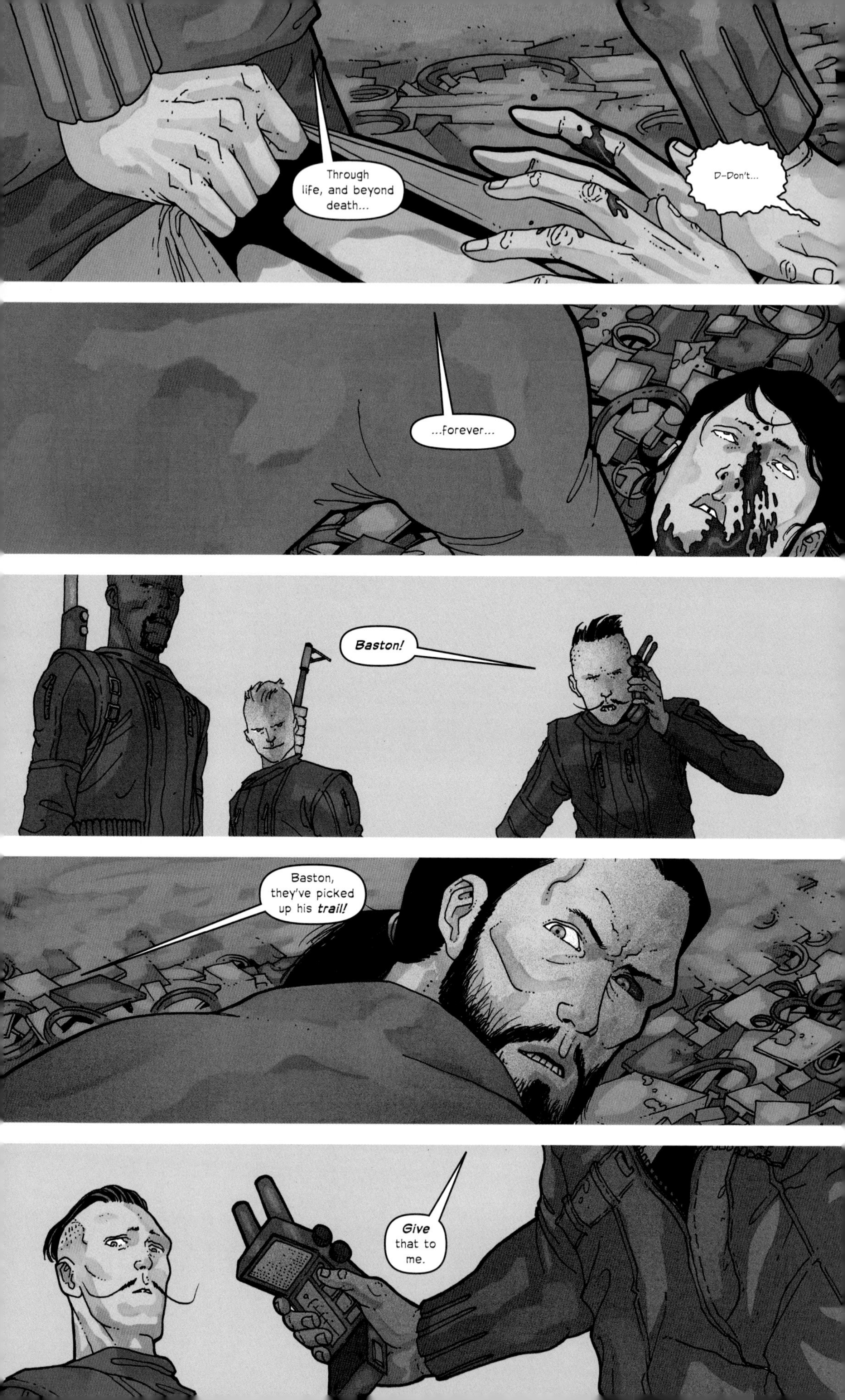
Through life, and beyond death...
D-Don't...
...forever...
Baston!
Baston, they've picked up his trail!
Give that to me.

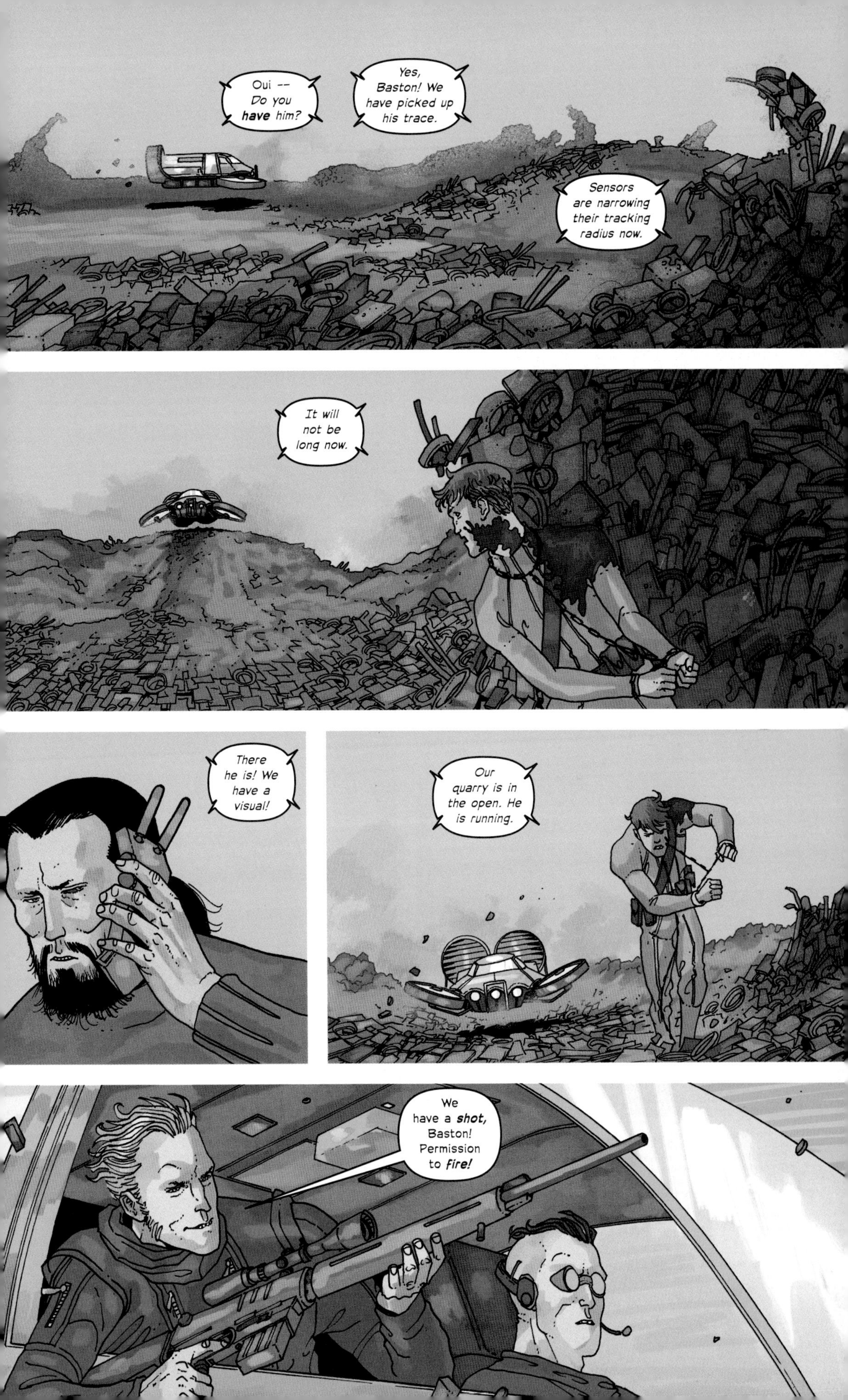
Oui -- Do you **have** him?
Yes, Baston! We have picked up his trace.
Sensors are narrowing their tracking radius now.
It will not be long now.
There he is! We have a visual!
Our quarry is in the open. He is running.
We have a ***shot,*** Baston! Permission to ***fire!***

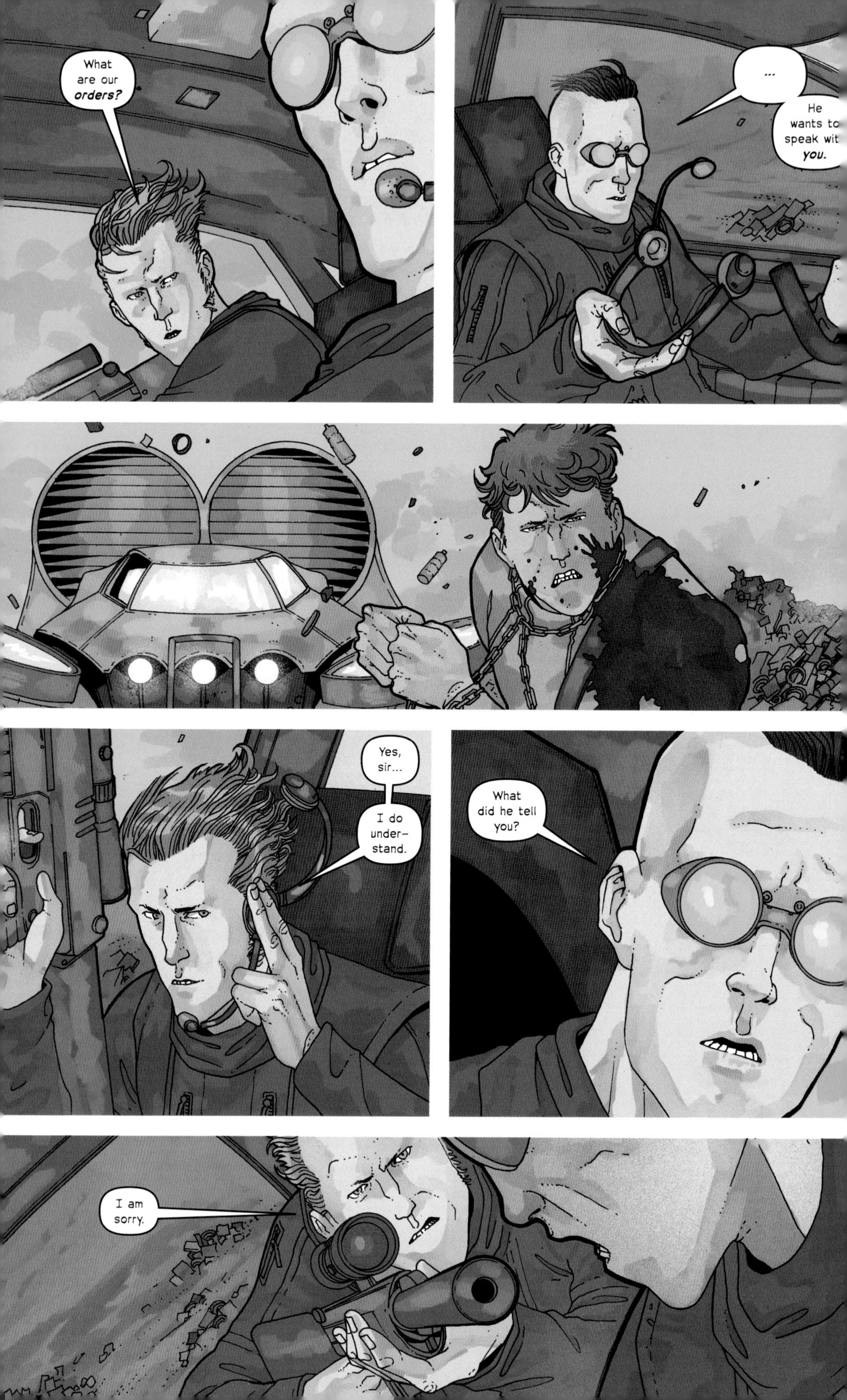
What are our orders?
...
He wants to speak wit you.
Yes, sir...
I do under-stand.
What did he tell you?
I am sorry.

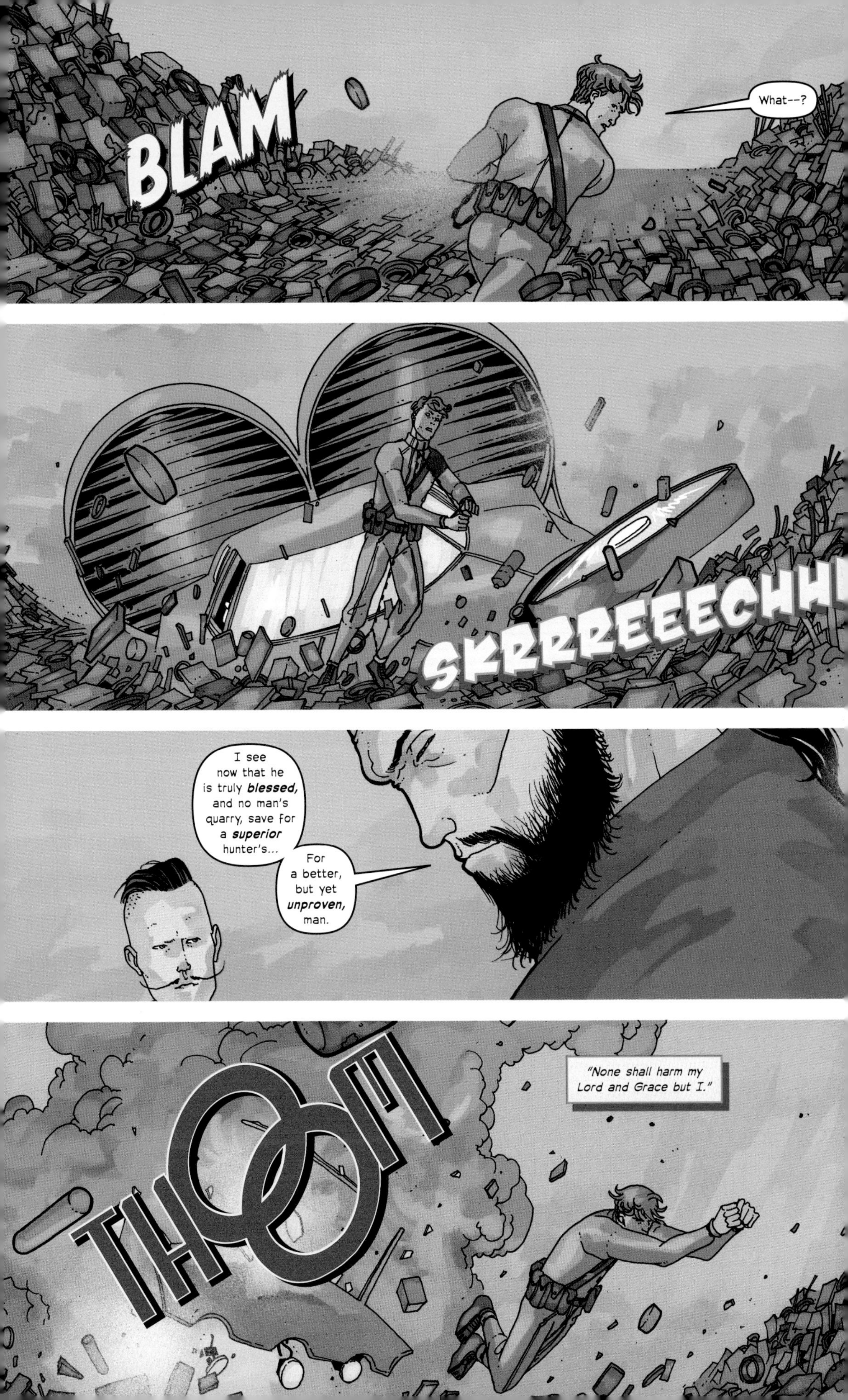

BLAM
What--?
SKRRREEEECHH
I see now that he is truly *blessed,* and no man's quarry, save for a *superior* hunter's...
For a better, but yet *unproven,* man.
THOOM
"None shall harm my Lord and Grace but I."

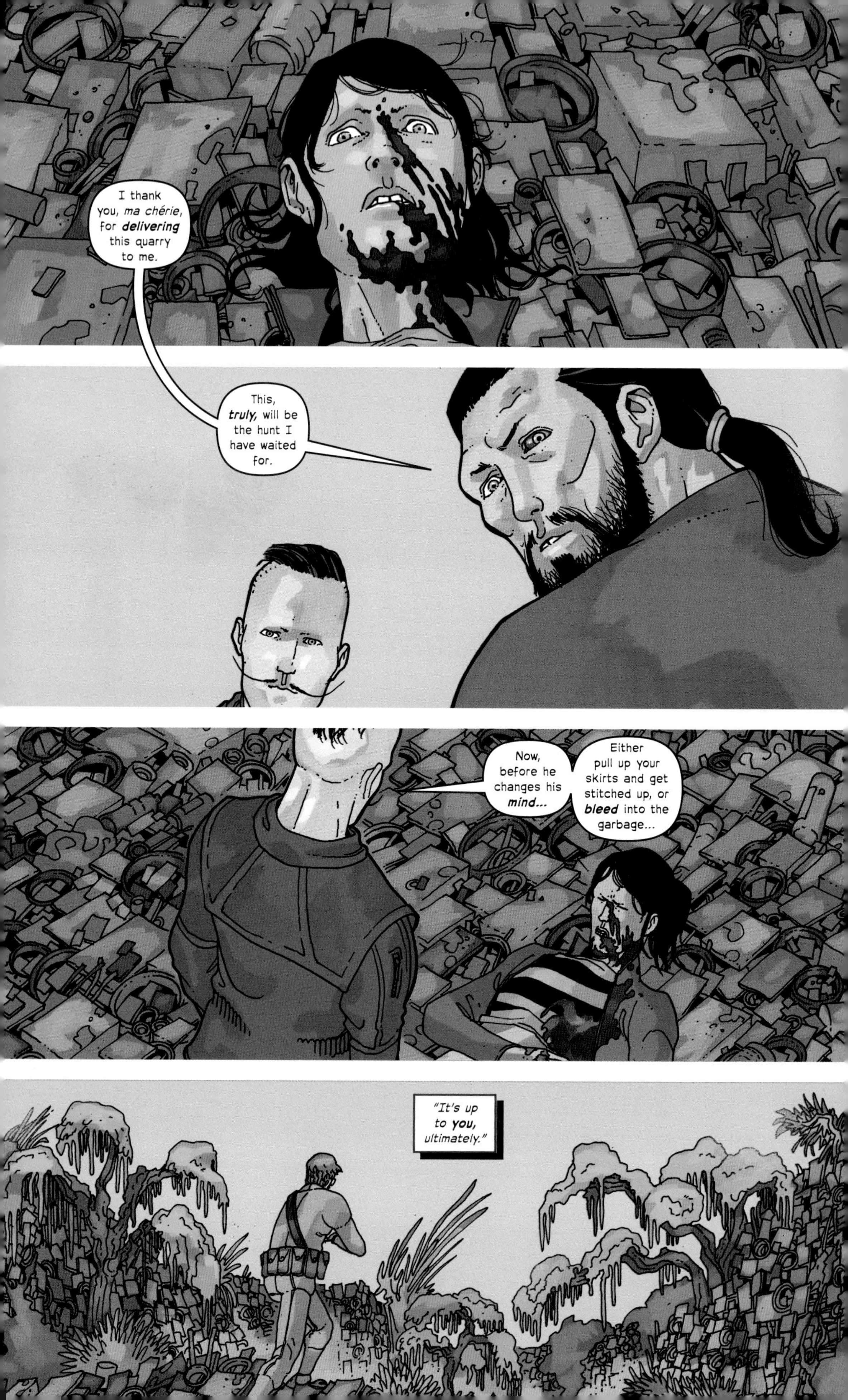
I thank you, *ma chérie,* for ***delivering*** this quarry to me.
This, ***truly,*** will be the hunt I have waited for.
Now, before he changes his ***mind...***
Either pull up your skirts and get stitched up, or ***bleed*** into the garbage...
*"It's up to **you,** ultimately."*

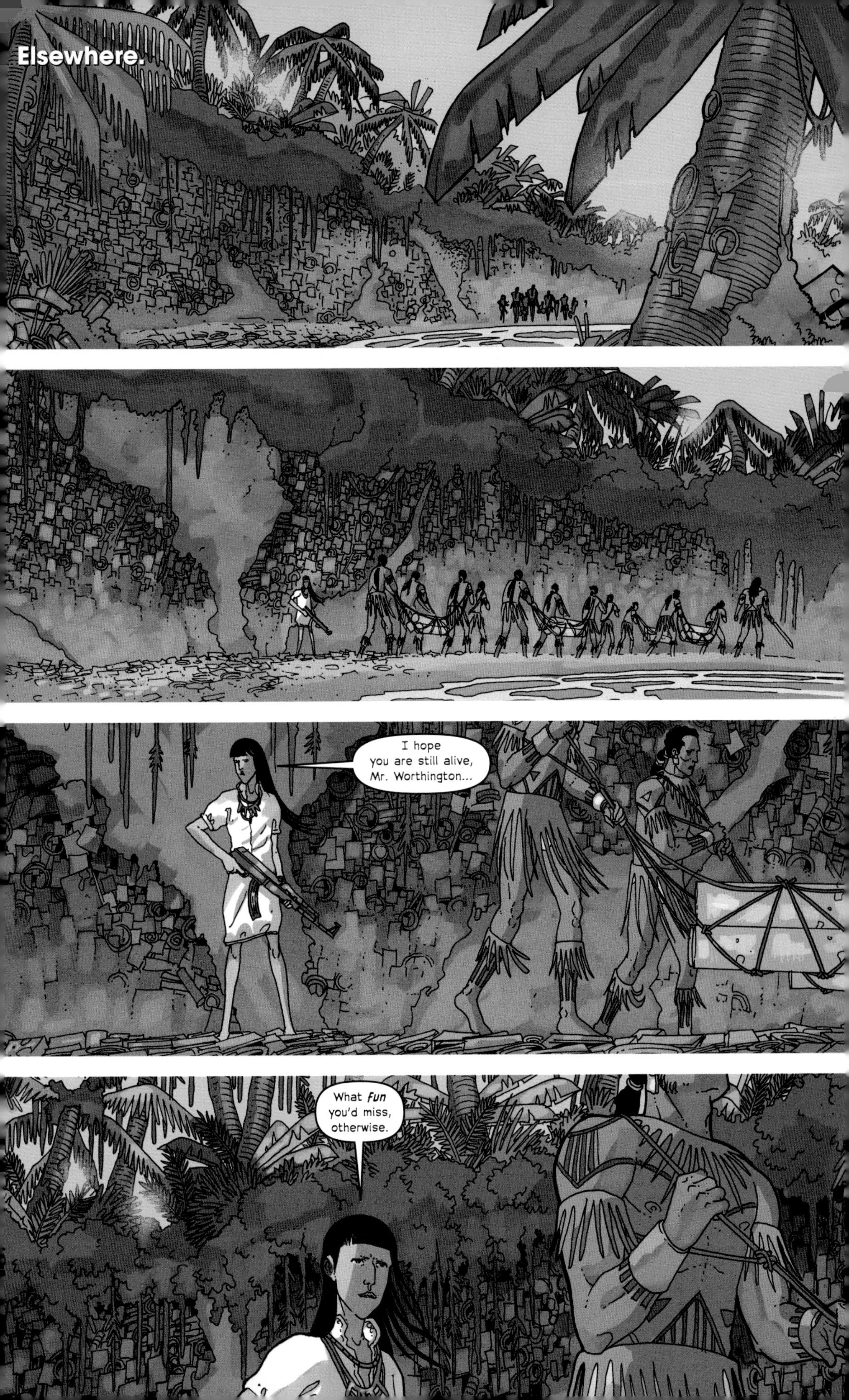
Elsewhere.
I hope you are still alive, Mr. Worthington...
What *fun* you'd miss, otherwise.

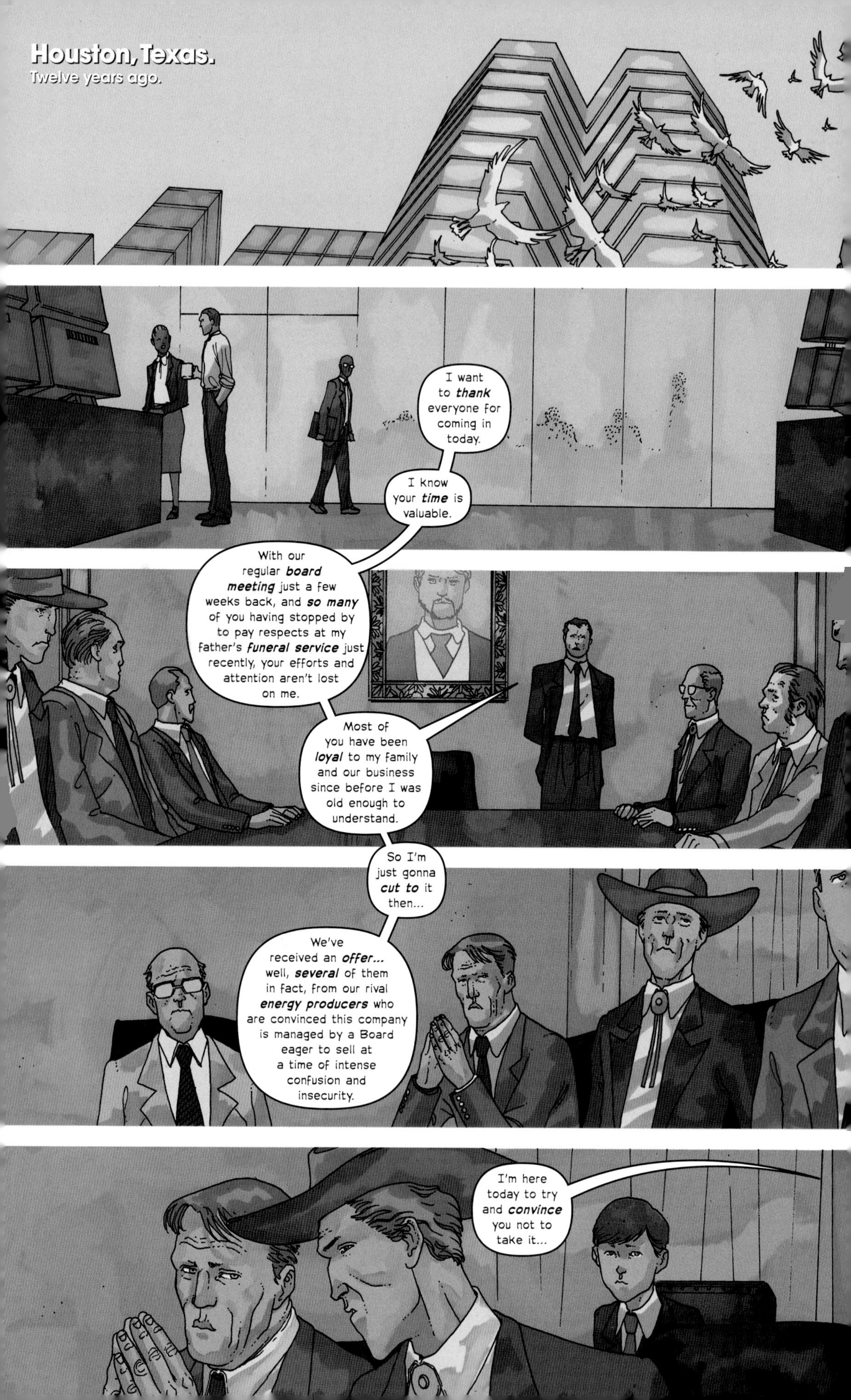
Houston, Texas.
Twelve years ago.
I want to thank everyone for coming in today.
I know your time is valuable.
With our regular board meeting just a few weeks back, and so many of you having stopped by to pay respects at my father's funeral service just recently, your efforts and attention aren't lost on me.
Most of you have been loyal to my family and our business since before I was old enough to understand.
So I'm just gonna cut to it then...
We've received an offer... well, several of them in fact, from our rival energy producers who are convinced this company is managed by a Board eager to sell at a time of intense confusion and insecurity.
I'm here today to try and convince you not to take it...

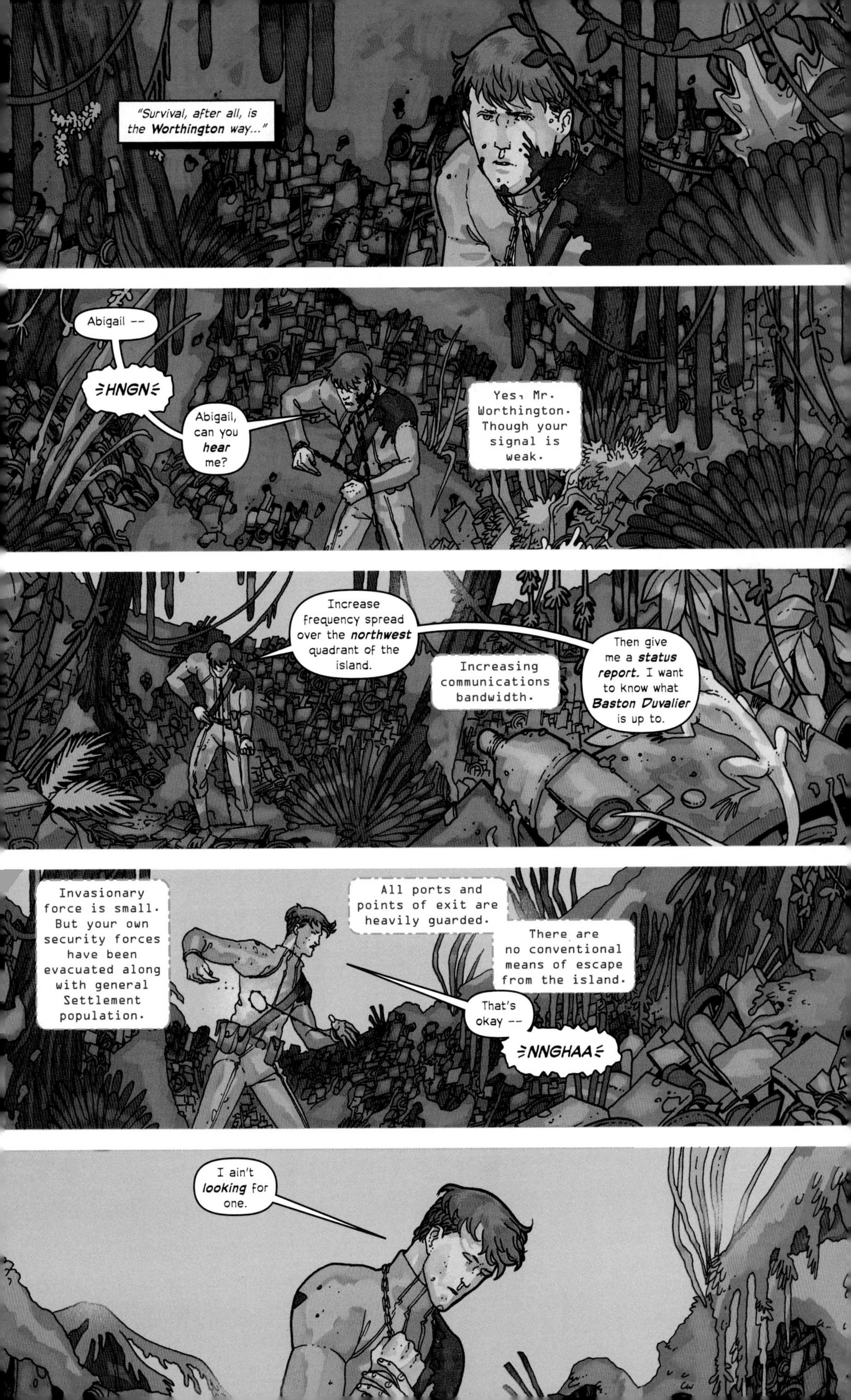

"Survival, after all, is the Worthington way..."
Abigail --
HNGN
Abigail, can you hear me?
Yes, Mr. Worthington. Though your signal is weak.
Increase frequency spread over the northwest quadrant of the island.
Increasing communications bandwidth.
Then give me a status report. I want to know what Baston Duvalier is up to.
Invasionary force is small. But your own security forces have been evacuated along with general Settlement population.
All ports and points of exit are heavily guarded.
There are no conventional means of escape from the island.
That's okay --
NNGHAA
I ain't looking for one.

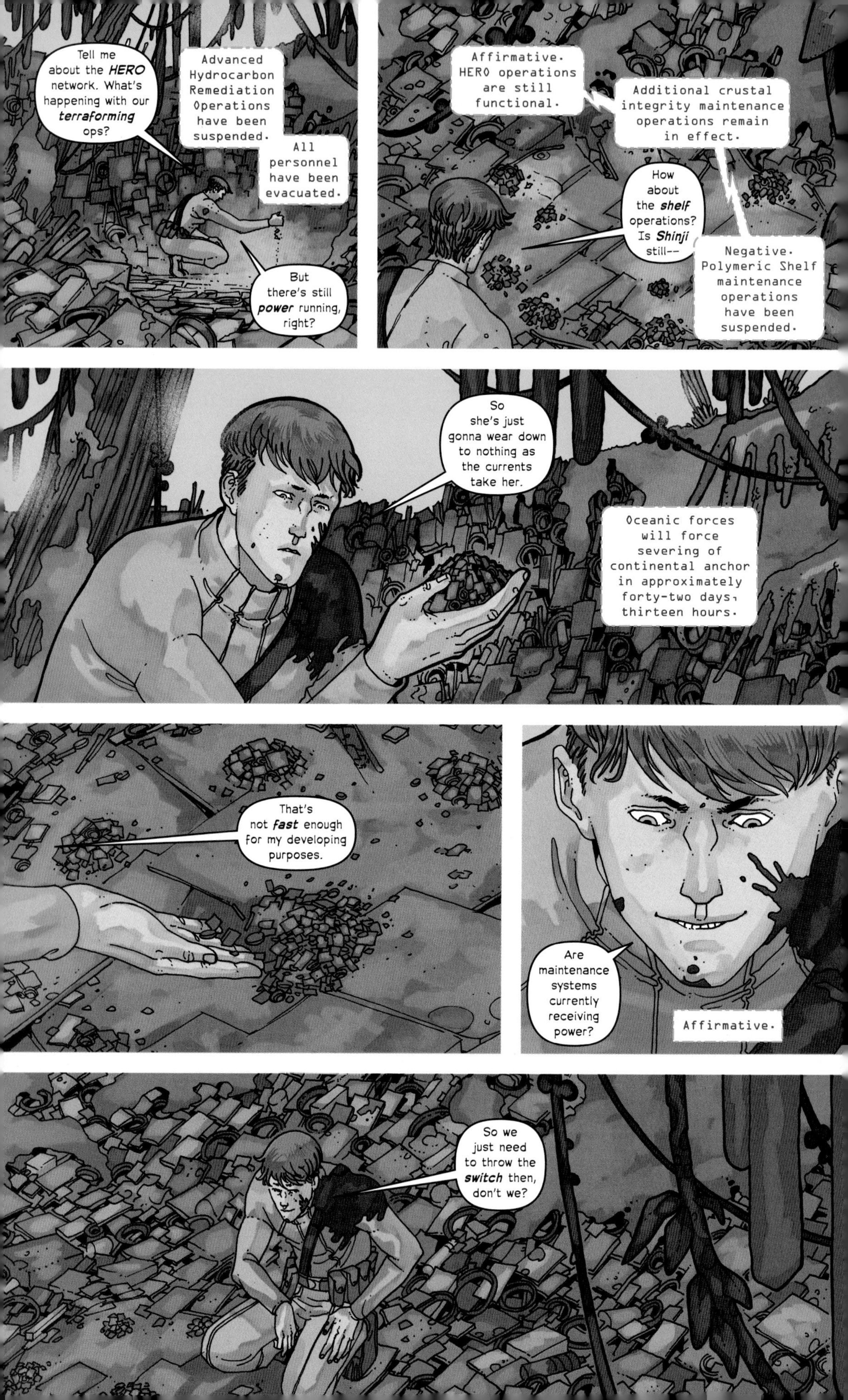

Tell me about the *HERO* network. What's happening with our *terraforming* ops?
Advanced Hydrocarbon Remediation Operations have been suspended.
All personnel have been evacuated.
But there's still *power* running, right?
Affirmative. HERO operations are still functional.
Additional crustal integrity maintenance operations remain in effect.
How about the *shelf* operations? Is *Shinji* still--
Negative. Polymeric Shelf maintenance operations have been suspended.
So she's just gonna wear down to nothing as the currents take her.
Oceanic forces will force severing of continental anchor in approximately forty-two days, thirteen hours.
That's not *fast* enough for my developing purposes.
Are maintenance systems currently receiving power?
Affirmative.
So we just need to throw the *switch* then, don't we?

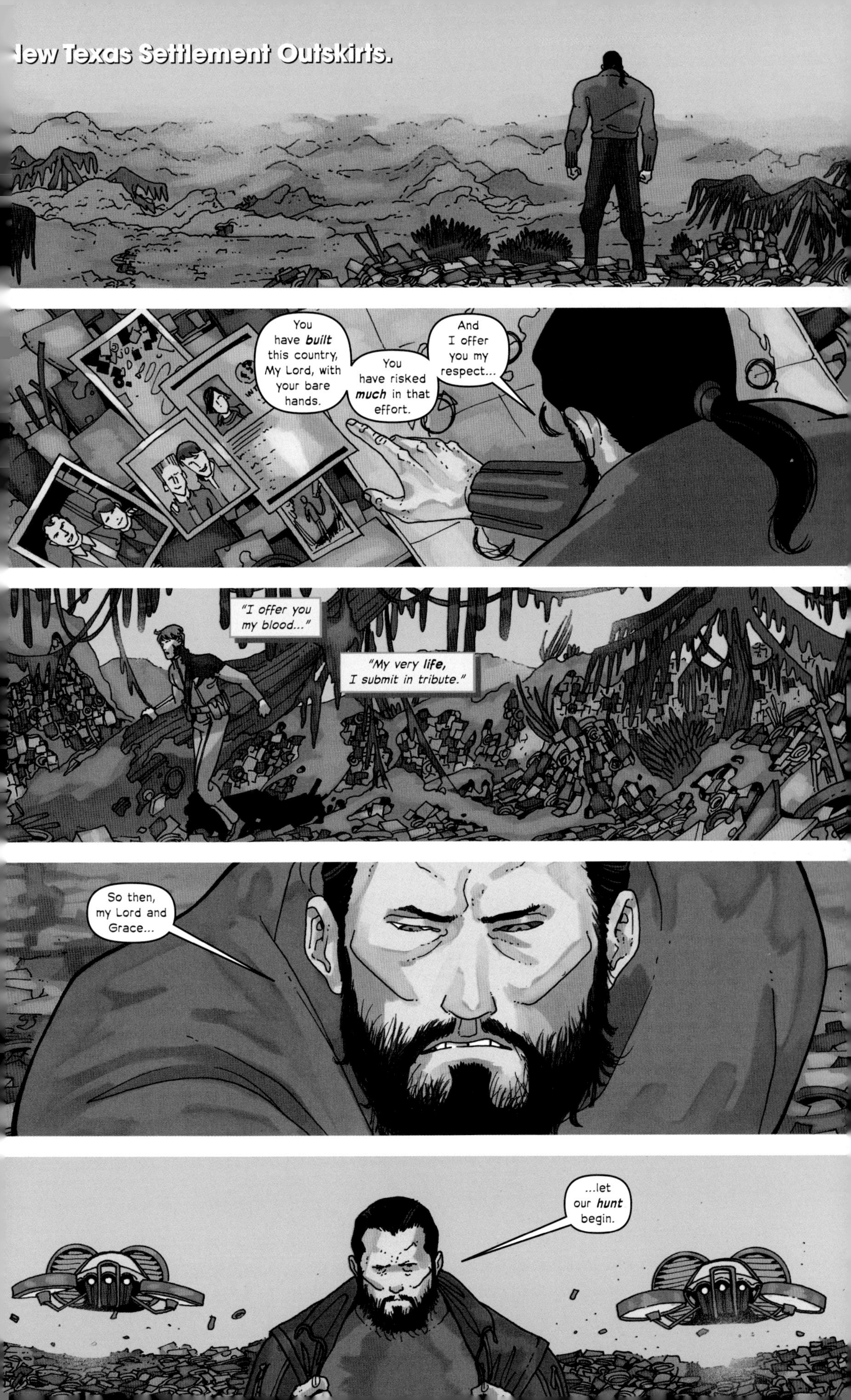

New Texas Settlement Outskirts.
You have built this country, My Lord, with your bare hands.
You have risked much in that effort.
And I offer you my respect...
"I offer you my blood..."
"My very life, I submit in tribute."
So then, my Lord and Grace...
...let our hunt begin.

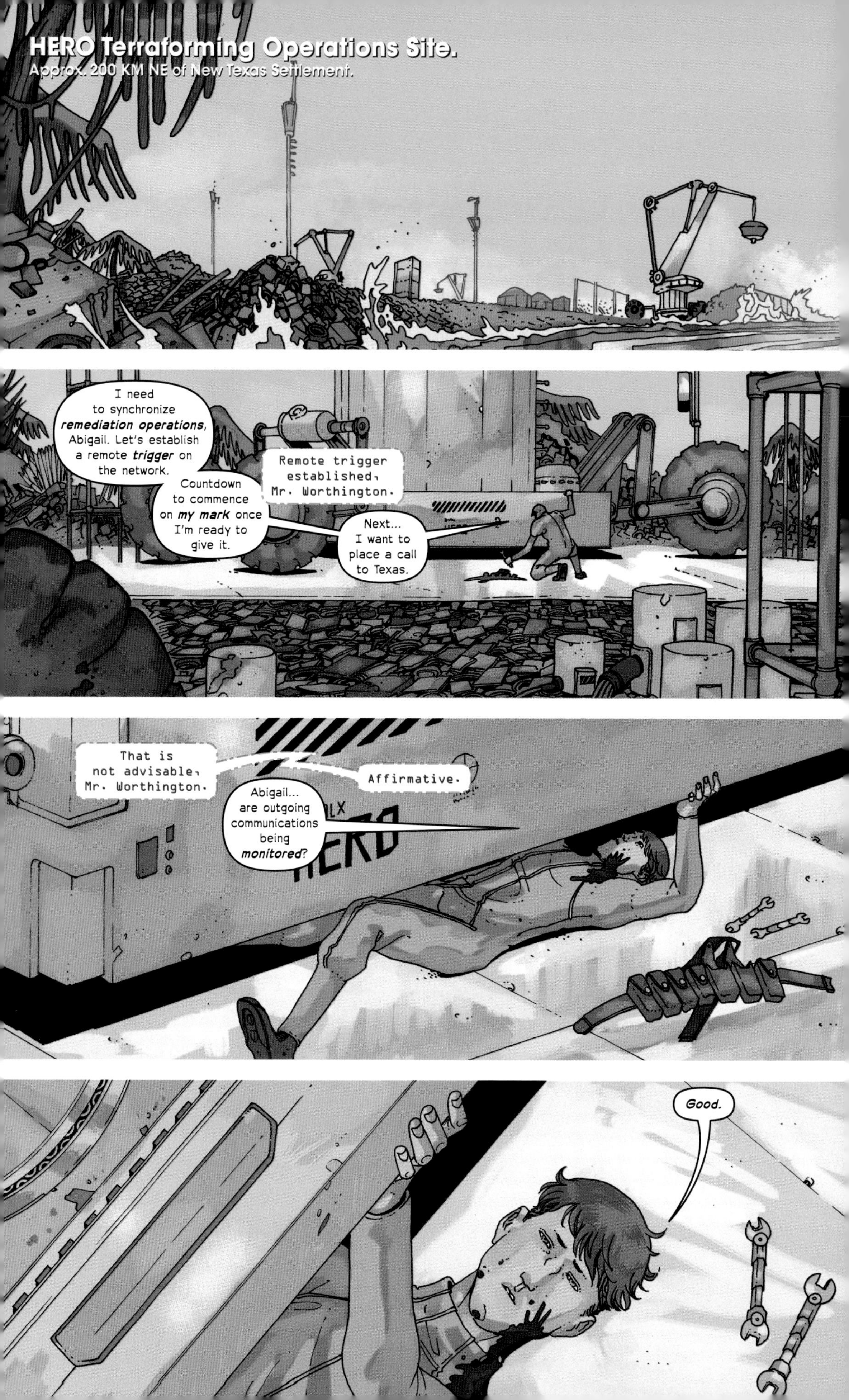
HERO Terraforming Operations Site.
Approx. 200 KM NE of New Texas Settlement.
I need to synchronize *remediation operations*, Abigail. Let's establish a remote *trigger* on the network.
Countdown to commence on *my mark* once I'm ready to give it.
Remote trigger established, Mr. Worthington.
Next... I want to place a call to Texas.
That is not advisable, Mr. Worthington.
Abigail... are outgoing communications being *monitored*?
Affirmative.
HERO
Good.

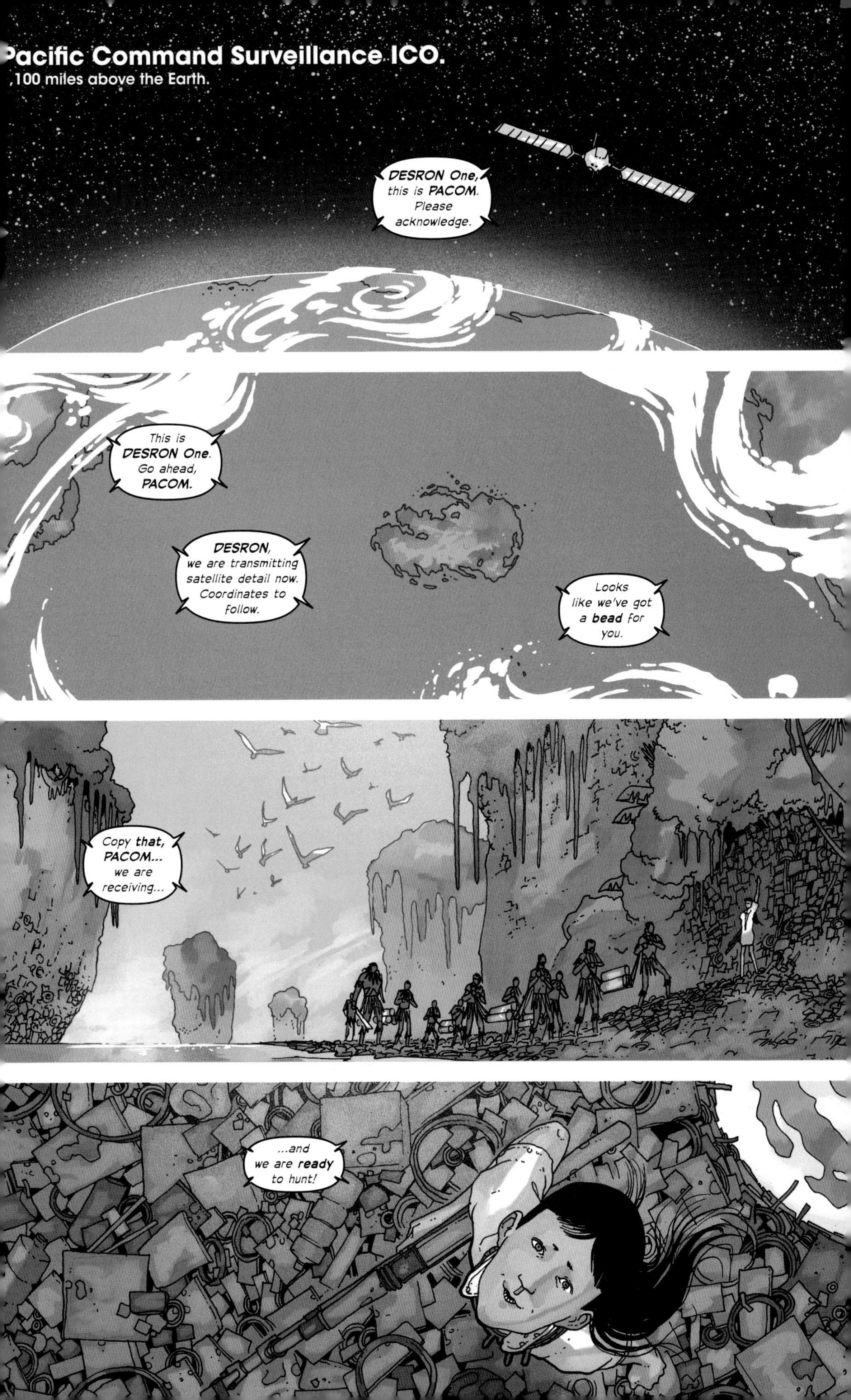
Pacific Command Surveillance ICO.
,100 miles above the Earth.
DESRON One, this is PACOM. Please acknowledge.
This is DESRON One. Go ahead, PACOM.
DESRON, we are transmitting satellite detail now. Coordinates to follow.
Looks like we've got a bead for you.
Copy that, PACOM... we are receiving...
...and we are ready to hunt!

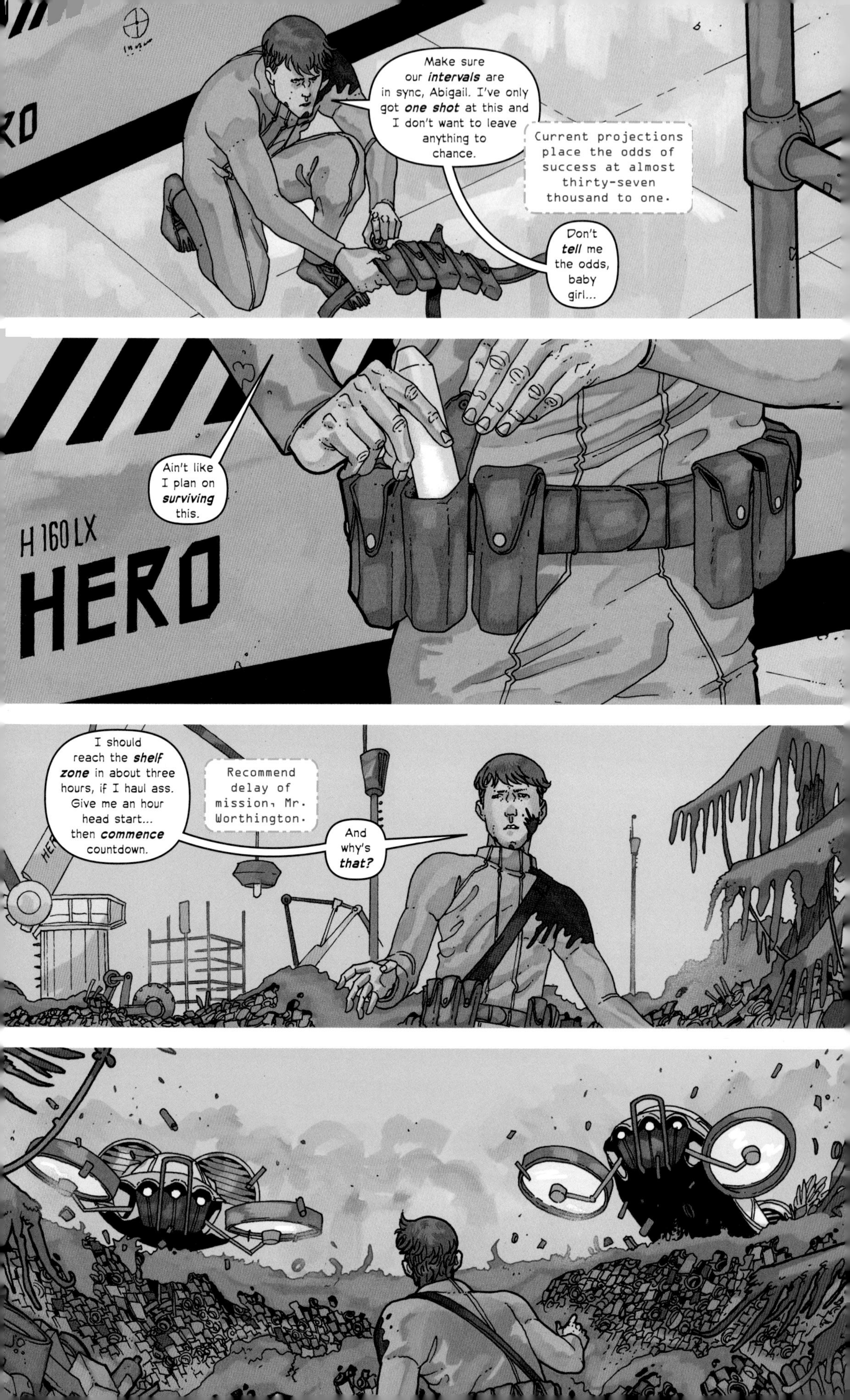

Make sure our intervals are in sync, Abigail. I've only got one shot at this and I don't want to leave anything to chance.
Current projections place the odds of success at almost thirty-seven thousand to one.
Don't tell me the odds, baby girl...
Ain't like I plan on surviving this.
H 160 LX
HERO
I should reach the shelf zone in about three hours, if I haul ass. Give me an hour head start... then commence countdown.
Recommend delay of mission, Mr. Worthington.
And why's that?

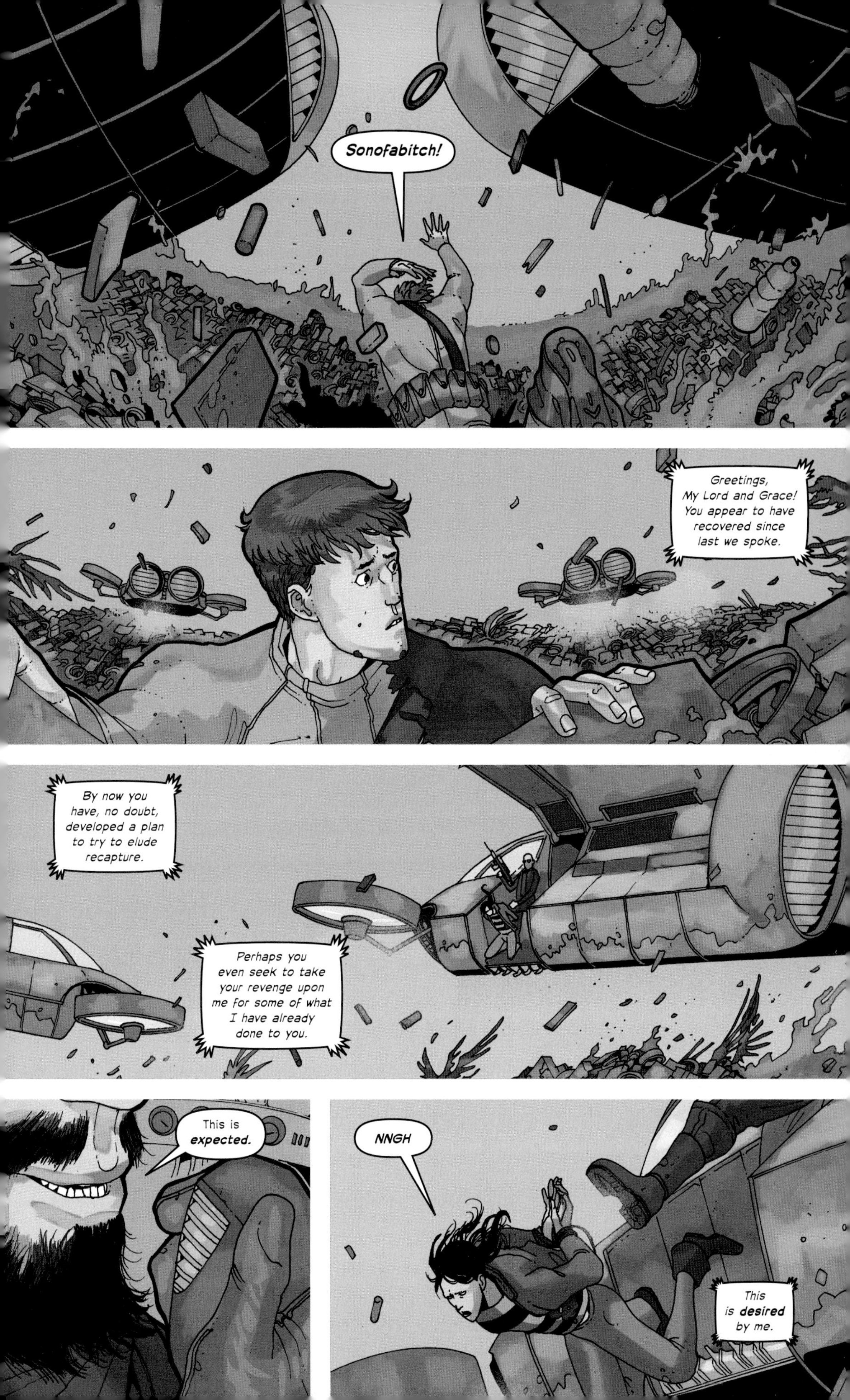
Sonofabitch!
Greetings, My Lord and Grace! You appear to have recovered since last we spoke.
By now you have, no doubt, developed a plan to try to elude recapture.
Perhaps you even seek to take your revenge upon me for some of what I have already done to you.
This is expected.
NNGH
This is desired by me.

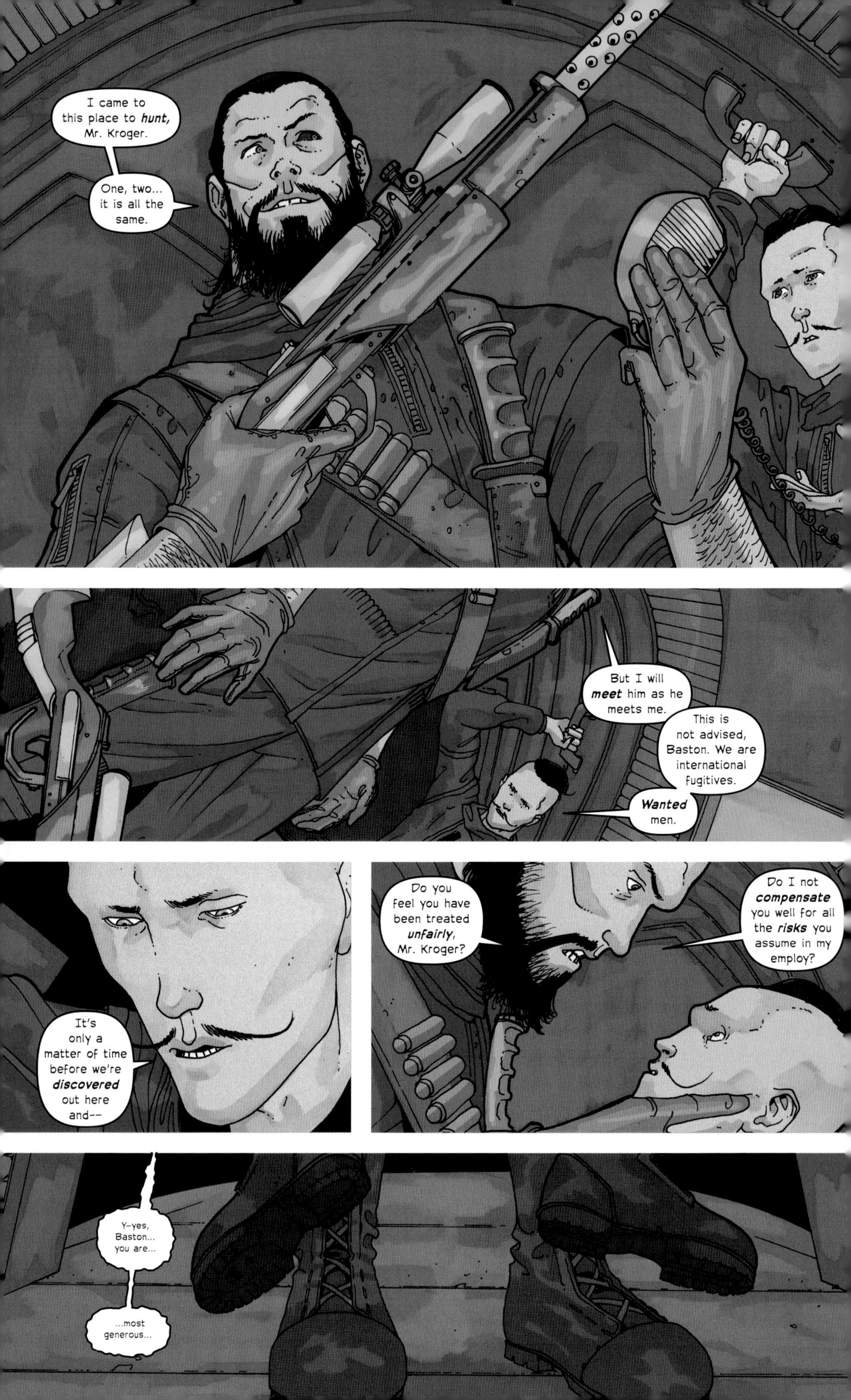
I came to this place to *hunt,* Mr. Kroger.
One, two... it is all the same.
But I will *meet* him as he meets me.
This is not advised, Baston. We are international fugitives.
Wanted men.
It's only a matter of time before we're *discovered* out here and--
Do you feel you have been treated *unfairly*, Mr. Kroger?
Do I not *compensate* you well for all the *risks* you assume in my employ?
Y-yes, Baston... you are...
...most generous...

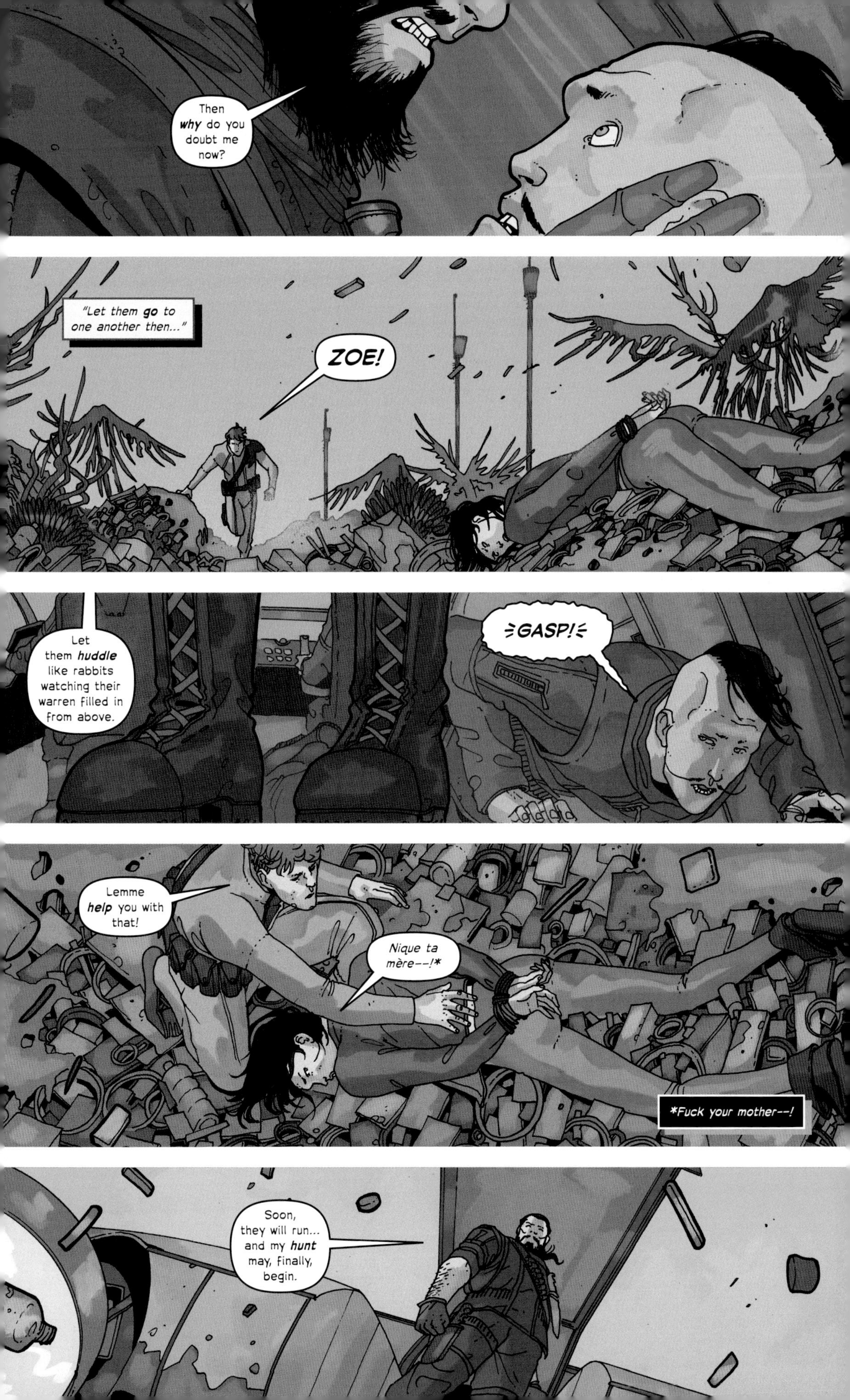
Then why do you doubt me now?
"Let them go to one another then..."
ZOE!
Let them huddle like rabbits watching their warren filled in from above.
GASP!
Lemme help you with that!
Nique ta mère--!*
*Fuck your mother--!
Soon, they will run... and my hunt may, finally, begin.

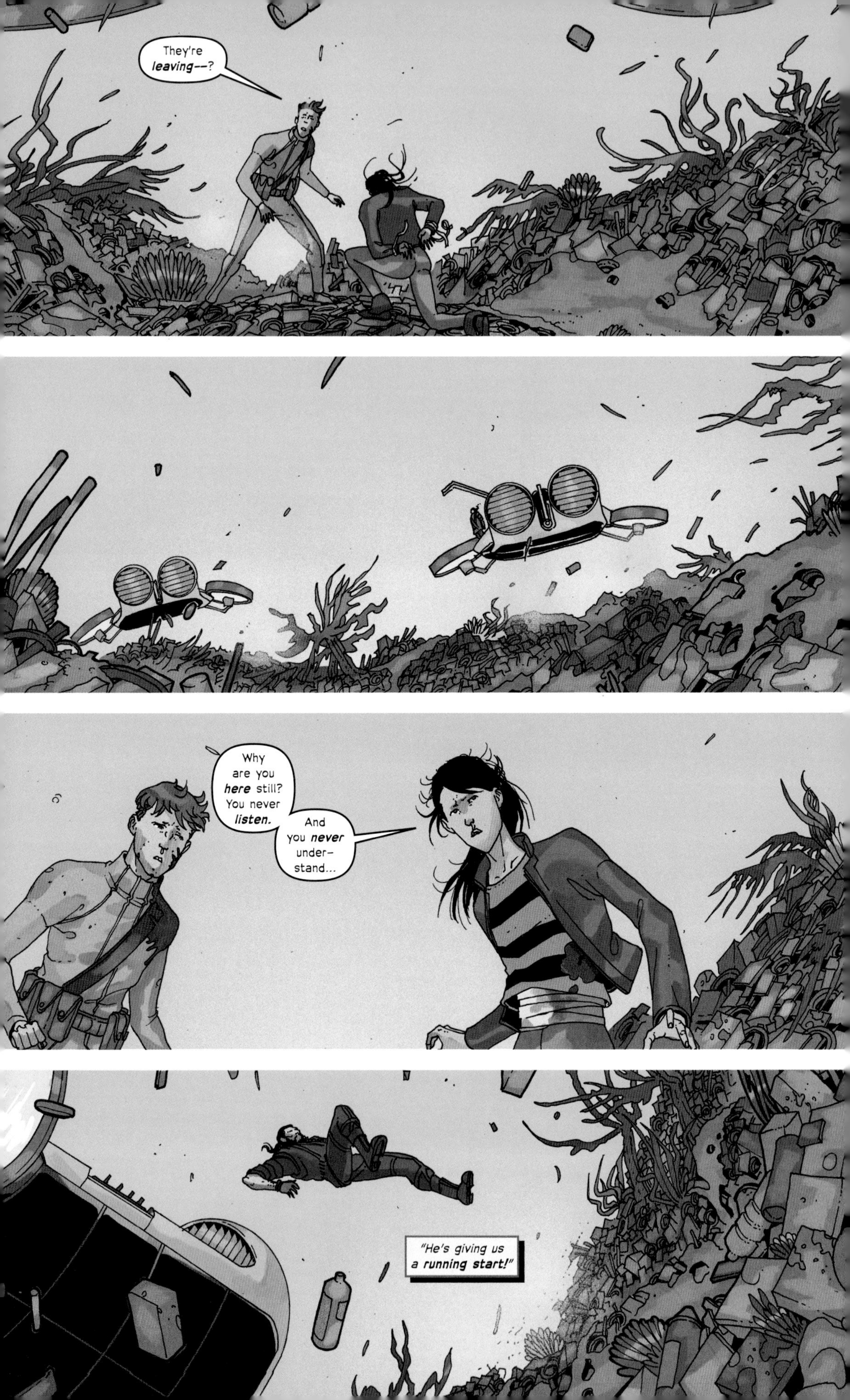
They're *leaving--*?
Why are you *here* still? You never *listen.*
And you *never* under-stand...
"He's giving us a *running start!*"

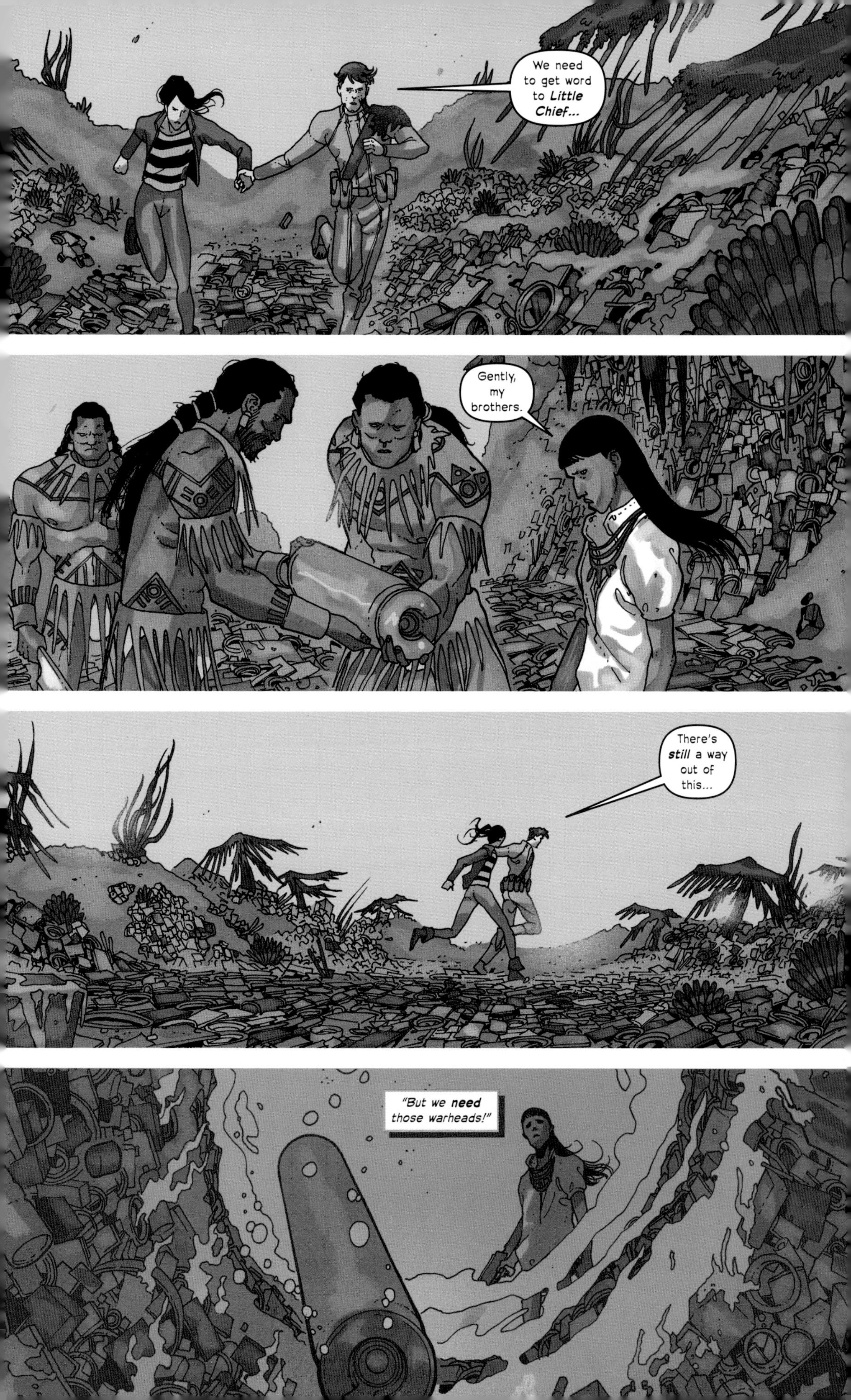
We need to get word to *Little Chief...*
Gently, my brothers.
There's *still* a way out of this...
*"But we **need** those warheads!"*

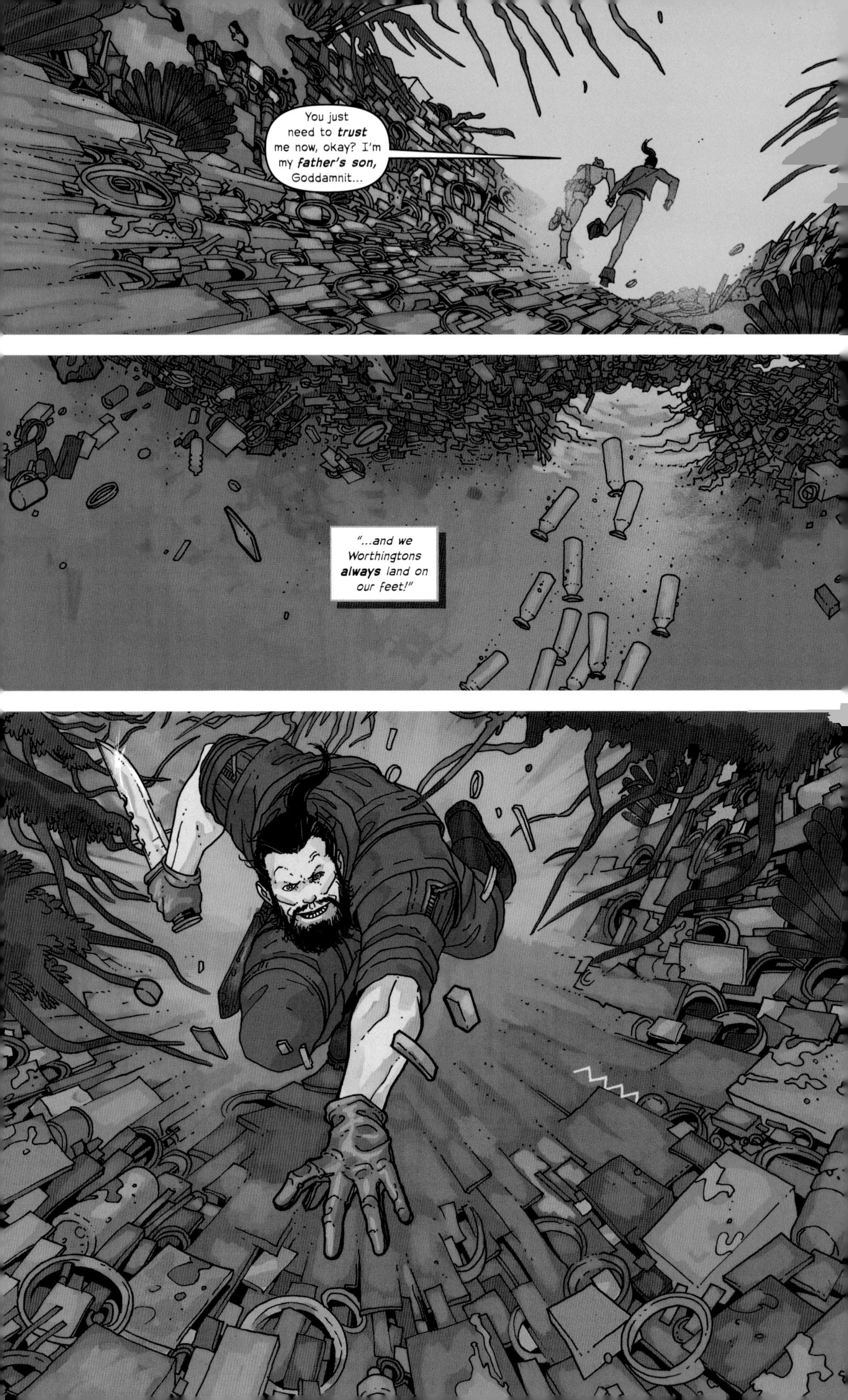
You just need to trust me now, okay? I'm my father's son, Goddamnit...
"...and we Worthingtons always land on our feet!"

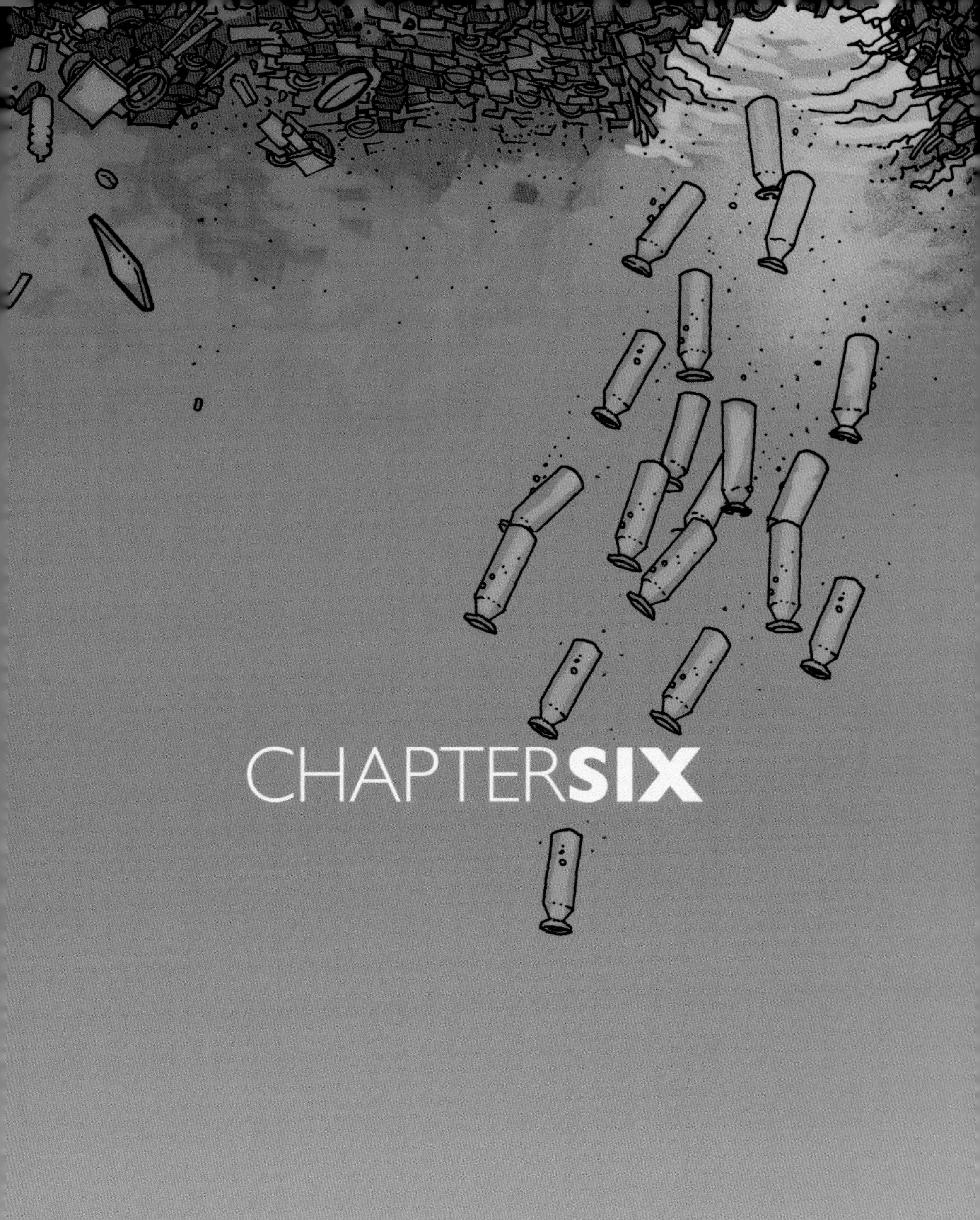

CHAPTER SIX

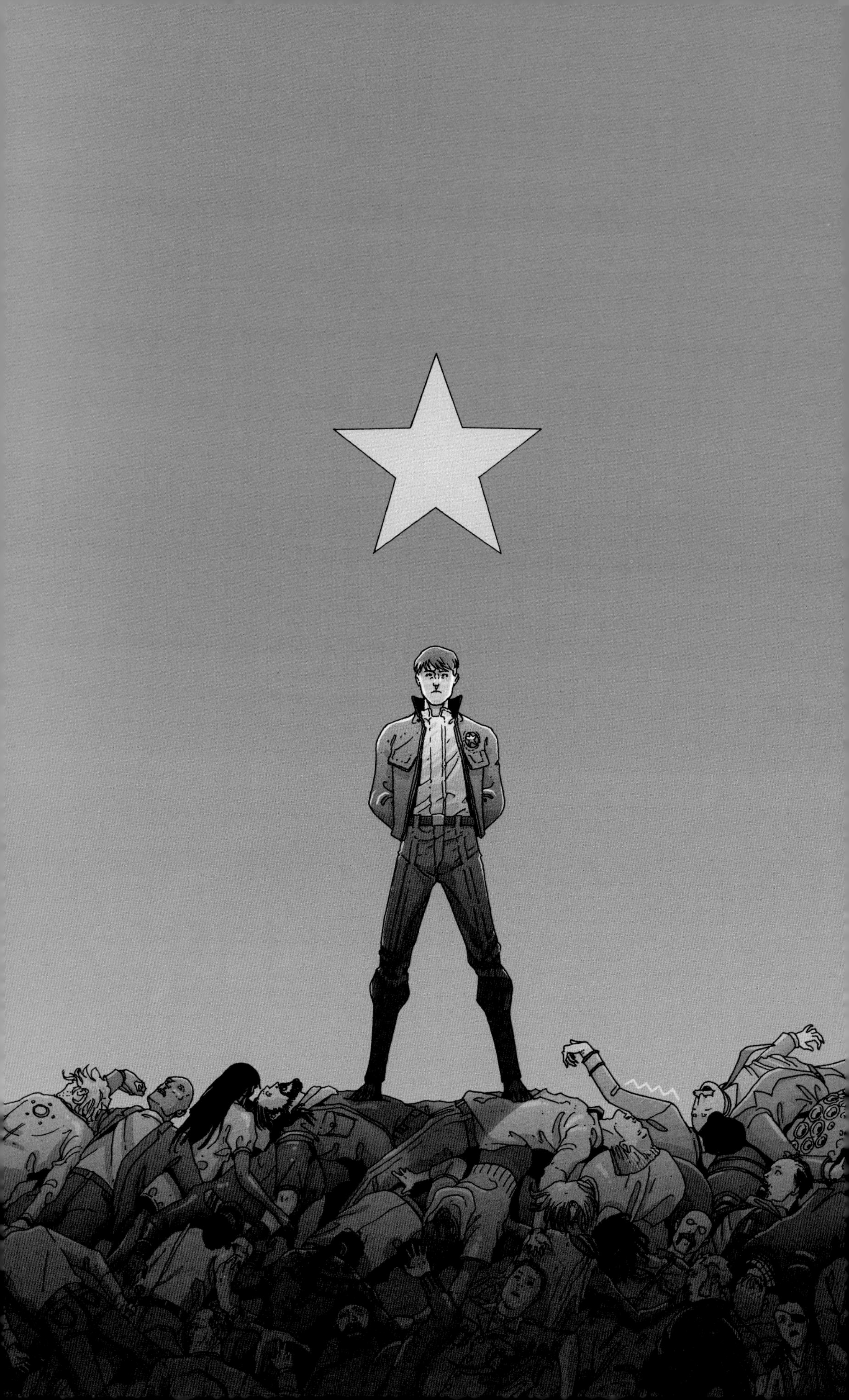

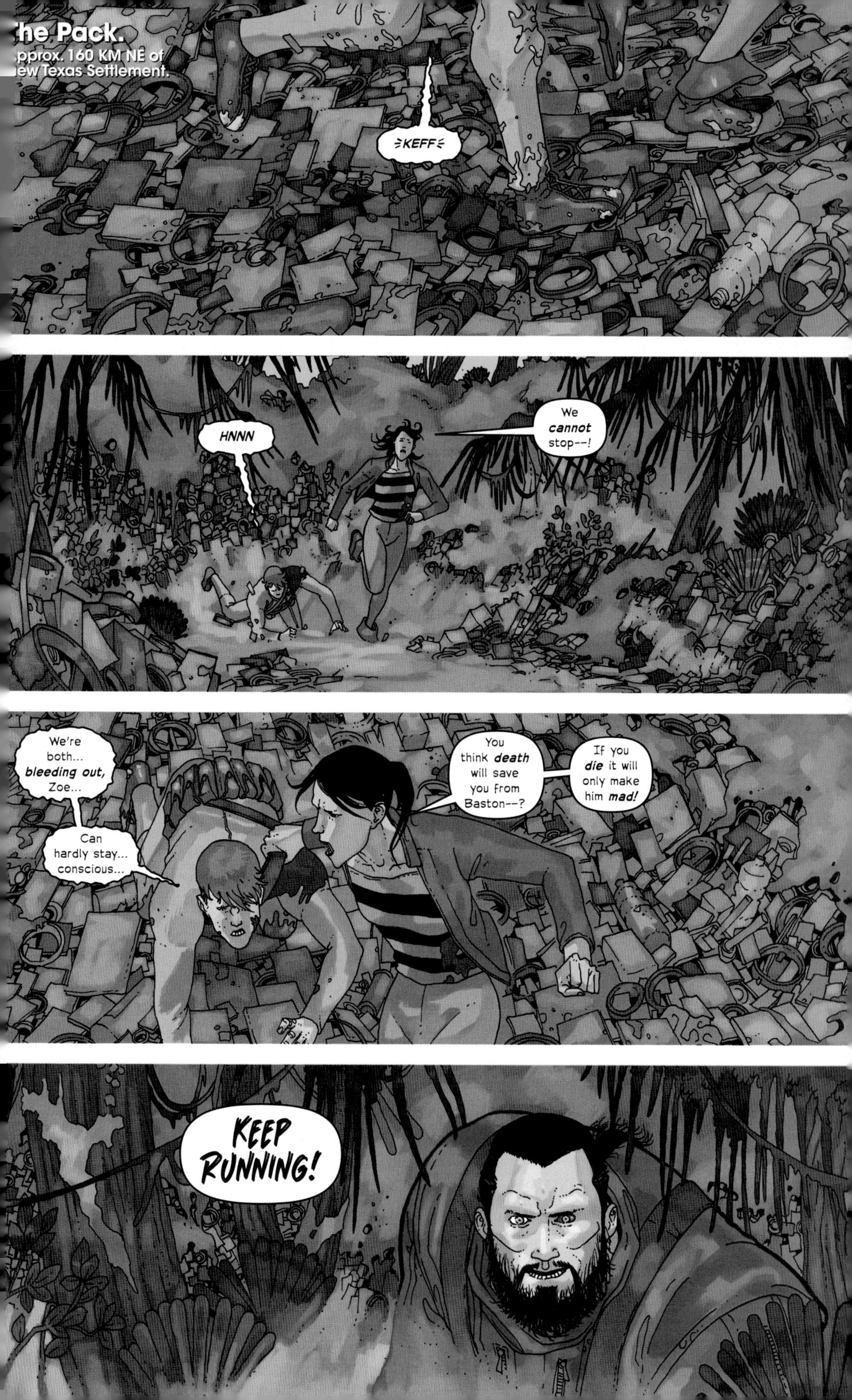
he Pack.
pprox. 160 KM NE of
ew Texas Settlement.
KEFF
HNNN
We cannot stop--!
We're both... bleeding out, Zoe...
Can hardly stay... conscious...
You think death will save you from Baston--?
If you die it will only make him mad!
KEEP RUNNING!

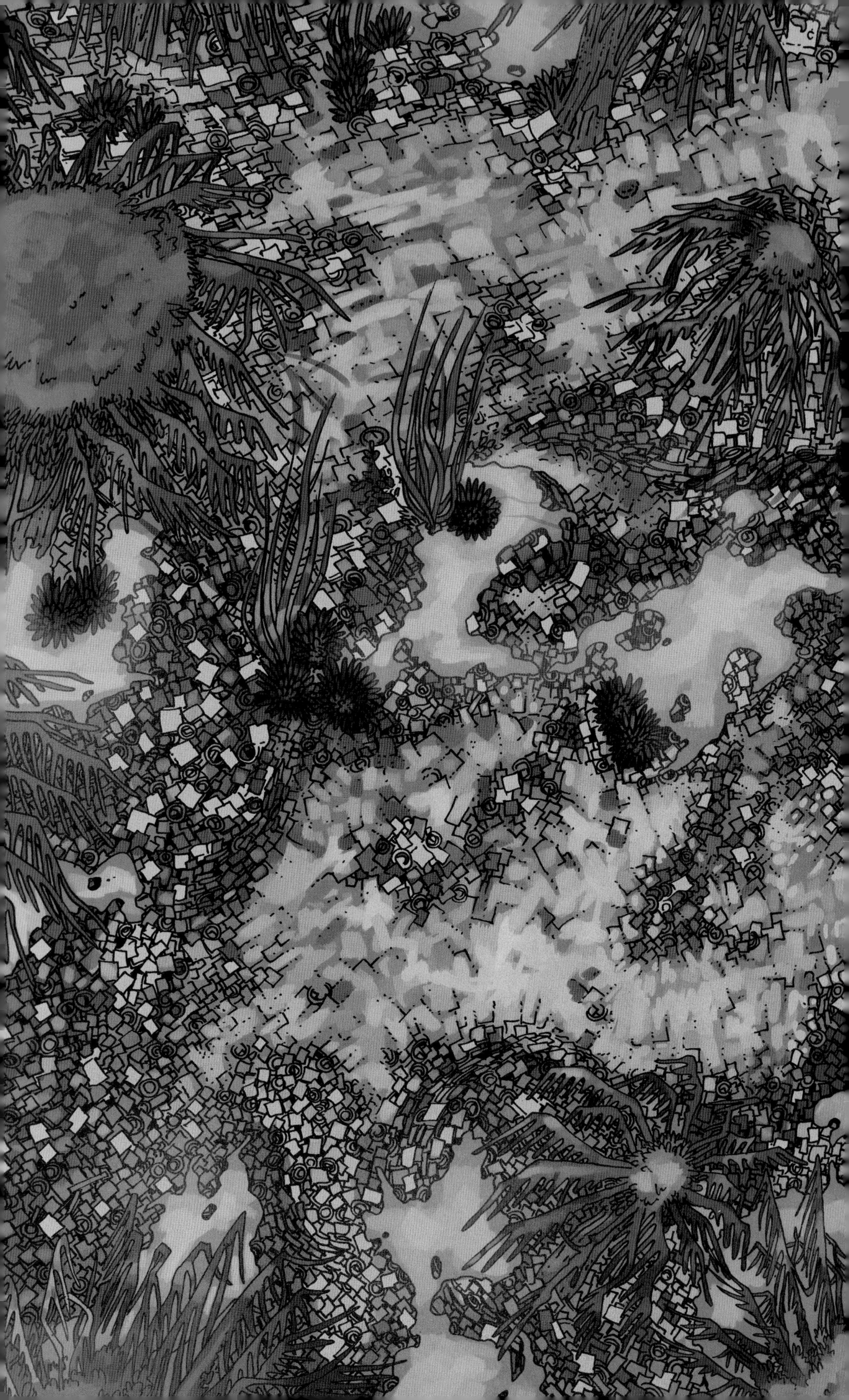

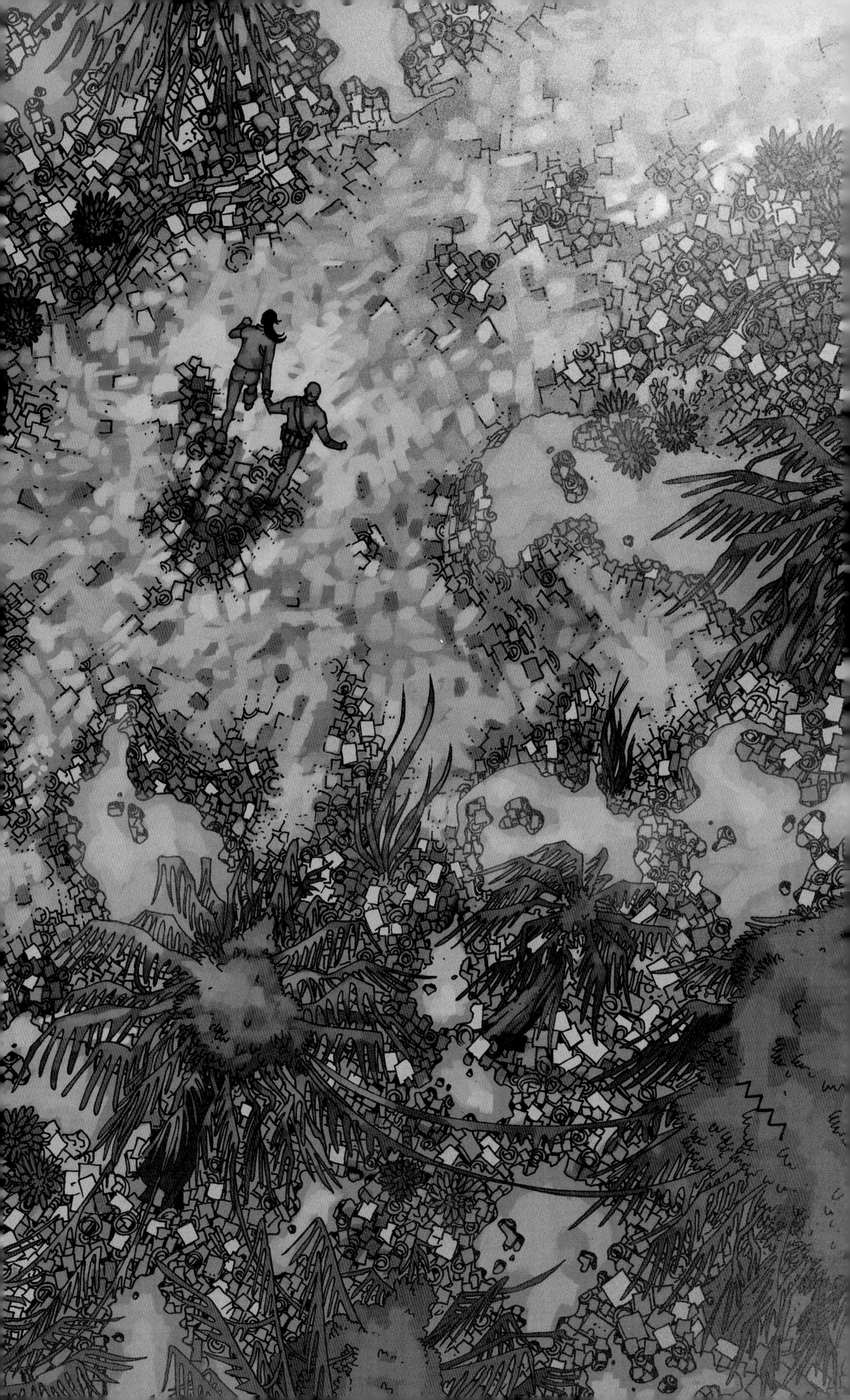

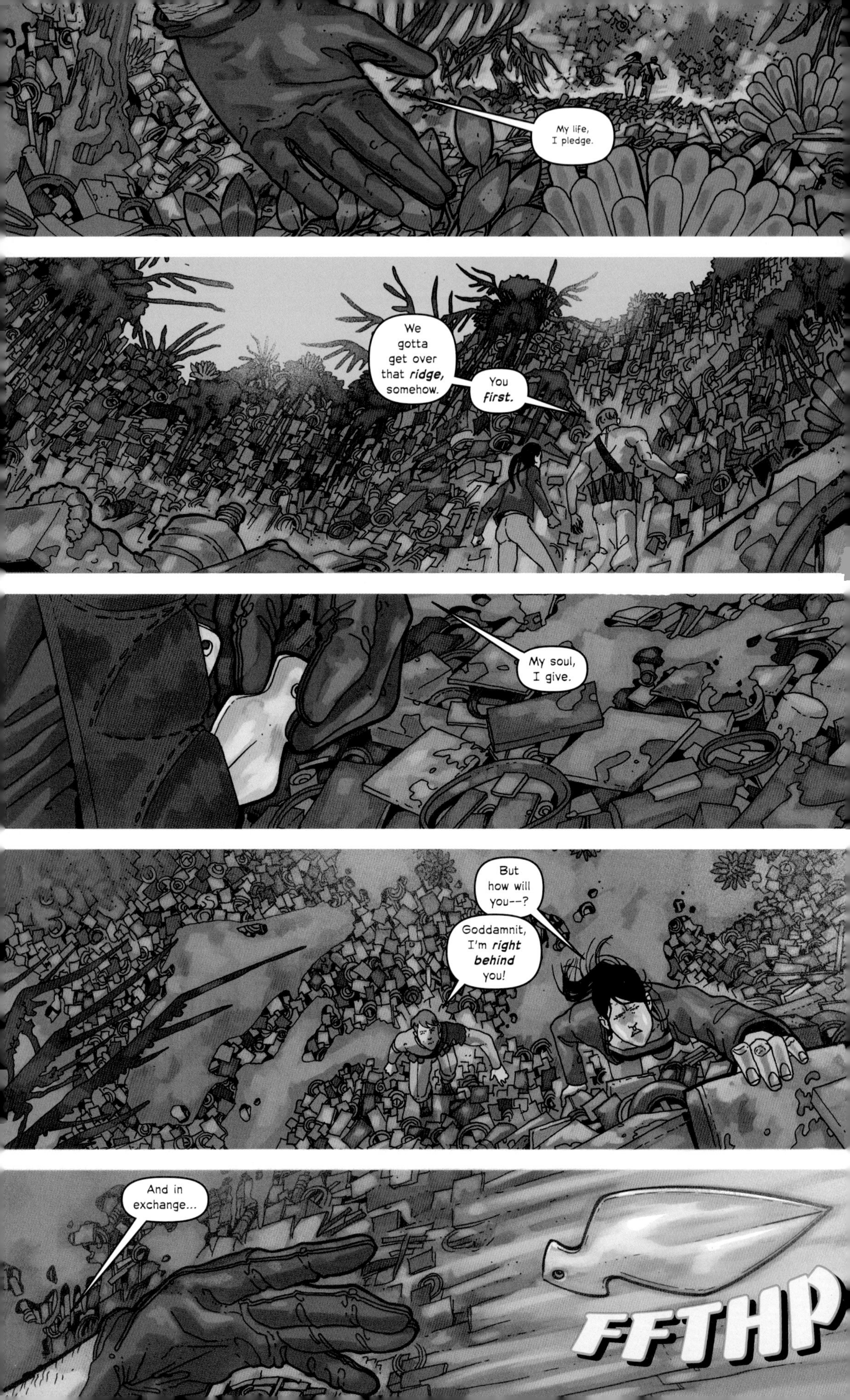
My life, I pledge.
We gotta get over that *ridge,* somehow.
You *first.*
My soul, I give.
But how will you--?
Goddamnit, I'm *right behind* you!
And in exchange...
FFTHP

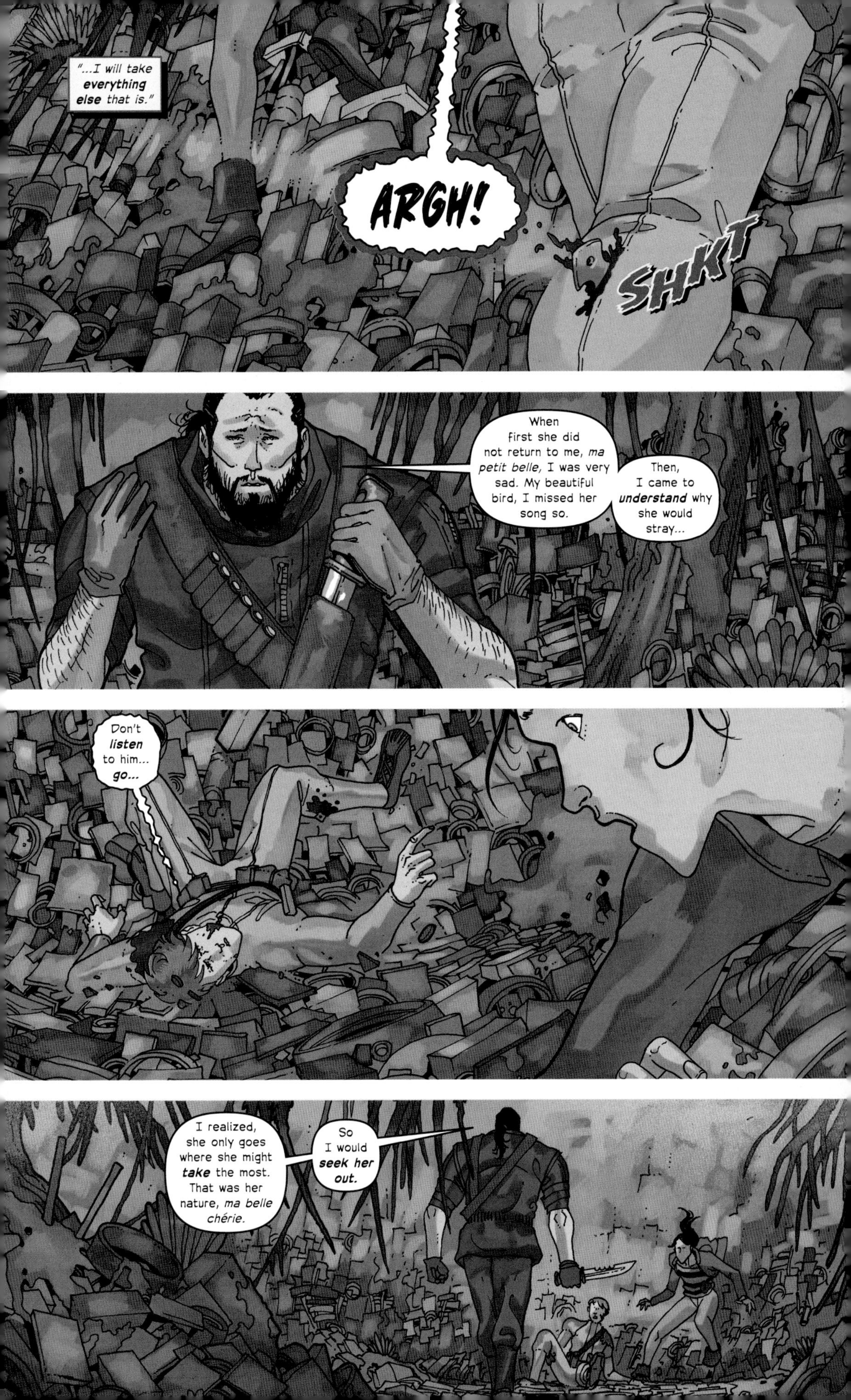
"...I will take everything else that is."
ARGH!
SHKT
When first she did not return to me, ma petit belle, I was very sad. My beautiful bird, I missed her song so.
Then, I came to understand why she would stray...
Don't listen to him... go...
I realized, she only goes where she might take the most. That was her nature, ma belle chérie.
So I would seek her out.

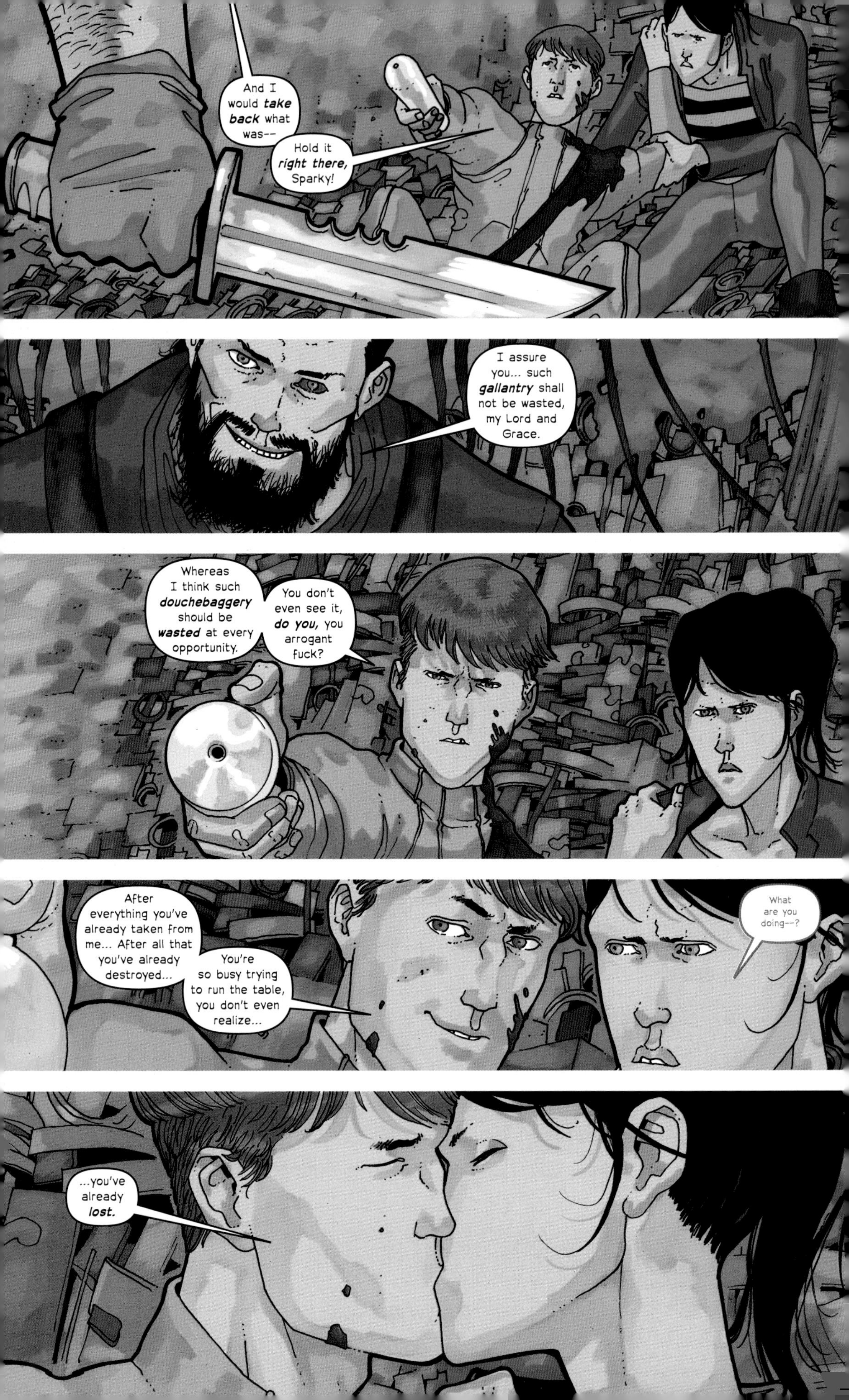

And I would take back what was--
Hold it right there, Sparky!
I assure you... such gallantry shall not be wasted, my Lord and Grace.
Whereas I think such douchebaggery should be wasted at every opportunity.
You don't even see it, do you, you arrogant fuck?
After everything you've already taken from me... After all that you've already destroyed...
You're so busy trying to run the table, you don't even realize...
What are you doing--?
...you've already lost.

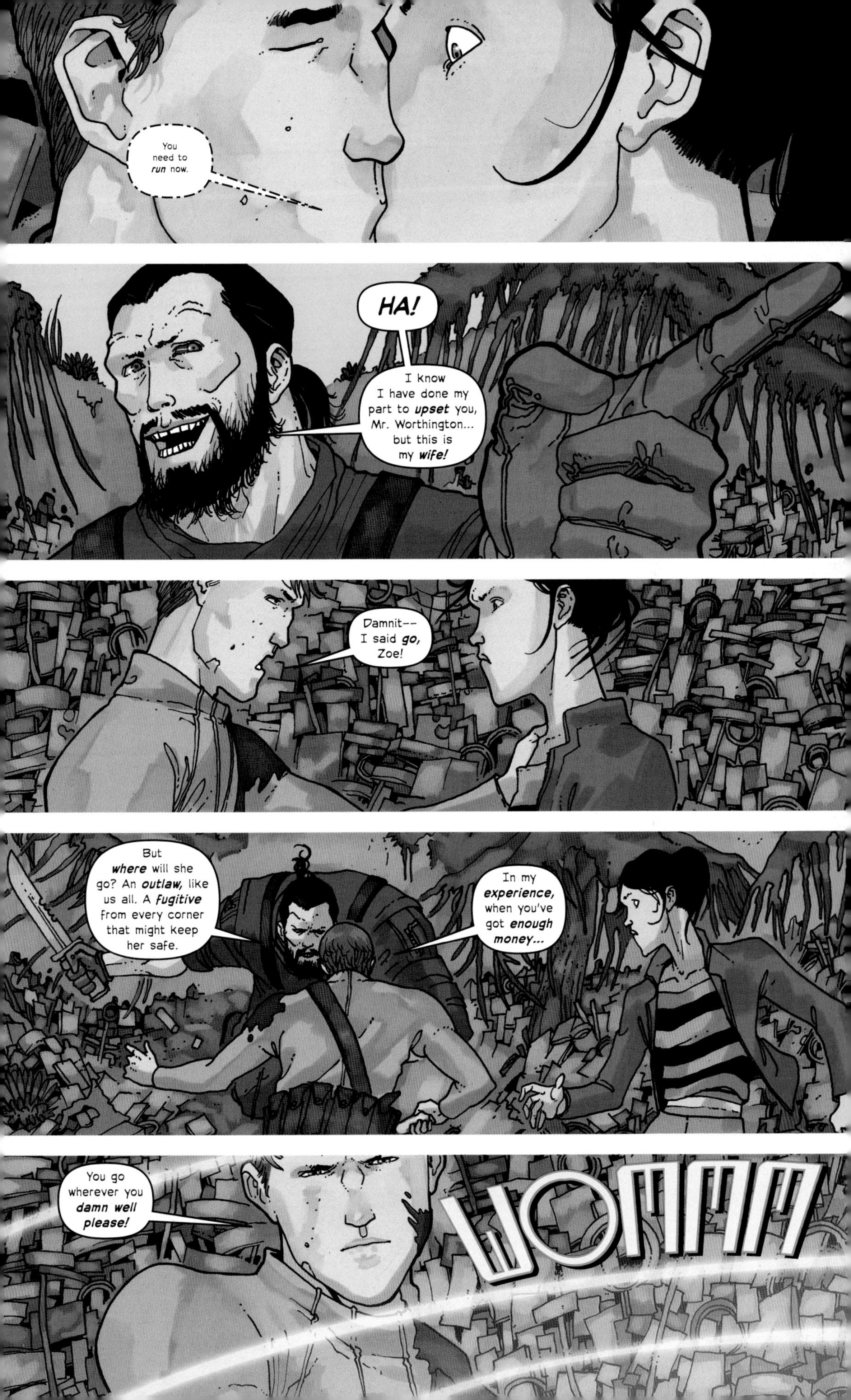
You need to *run* now.
HA!
I know I have done my part to ***upset*** you, Mr. Worthington... but this is my ***wife!***
Damnit-- I said ***go,*** Zoe!
But ***where*** will she go? An ***outlaw,*** like us all. A ***fugitive*** from every corner that might keep her safe.
In my ***experience,*** when you've got ***enough money...***
You go wherever you ***damn well please!***
WOMMM

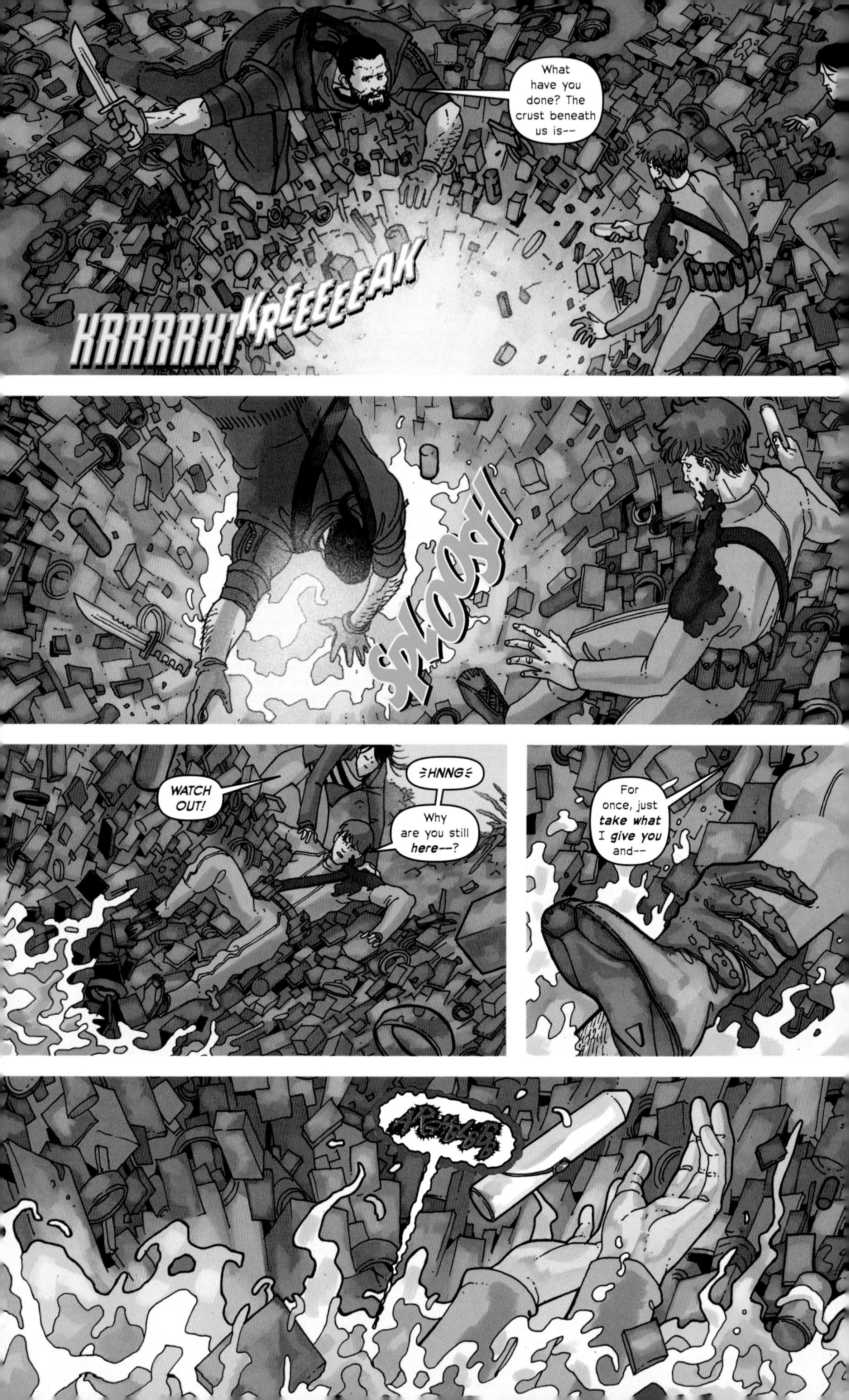
What have you done? The crust beneath us is--
KRRRRKT KREEEEEAK
SPLOOSH
WATCH OUT!
HNNG
Why are you still *here*--?
For once, just *take what* I *give you* and--

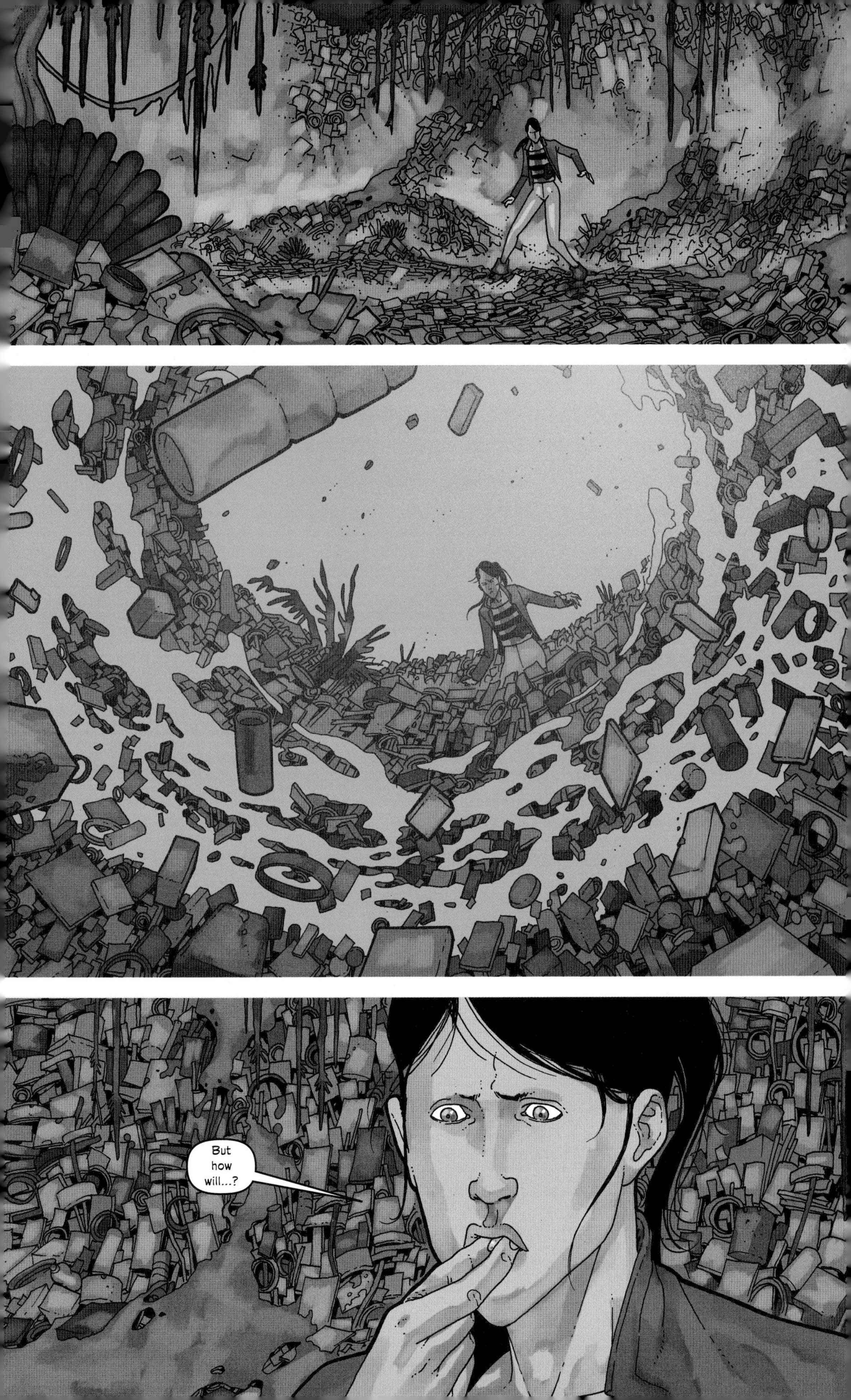
But how will...?

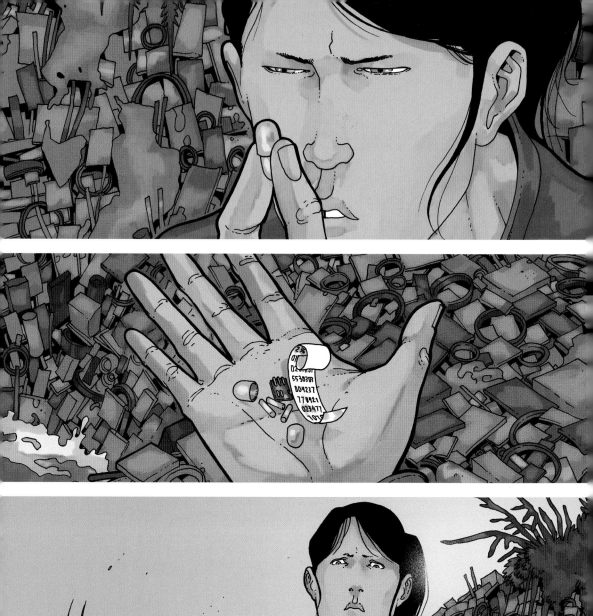

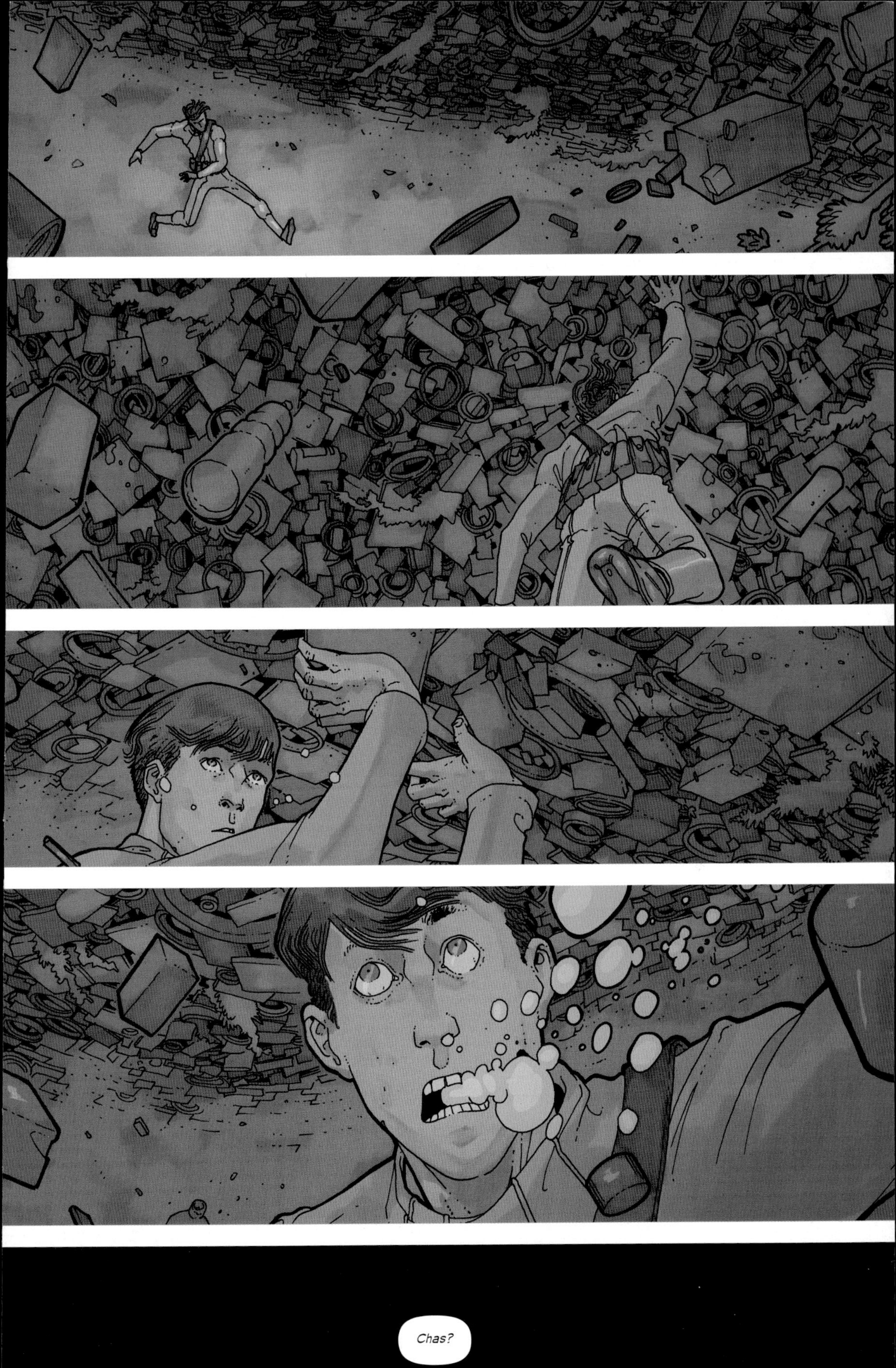
Chas?

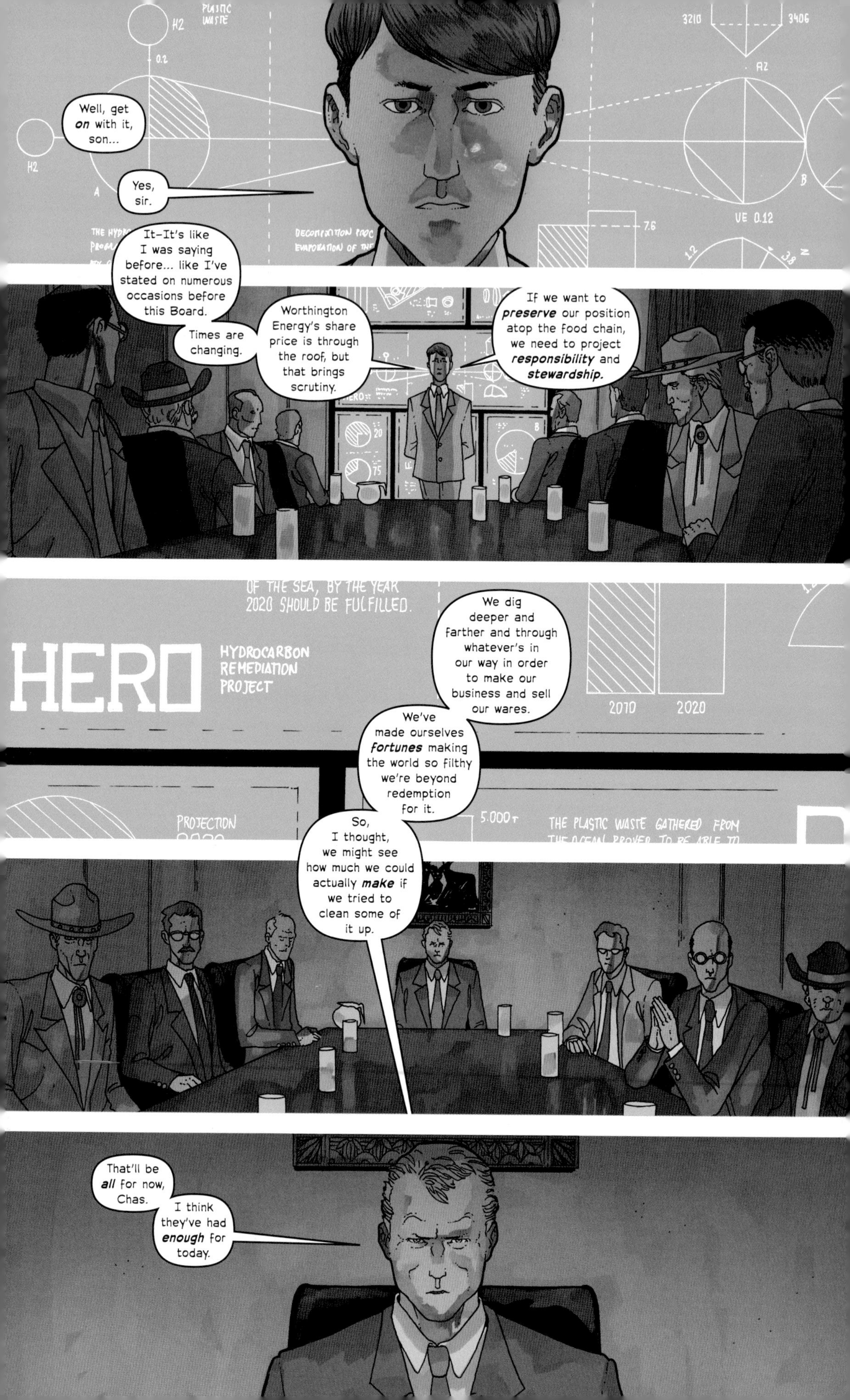
Well, get *on* with it, son...
Yes, sir.
It–It's like I was saying before... like I've stated on numerous occasions before this Board.
Times are changing.
Worthington Energy's share price is through the roof, but that brings scrutiny.
If we want to *preserve* our position atop the food chain, we need to project *responsibility* and *stewardship.*
OF THE SEA, BY THE YEAR 2020 SHOULD BE FULFILLED.
HERO
HYDROCARBON REMEDIATION PROJECT
2010
2020
We dig deeper and farther and through whatever's in our way in order to make our business and sell our wares.
We've made ourselves *fortunes* making the world so filthy we're beyond redemption for it.
PROJECTION
5.000 T
THE PLASTIC WASTE GATHERED FROM
So, I thought, we might see how much we could actually *make* if we tried to clean some of it up.
That'll be *all* for now, Chas.
I think they've had *enough* for today.

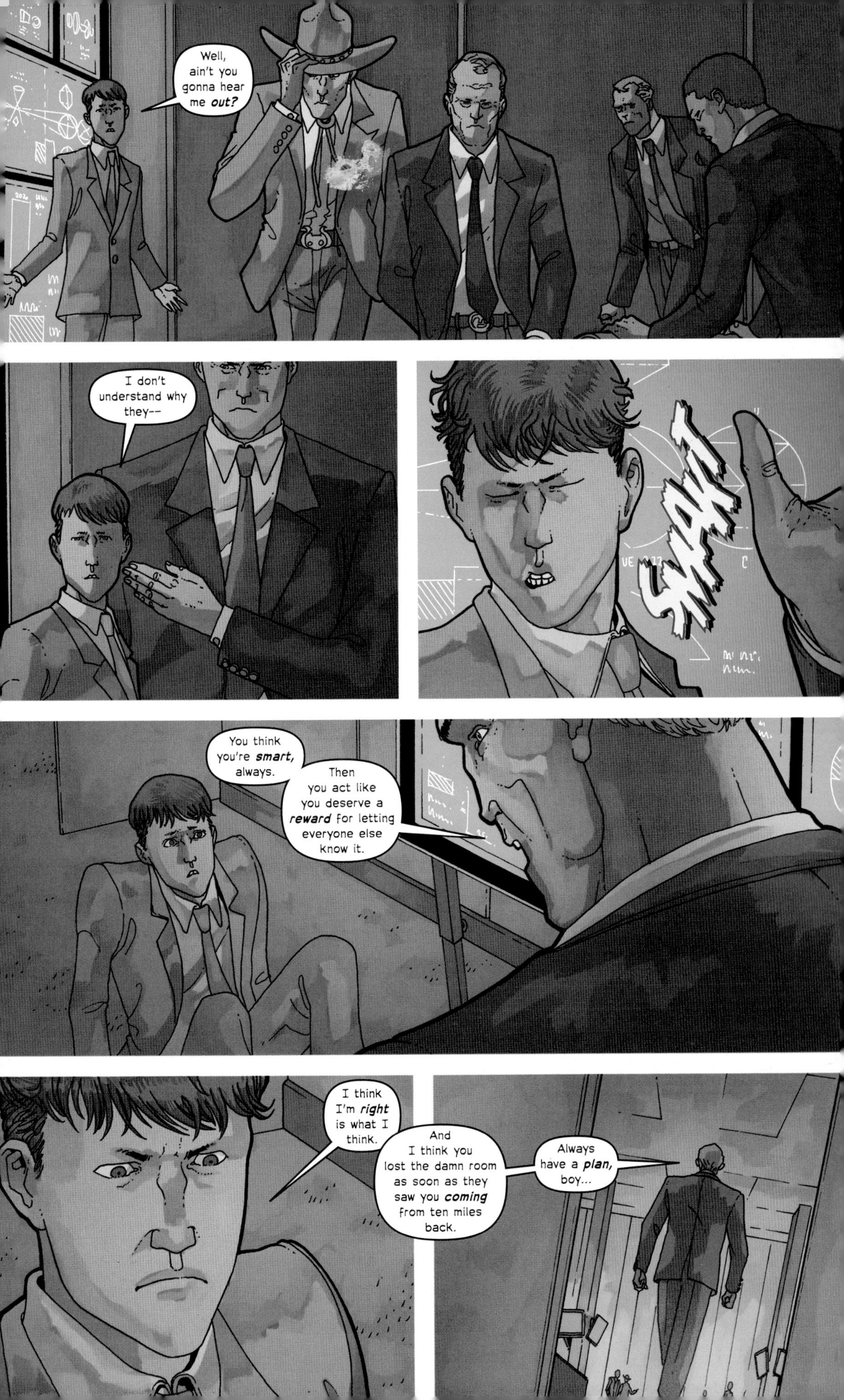

Well, ain't you gonna hear me *out?*
I don't understand why they--
SMACK
You think you're *smart,* always.
Then you act like you deserve a *reward* for letting everyone else know it.
I think I'm *right* is what I think.
And I think you lost the damn room as soon as they saw you *coming* from ten miles back.
Always have a *plan,* boy...

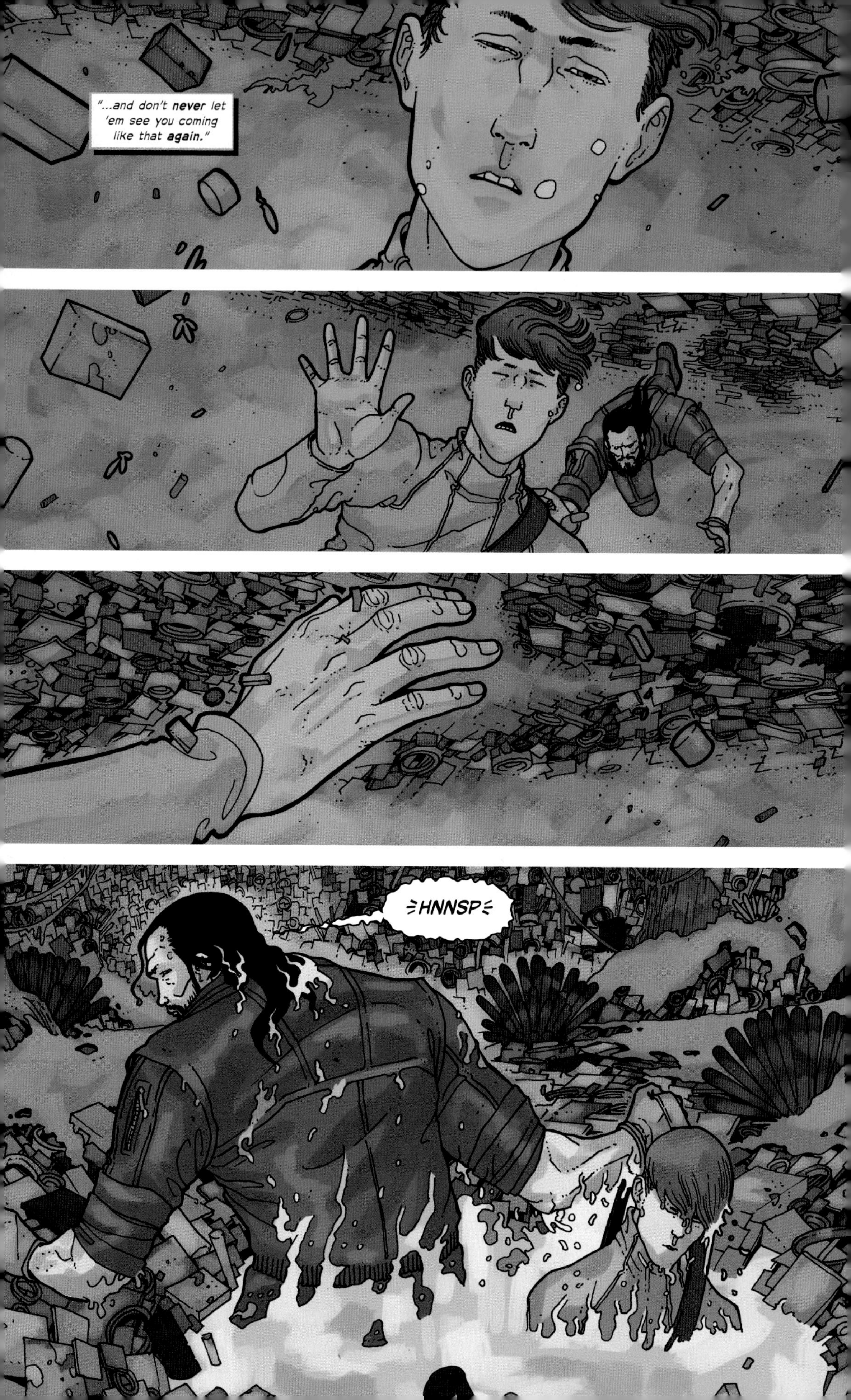
"...and don't **never** let 'em see you coming like that **again.**"
HNNSP

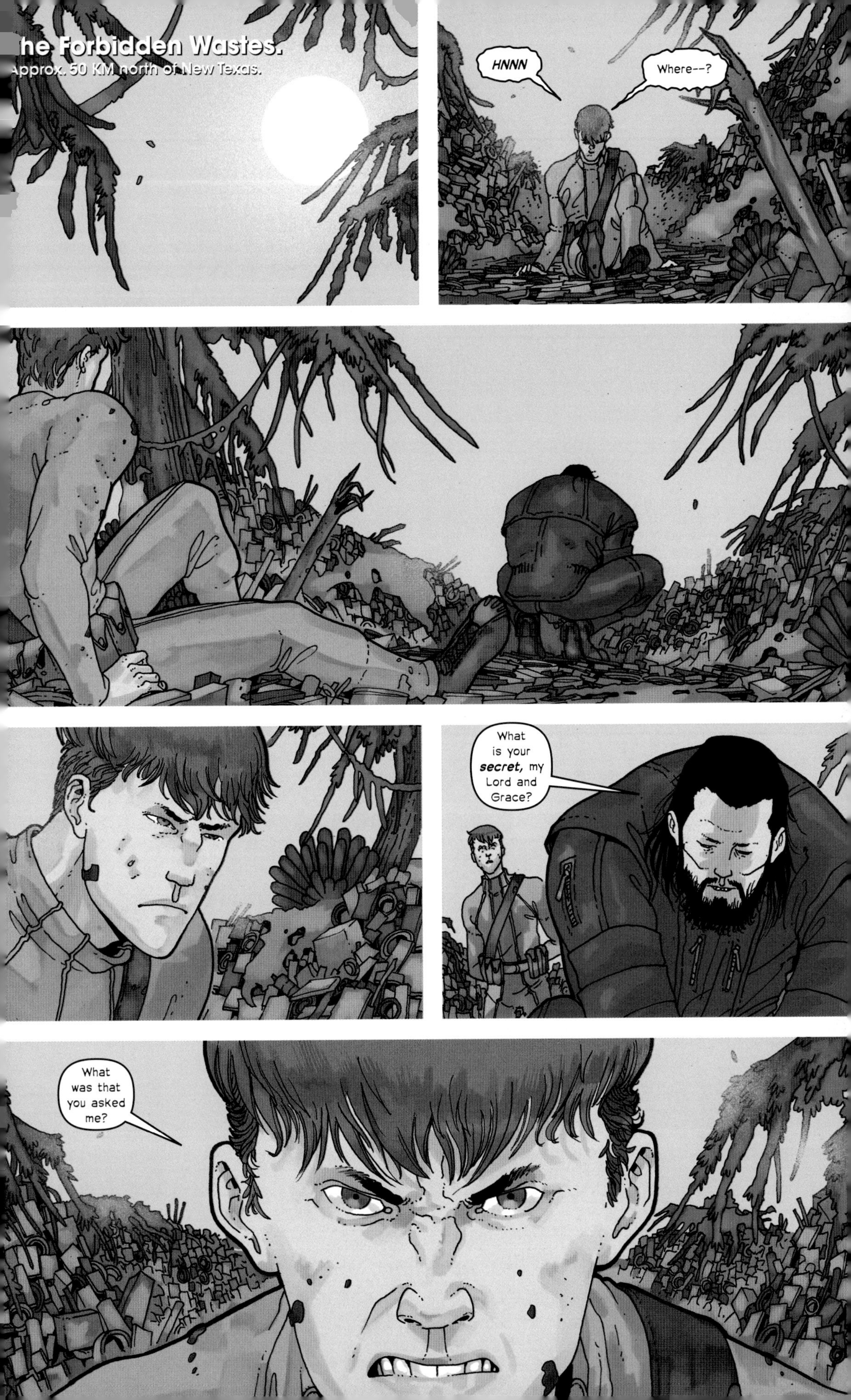
he Forbidden Wastes.
Approx. 50 KM north of New Texas.
HNNN
Where--?
What is your **secret,** my Lord and Grace?
What was that you asked me?

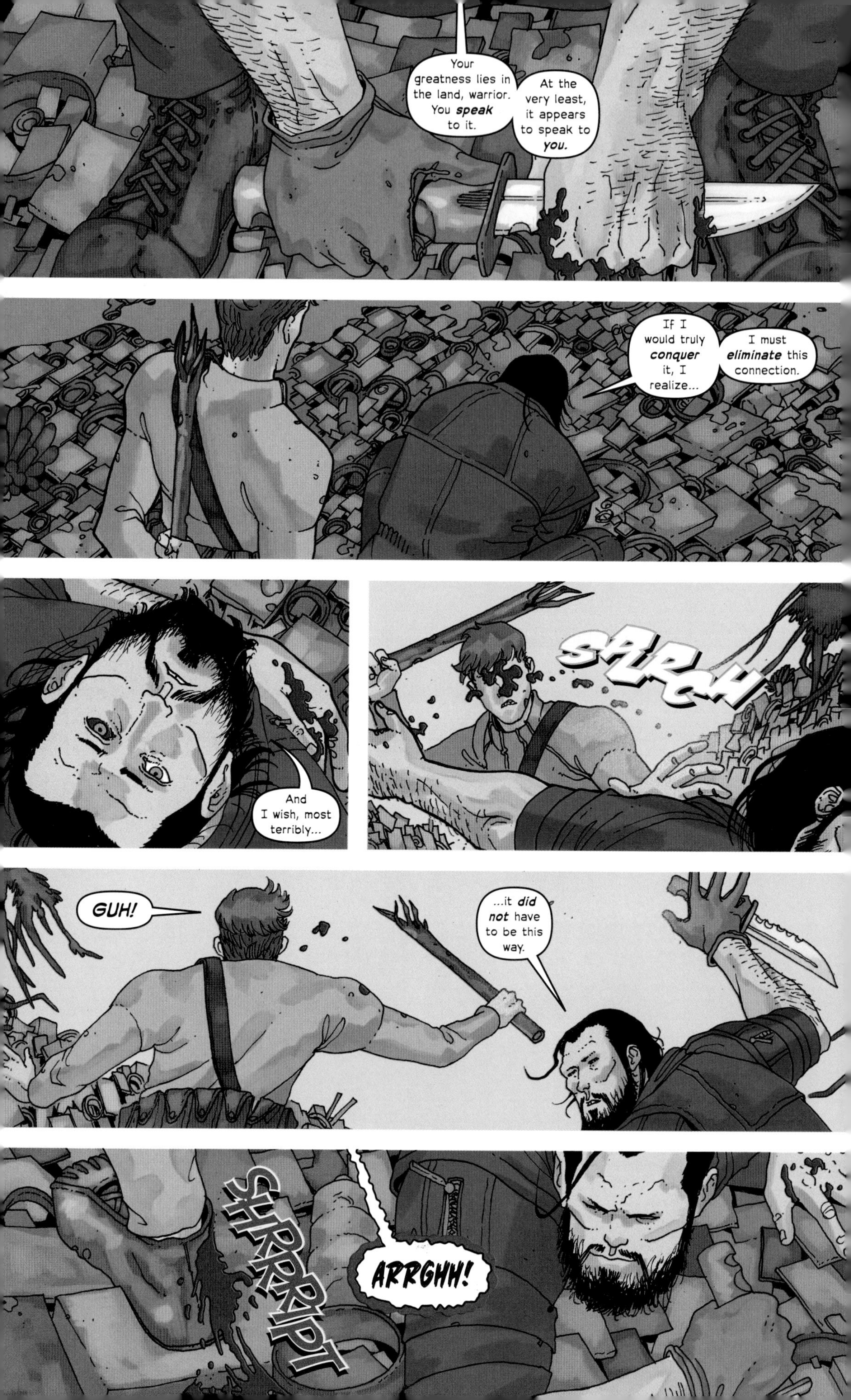
Your greatness lies in the land, warrior. You speak to it.
At the very least, it appears to speak to you.
If I would truly conquer it, I realize...
I must eliminate this connection.
And I wish, most terribly...
SPLRCH
GUH!
...it did not have to be this way.
SHRRIPT
ARRGHH!

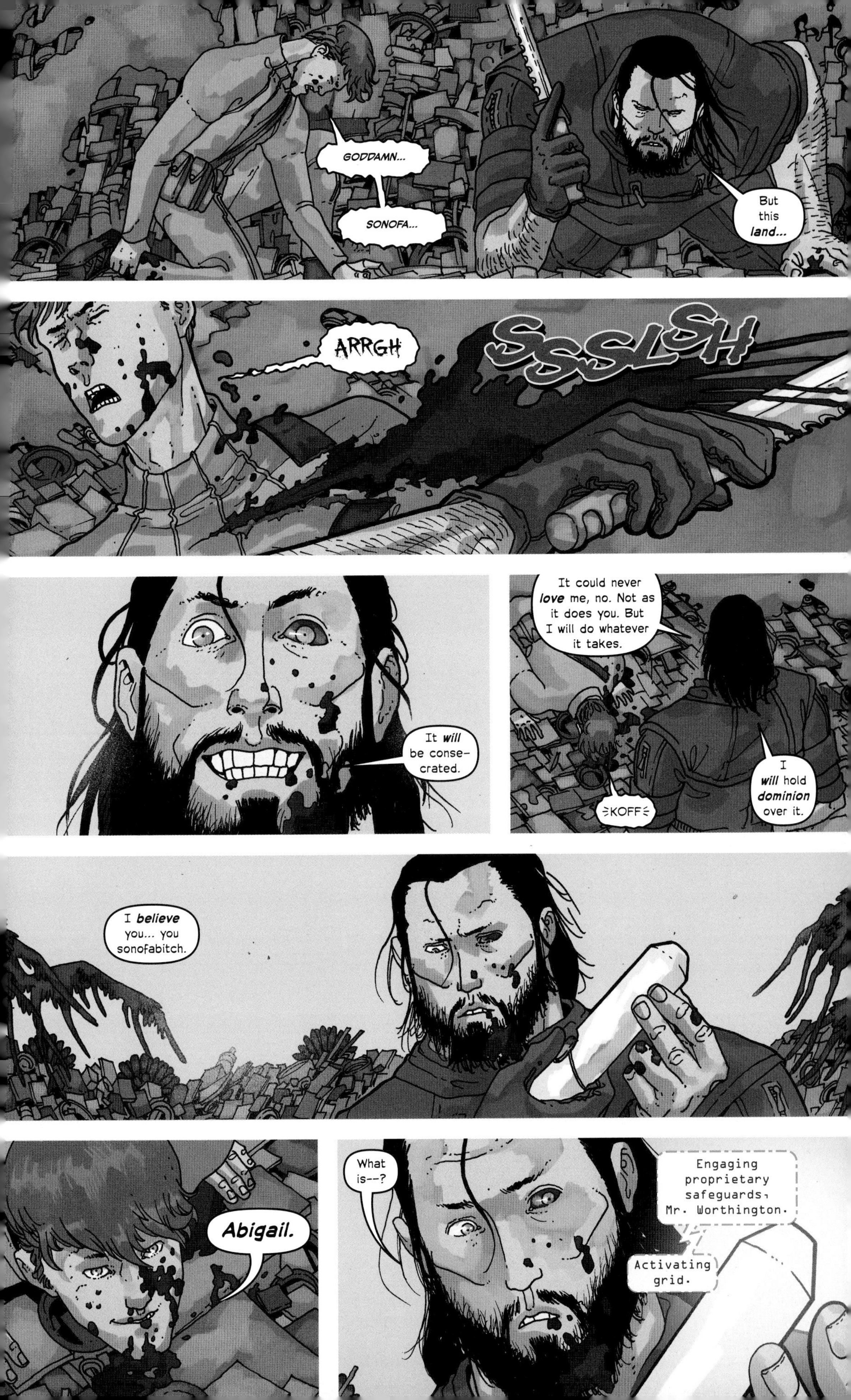
GODDAMN...
SONOFA...
But this land...
ARRGH
SSSLSH
It will be conse-crated.
It could never love me, no. Not as it does you. But I will do whatever it takes.
KOFF
I will hold dominion over it.
I believe you... you sonofabitch.
Abigail.
What is--?
Engaging proprietary safeguards, Mr. Worthington.
Activating grid.

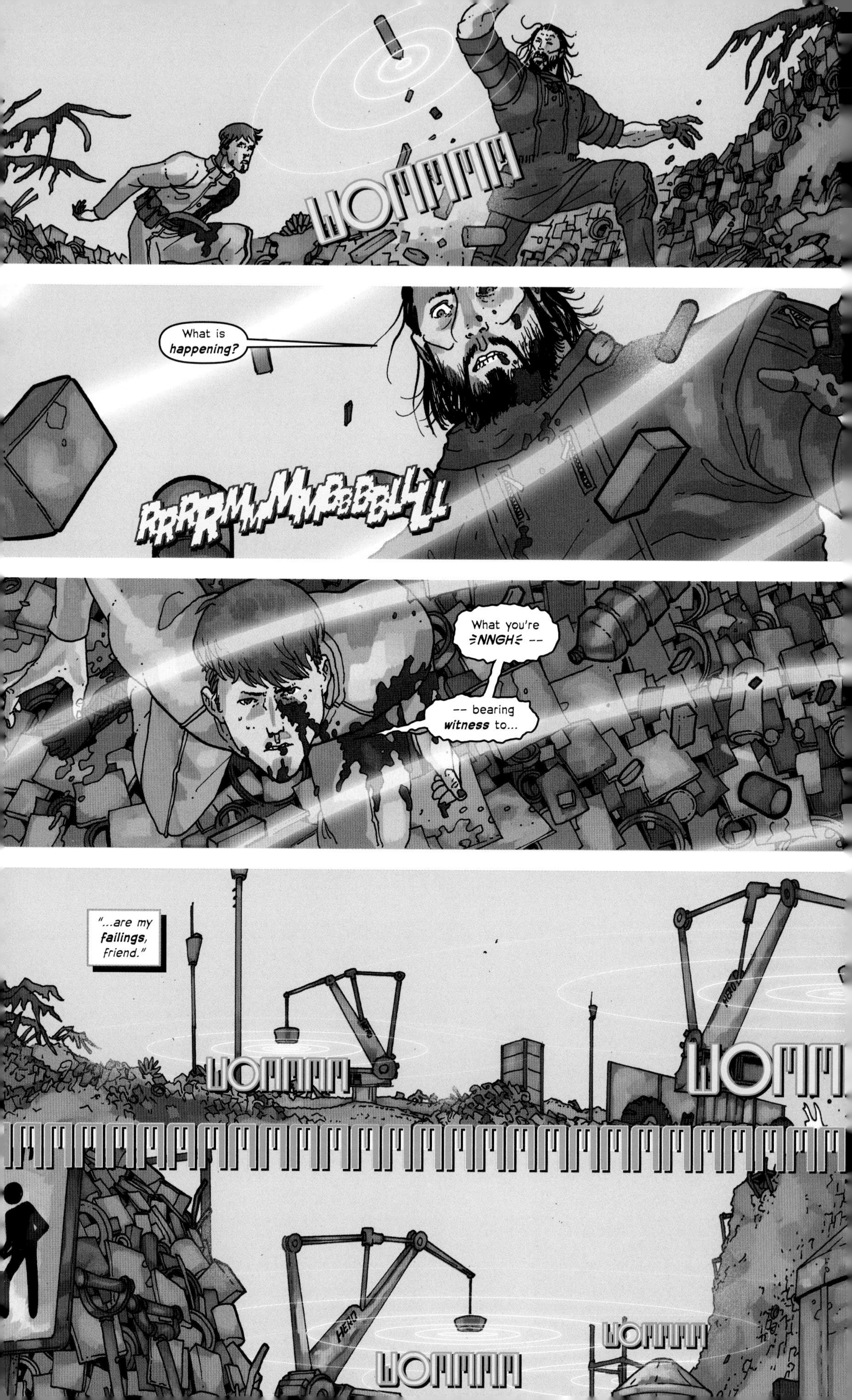
WOMMMM
What is *happening?*
RRRRMMMMBBBLLL
What you're ≶NNGH≶ --
-- bearing *witness* to...
"...are my *failings*, friend."
WOMMMM
WOMM
MMMMMMMMMMMMMMMMMMMMMMMMMMMMMM
WOMMMM
WOMMMM

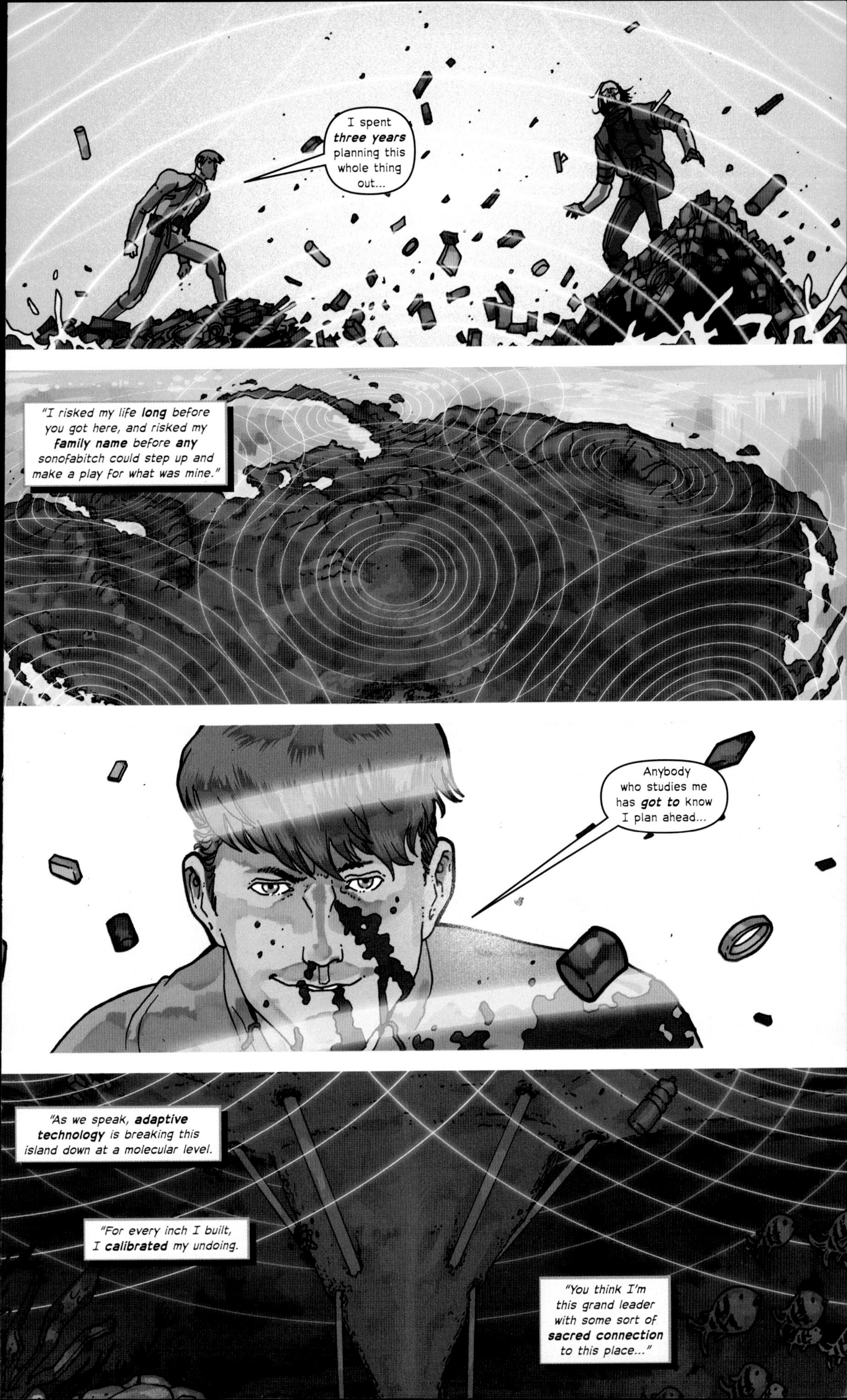
I spent *three years* planning this whole thing out...
"I risked my life **long** before you got here, and risked my **family name** before **any** sonofabitch could step up and make a play for what was mine."
Anybody who studies me has ***got to*** know I plan ahead...
"As we speak, **adaptive technology** is breaking this island down at a molecular level.
"For every inch I built, I **calibrated** my undoing.
"You think I'm this grand leader with some sort of **sacred connection** to this place..."

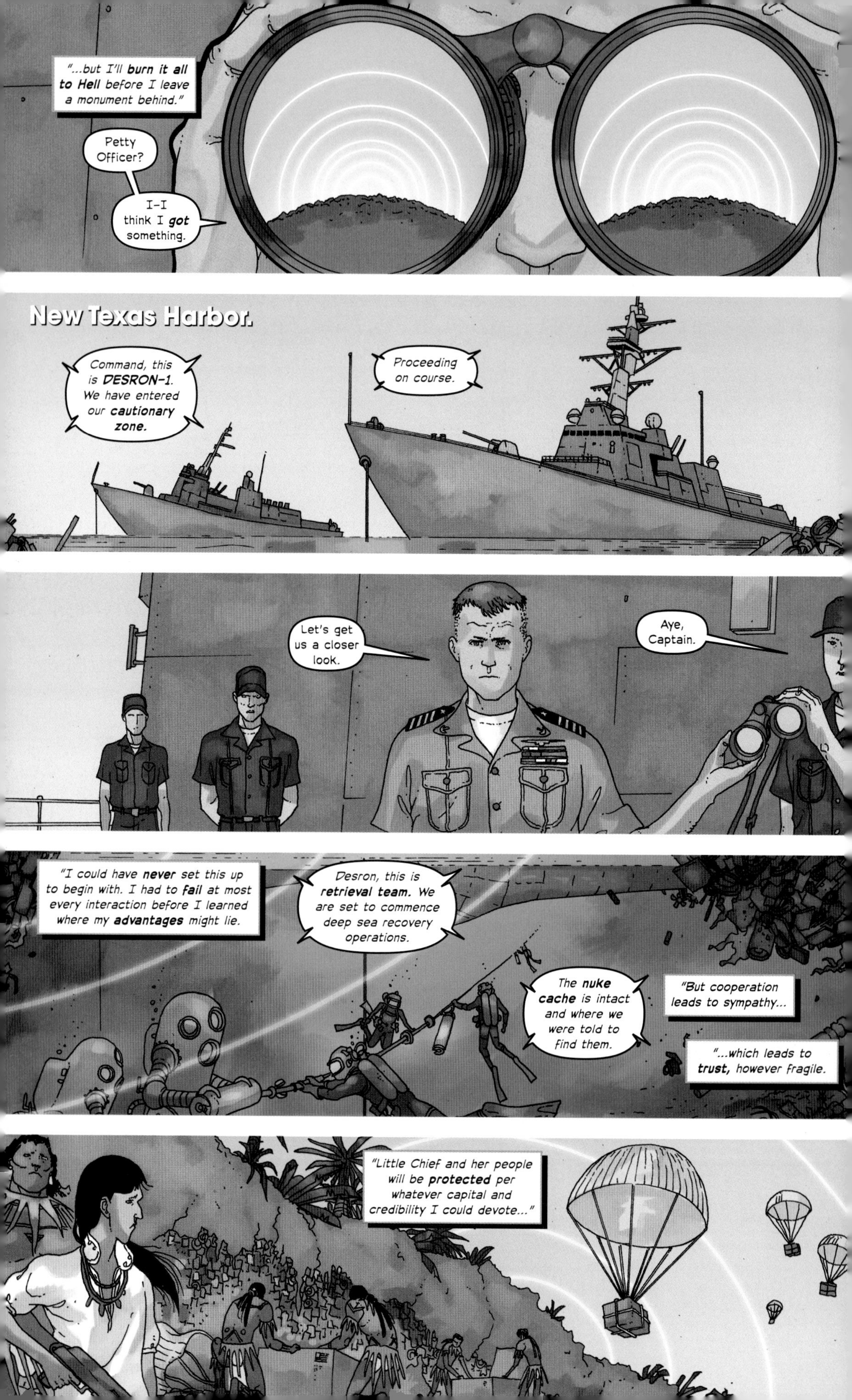

"...but I'll **burn it all to Hell** before I leave a monument behind."
Petty Officer?
I-I think I **got** something.
New Texas Harbor.
Command, this is **DESRON-1**. We have entered our **cautionary zone.**
Proceeding on course.
Let's get us a closer look.
Aye, Captain.
"I could have **never** set this up to begin with. I had to **fail** at most every interaction before I learned where my **advantages** might lie.
Desron, this is **retrieval team.** We are set to commence deep sea recovery operations.
The **nuke cache** is intact and where we were told to find them.
"But cooperation leads to sympathy...
"...which leads to **trust,** however fragile.
"Little Chief and her people will be **protected** per whatever capital and credibility I could devote..."

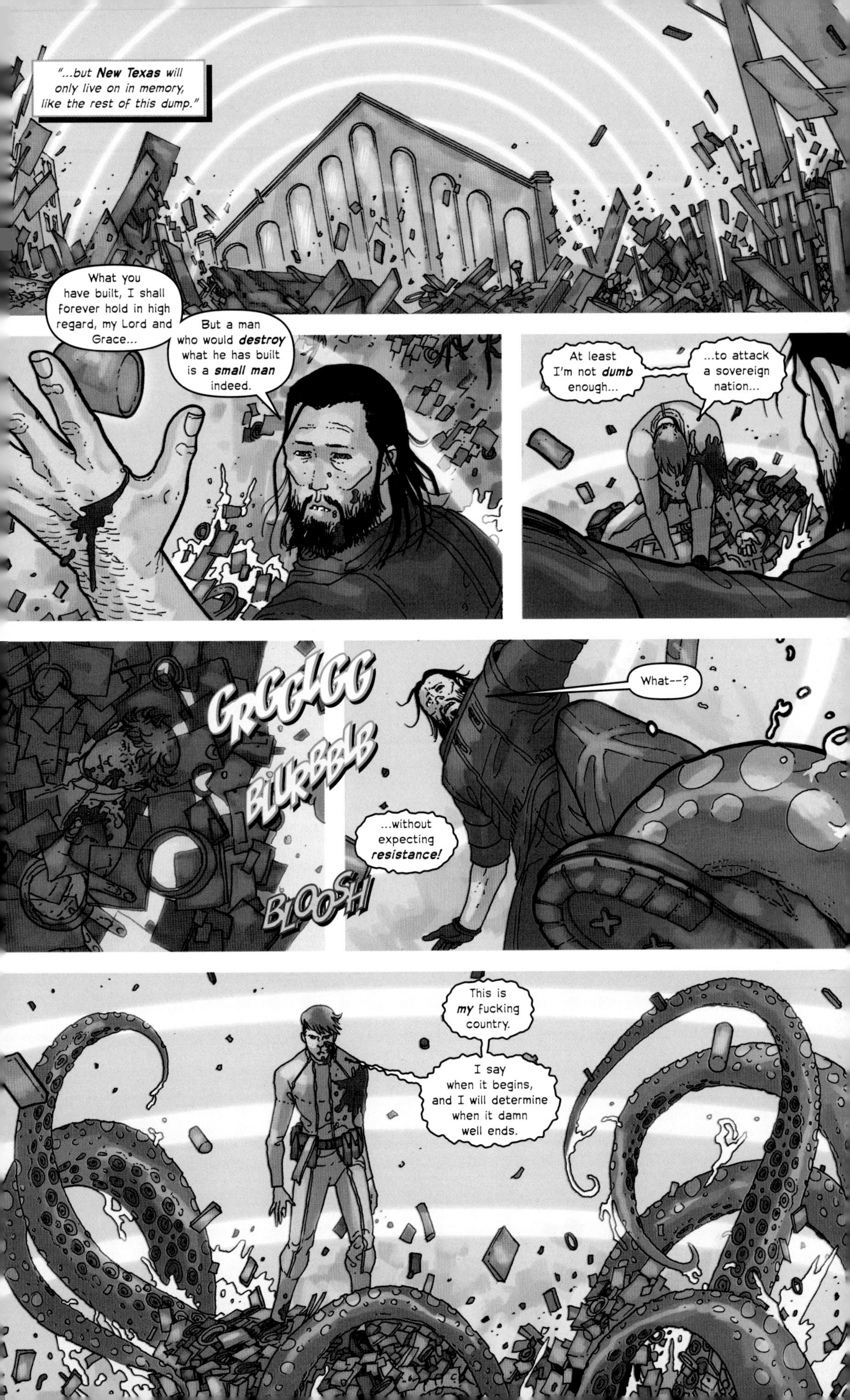

"...but **New Texas** will only live on in memory, like the rest of this dump."
What you have built, I shall forever hold in high regard, my Lord and Grace...
But a man who would ***destroy*** what he has built is a ***small man*** indeed.
At least I'm not ***dumb*** enough...
...to attack a sovereign nation...
GRGGLGG
BLURBBLB
BLOOSH
What--?
...without expecting ***resistance!***
This is ***my*** fucking country.
I say when it begins, and I will determine when it damn well ends.

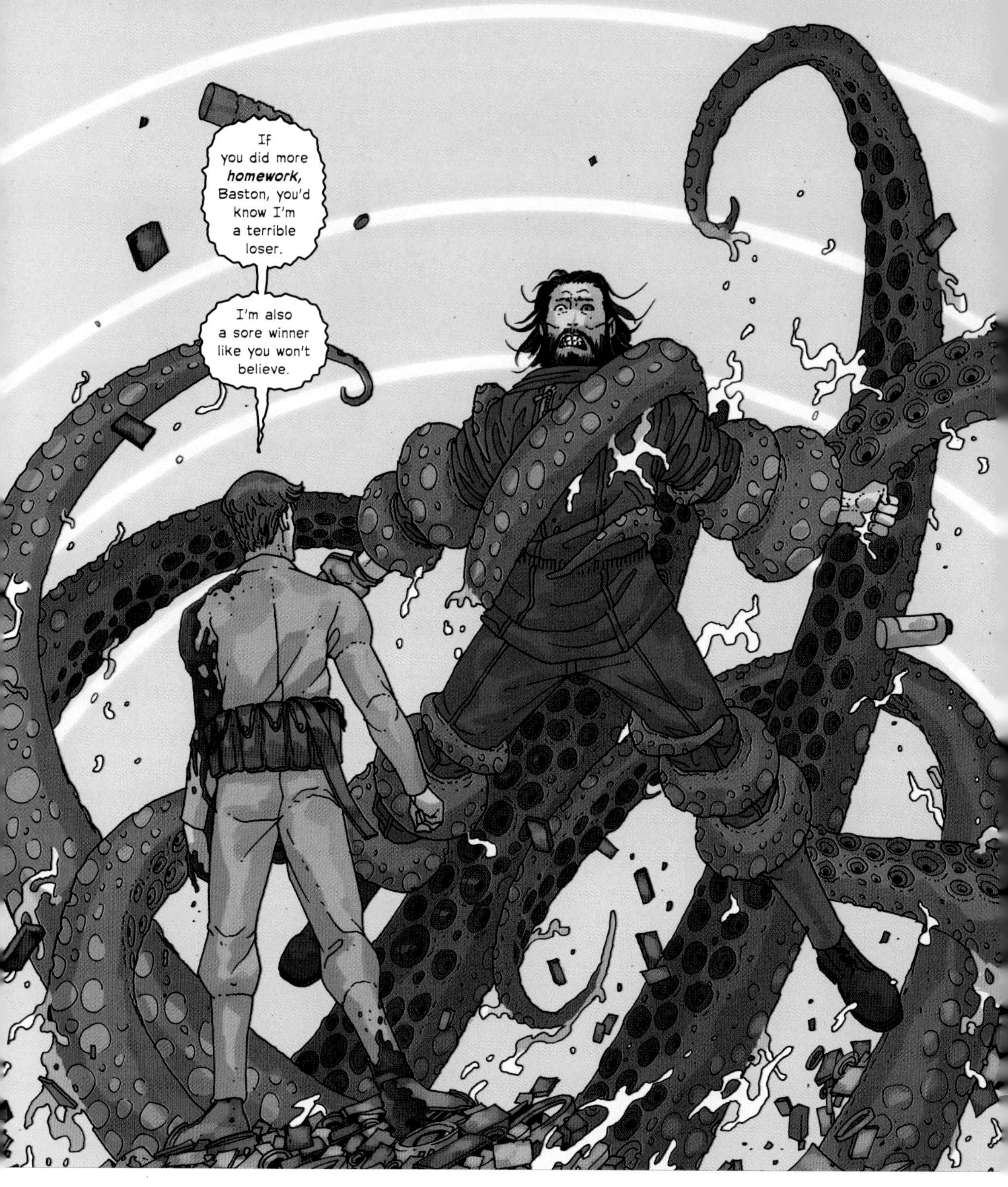
If you did more homework, Baston, you'd know I'm a terrible loser.
I'm also a sore winner like you won't believe.

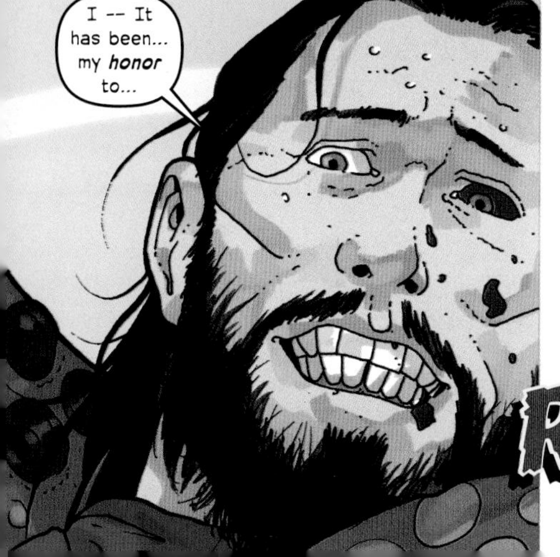
I -- It has been... my honor to...

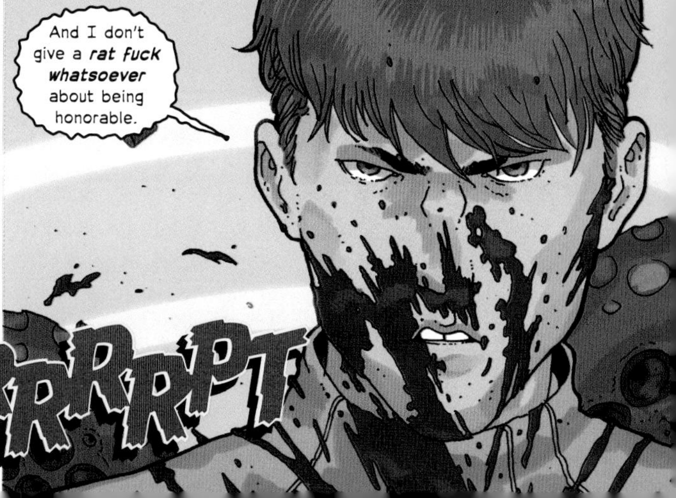
And I don't give a rat fuck whatsoever about being honorable.
RRRRPT

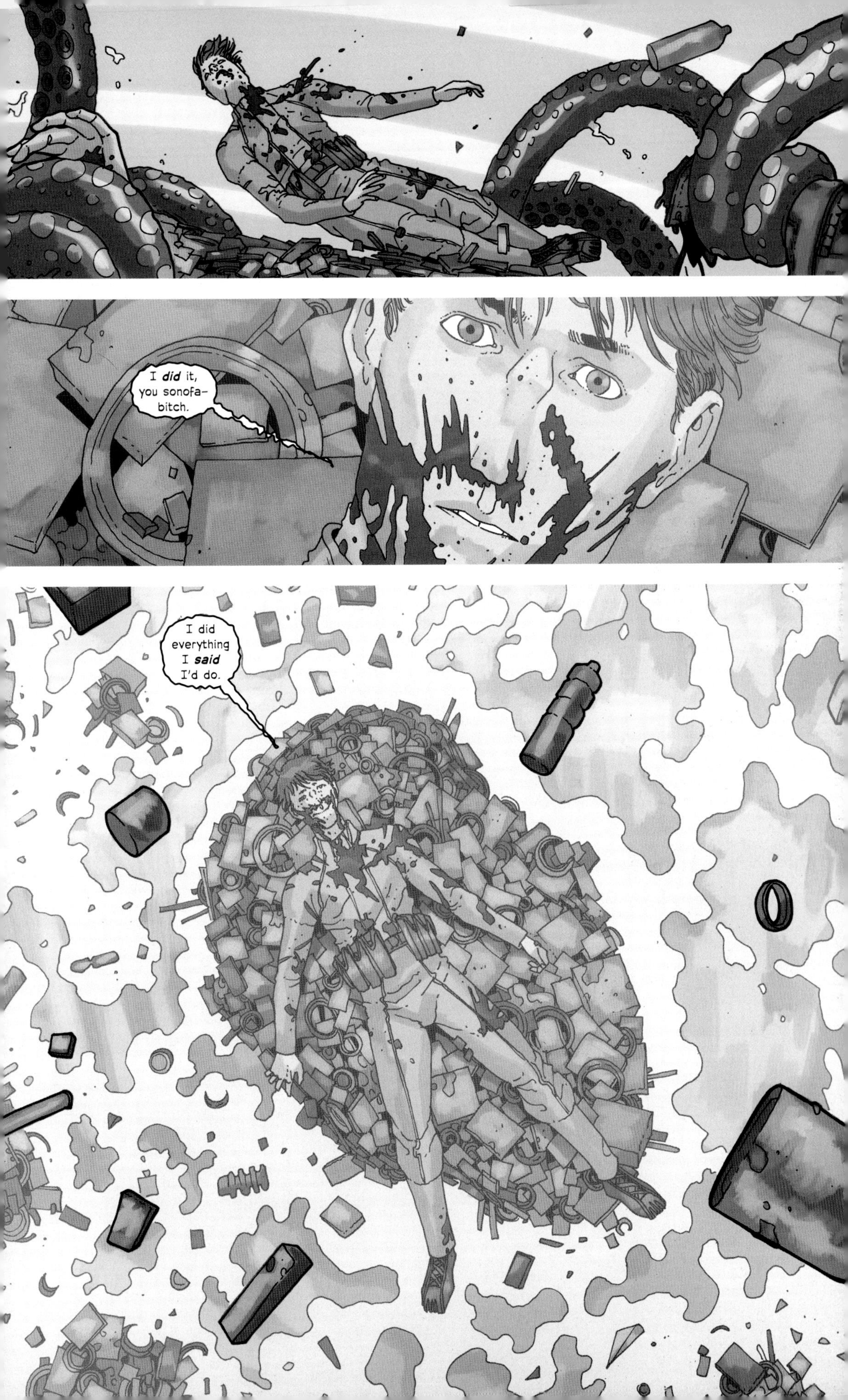
I **did** it, you sonofa-bitch.
I did everything I **said** I'd do.

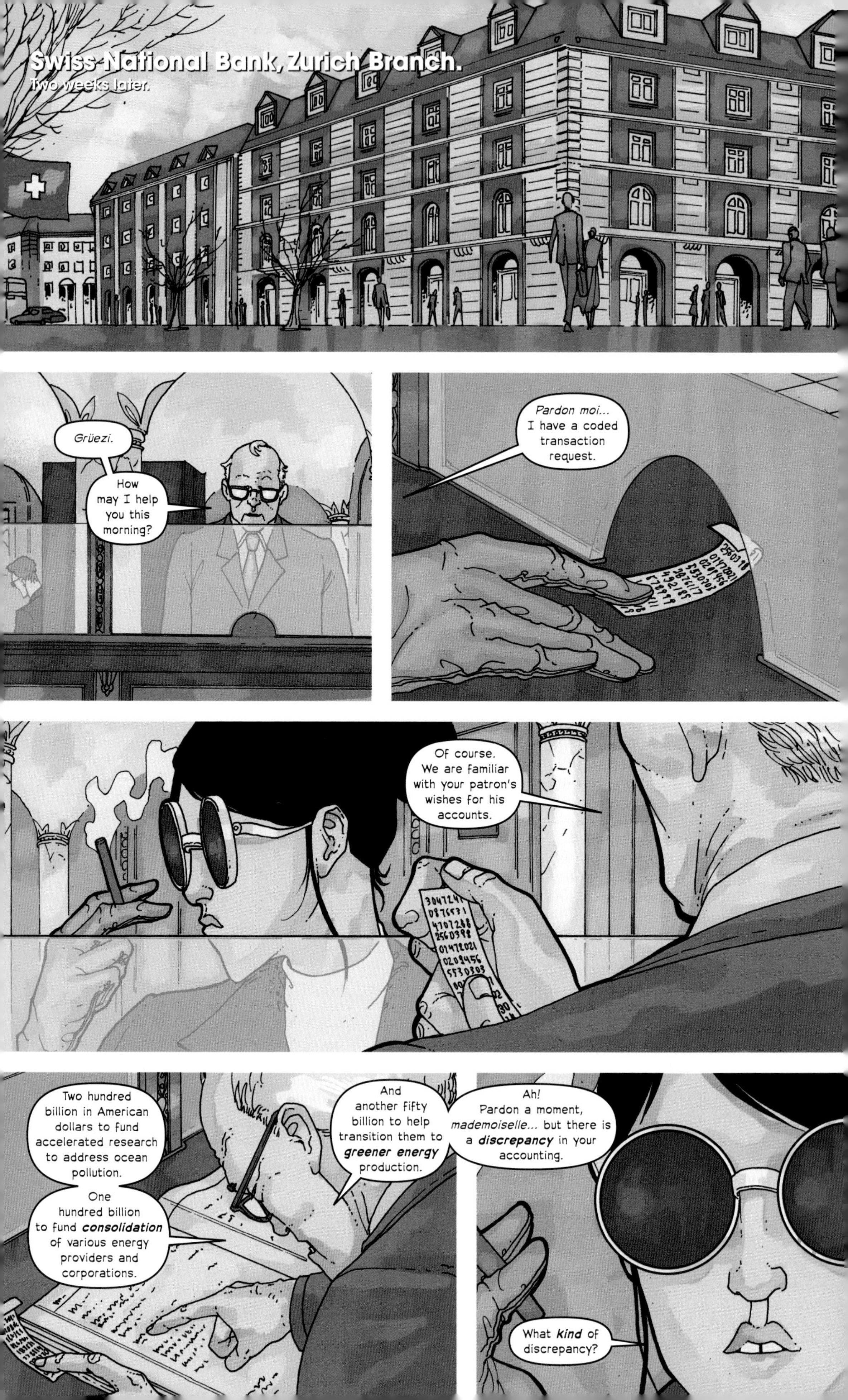
Swiss National Bank, Zurich Branch.
Two weeks later.
Grüezi.
How may I help you this morning?
Pardon moi... I have a coded transaction request.
Of course. We are familiar with your patron's wishes for his accounts.
Two hundred billion in American dollars to fund accelerated research to address ocean pollution.
One hundred billion to fund consolidation of various energy providers and corporations.
And another fifty billion to help transition them to greener energy production.
Ah! Pardon a moment, mademoiselle... but there is a discrepancy in your accounting.
What kind of discrepancy?

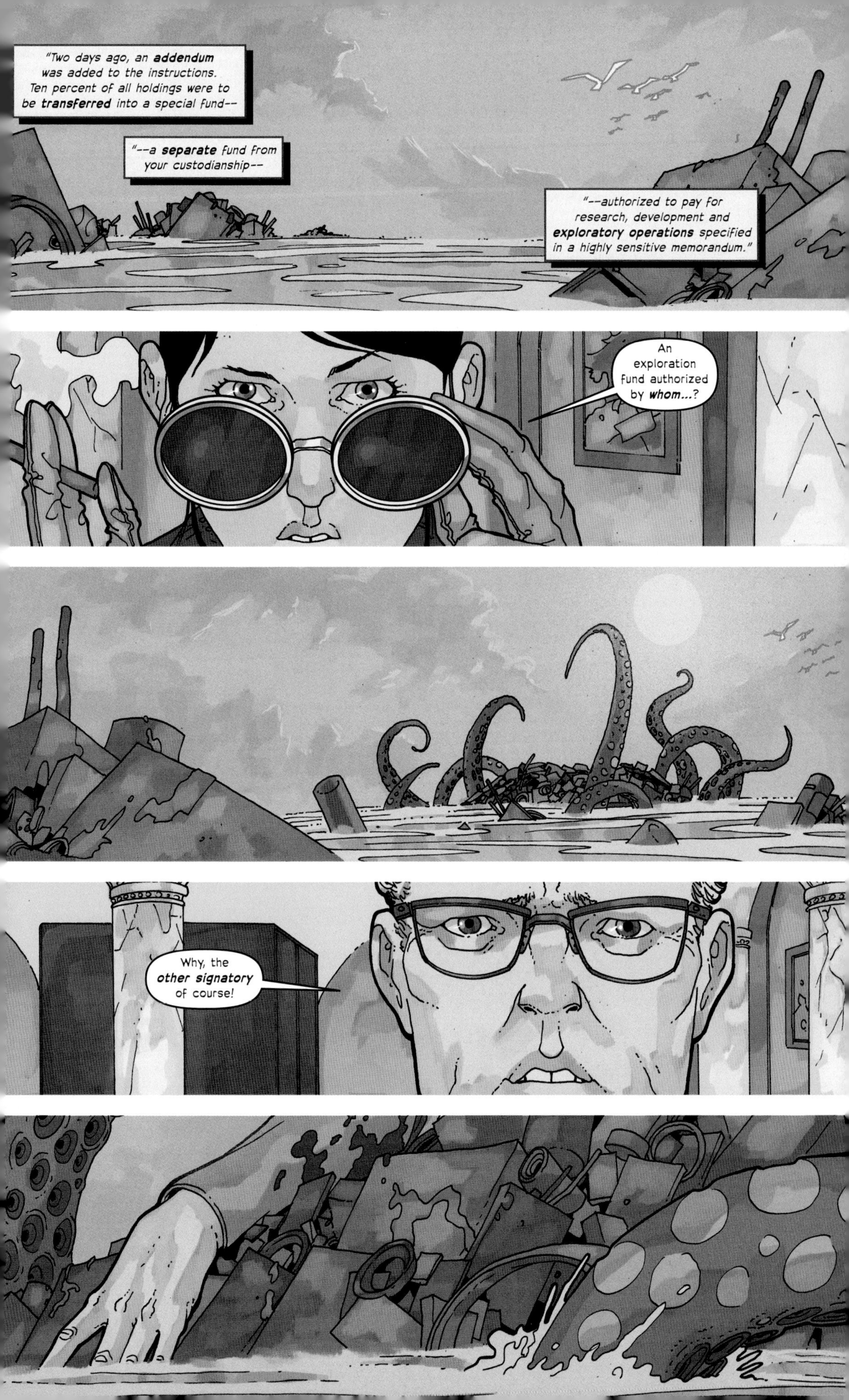
"Two days ago, an addendum was added to the instructions. Ten percent of all holdings were to be transferred into a special fund--
"--a separate fund from your custodianship--
"--authorized to pay for research, development and exploratory operations specified in a highly sensitive memorandum."
An exploration fund authorized by whom...?
Why, the other signatory of course!

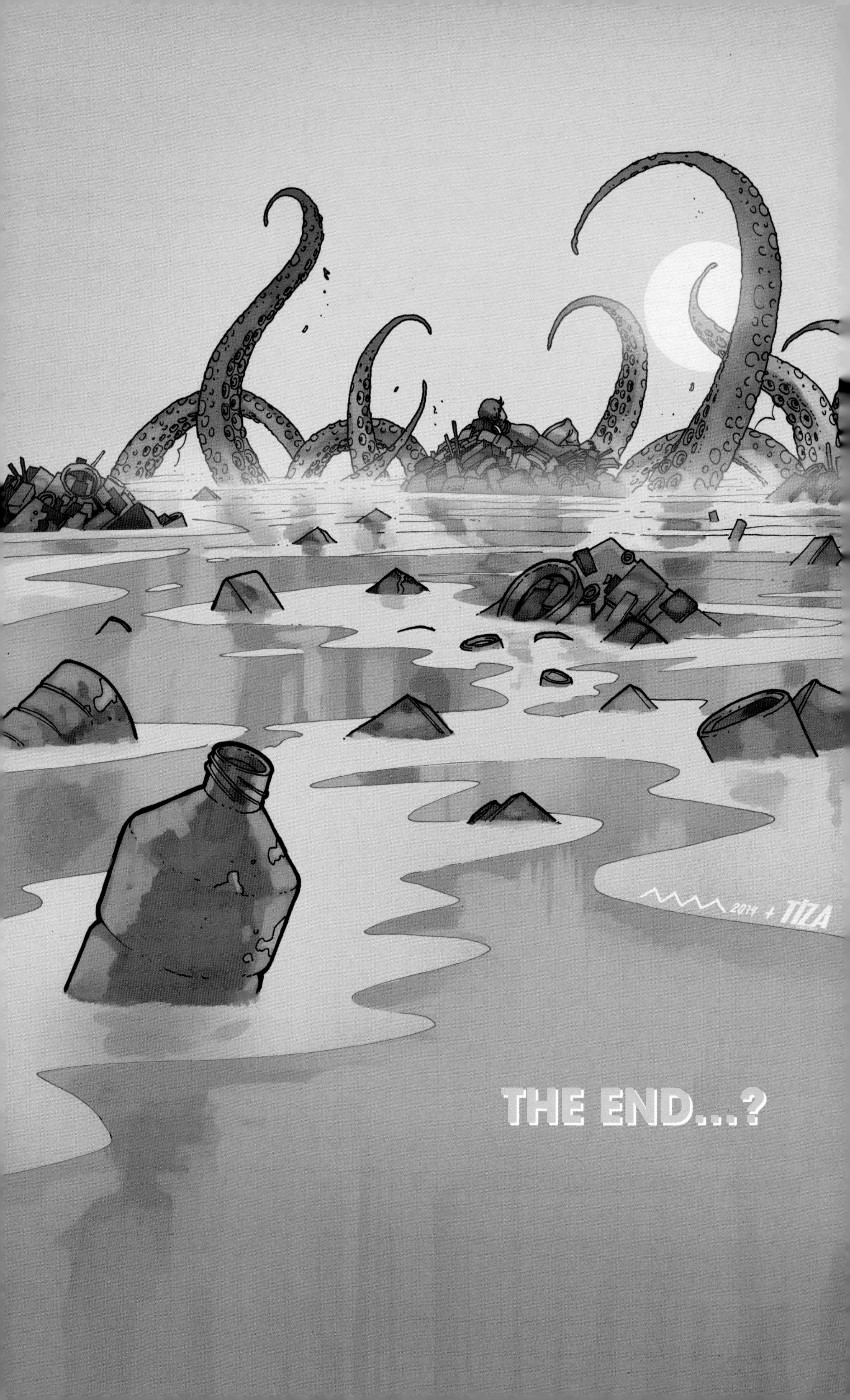
2014 + TIZA
THE END...?

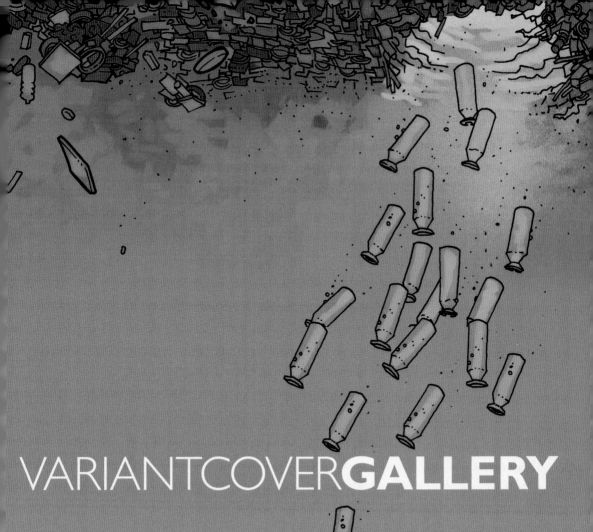

VARIANTCOVER**GALLERY**

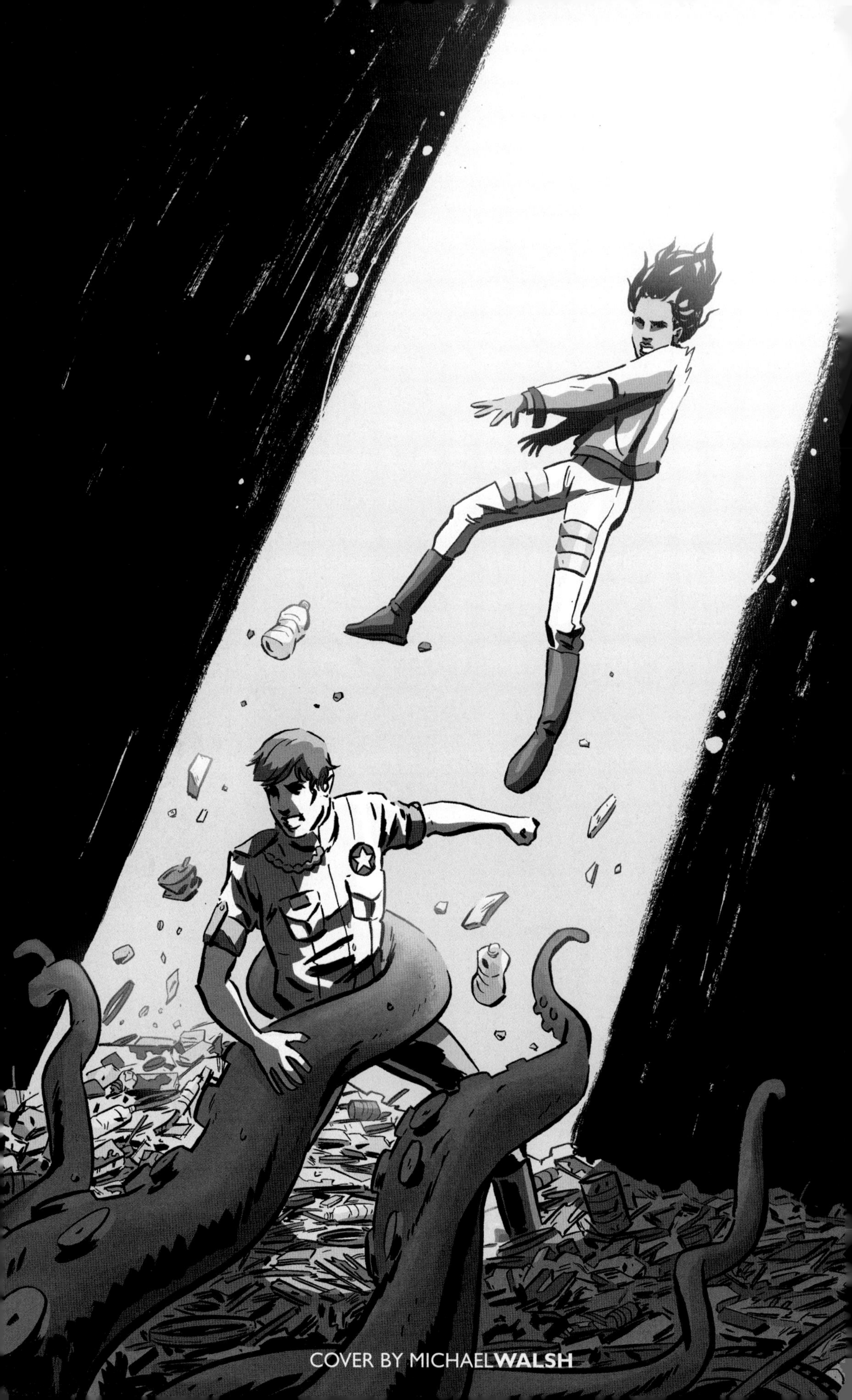

COVER BY MICHAEL**WALSH**

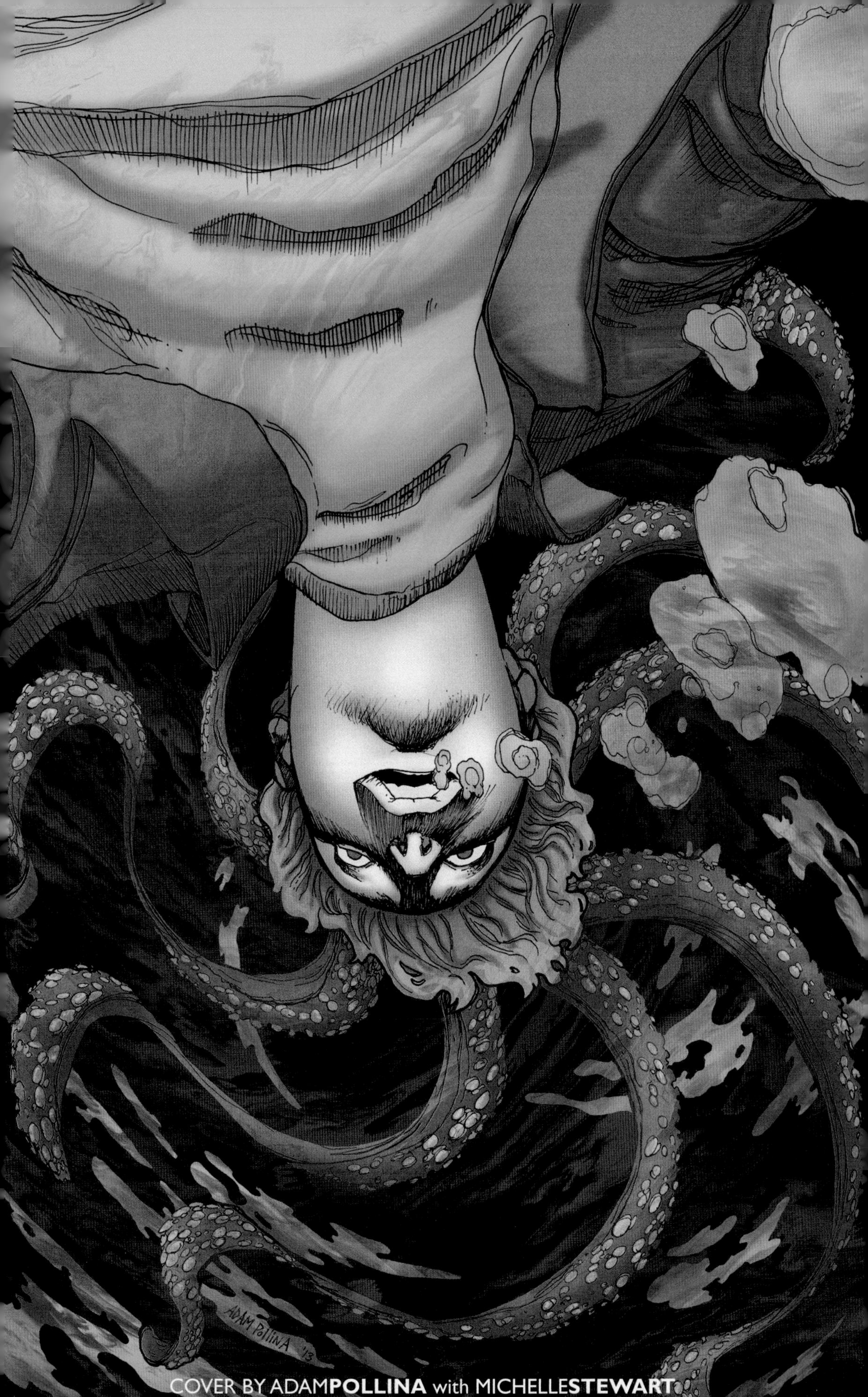
ADAM POLLINA '13

COVER BY ADAM**POLLINA** with MICHELLE**STEWART**

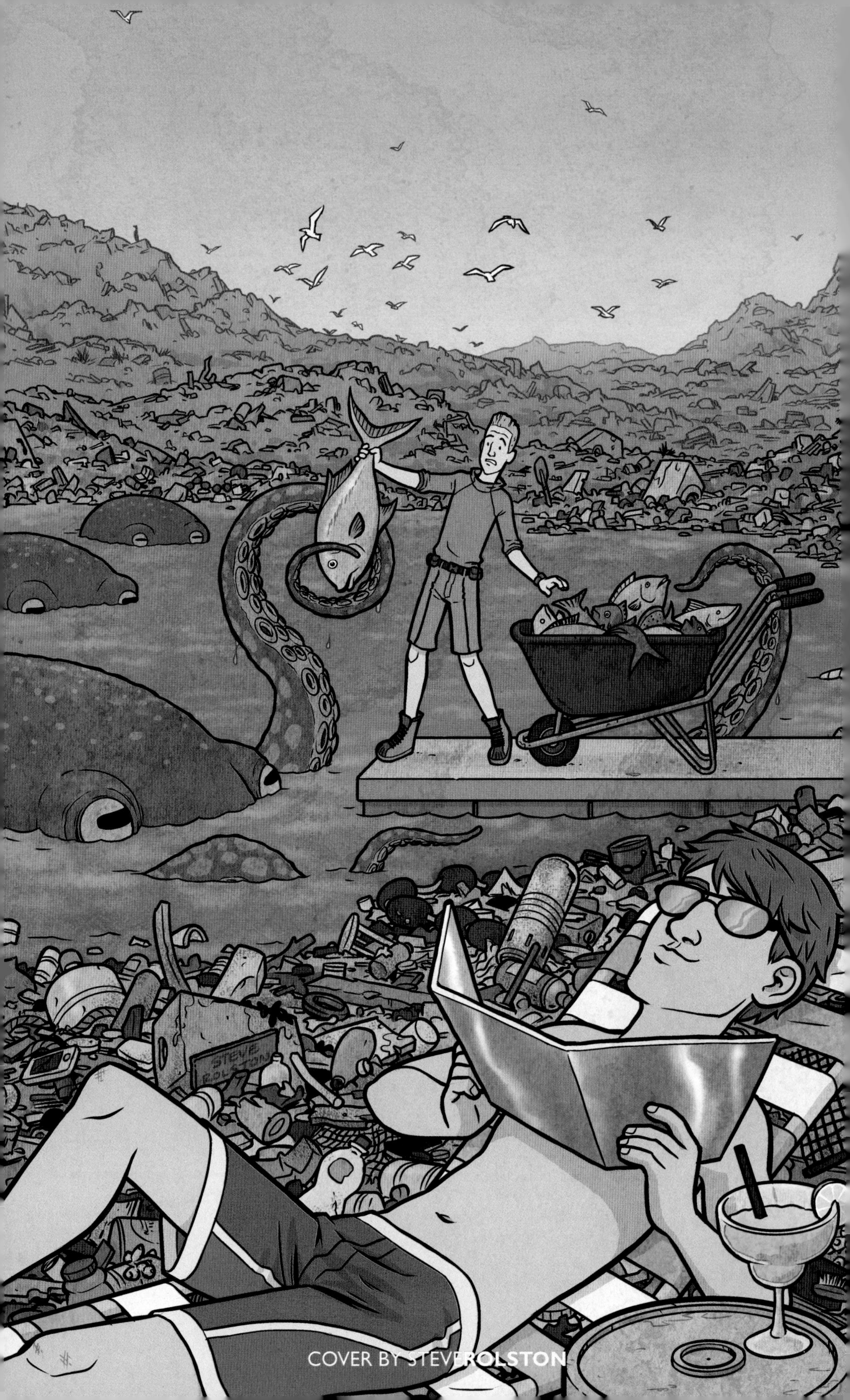
STEVE ROLSTON

COVER BY STEVE ROLSTON

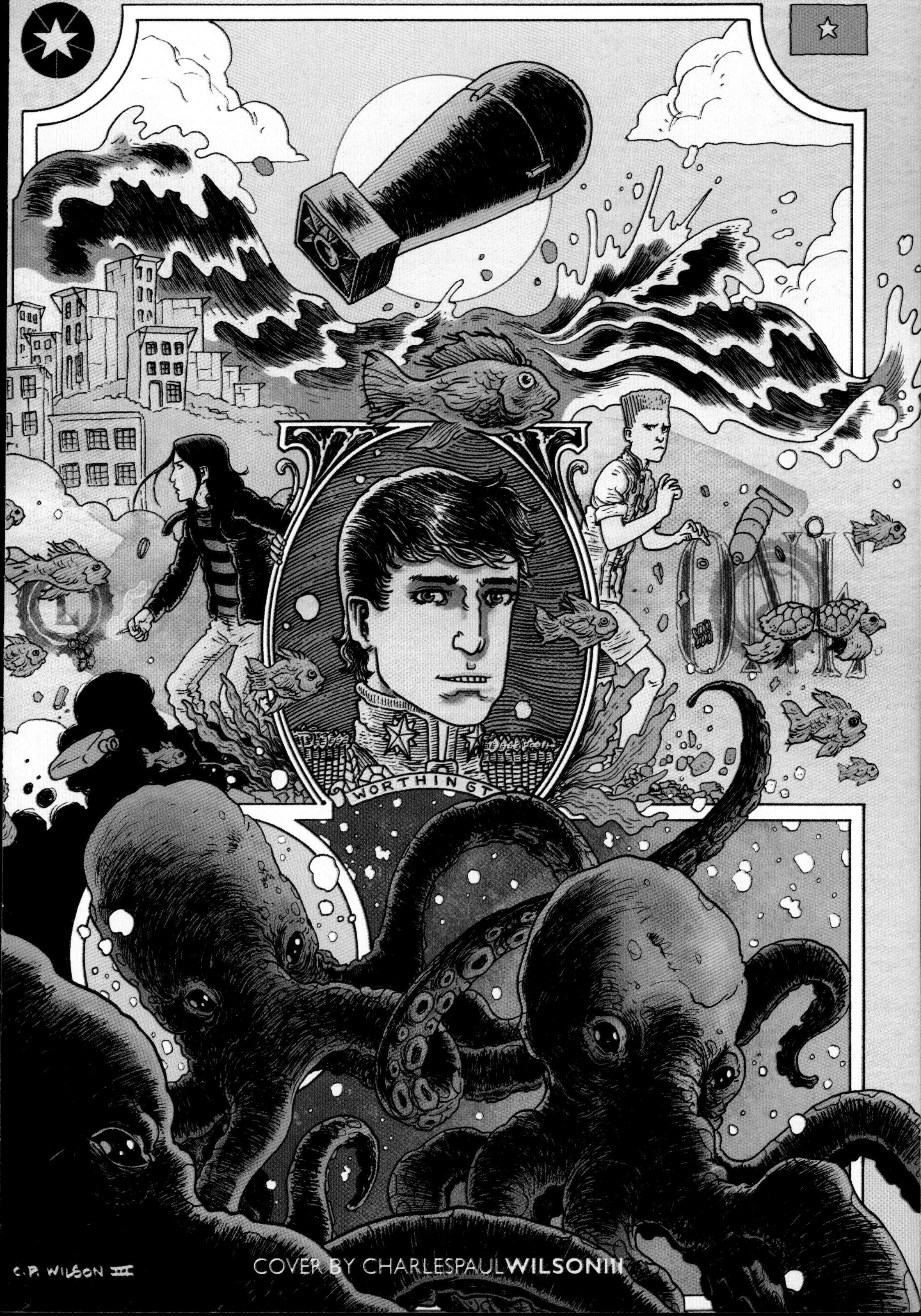
WORTHINGT
C.P. WILSON III

COVER BY CHARLESPAUL**WILSON**III

JOE HARRIS is the creator and writer of original comics and graphic novels such as *"Ghost Projekt,"* *"Spontaneous,"* *"Wars In Toyland"* and the upcoming, *"Death Defied"* for Oni Press. He writes the fan-favorite continuation of the paranormal investigations of Agents Mulder and Scully in *"The X-Files: Season 10"* as well as the brooding adventures of profiler Frank Black in *"Millennium,"* both for IDW.

A horror screenwriter and filmmaker, Harris conceived and co-wrote the Sony Pictures release, *"Darkness Falls"* after his short film, *"Tooth Fairy"* was acquired by Revolution Studios, and *"The Tripper,"* a political slasher movie co-written with David Arquette.

A native New Yorker, he lives in Manhattan.

MARTIN MORAZZO is an artist based in Argentina who first came to the attention of US comics readers through his gorgeous artwork on the award-winning webcomic Absolute Magnitude, which was published via DC's now defunct online imprint, Zuda. Morazzo lives in Buenos Aires, and when he isn't spending every waking minute drawing GREAT PACIFIC, he likes to spend time at the beach with his lovely wife, Victoria and his two children.

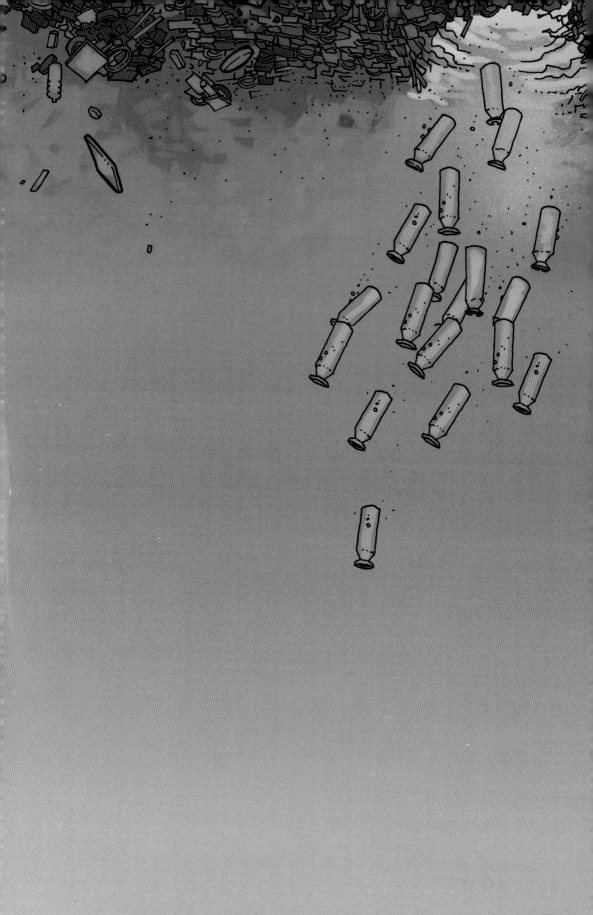